**Rais**
**in F**

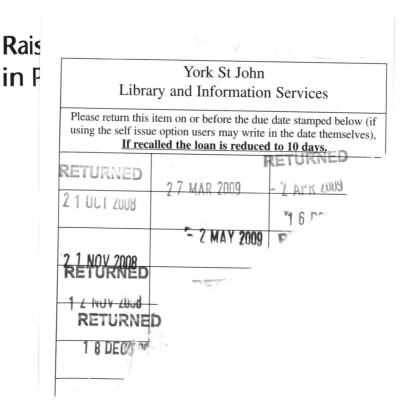

# Raising Boys' Achievement in Primary Schools

Towards an holistic approach

*Molly Warrington and Mike Younger*
*with Eve Bearne*

Open University Press

Open University Press
McGraw-Hill Education
McGraw-Hill House
Shoppenhangers Road
Maidenhead
Berkshire
England
SL6 2QL

email: enquiries@openup.co.uk
world wide web: www.openup.co.uk

and Two Penn Plaza, New York, NY 10121-2289, USA

First published 2006

A catalogue record of this book is available from the British Library

ISBN-10: 0335 216064 (pb) 0335 216072 (hb)
ISBN-13: 9780 335216 062 (pb) 9780 335216 079 (hb)

Library of Congress Cataloguing-in-Publication Data
CIP data applied for

Typeset by BookEns Ltd, Royston, Herts.
Printed in Poland by OZGraf S.A.
www.polskabook.pl

# Contents

# Acknowledgements

We have learnt a great deal in carrying out the research which has formed the substance of this book, and met many interesting and challenging people. We are indebted to them for their openness, their enthusiasm and beliefs in what they were doing, their commitment to the education of young children and their dedication to state education in England. Often unrecognized, they are the bedrock of the primary education system in this country, and we acknowledge in this book the power of their work in helping to transform primary education and open opportunity to all in their schools, staff as well as children. So, among many with whom we have worked, we offer a special thanks to Cathy and Shauna, John, Cheryl and Joan, Neena, Diane and Nina, Kirsty and Ted, Jean, Irene and Peter, Chris and Linda, and Mike, who have always responded with enthusiasm, unfailing tolerance and openness to our many requests. Particularly, we thank Karen and Pat, two exceptional women heading up outstanding schools, whom we have met on several occasions during the course of the project. Often working in difficult circumstances, their honesty, vision and determination – and their achievements and those of their pupils – have inspired us and shown what *is* possible. This book would be far less meaningful without the contributions of pupils and their distinctive voices about their education, their learning and the teaching they receive. We have talked with many of them over the last four years, and we are indebted to them, too, for their willingness to talk, for the clarity and the incisiveness of their insights, and for the pride and delight which many showed in their schools, their teachers and their own achievements.

A special thanks must go to our colleagues at Cambridge who have sustained and supported us during the course of the Raising Boys' Achievement Project: to John Gray and Jean Rudduck, our co-directors, to our research associates, Ros McLellan and Pat Bricheno, to Suzanne Carter and Jen Reynolds, both primary school teachers seconded to the project and to our colleague, Ruth Kershner. The outcomes of the project would have been significantly poorer without their experience, their dedication and the challenges and encouragements they have offered us.

The Raising Boys' Achievement Project was funded by the Department for Education and Skills, and we should like to acknowledge here both financial support, and also the support of our steering group. Under Judy Sebba's able guidance and chairing, they offered continual support, questions and fresh challenges, and were prepared to be flexible and responsive in the light of new evidence.

We would also like to thank Karen Fowler, Headteacher, and Jason Cobb, teacher/photographer, from Michael Faraday School, Southwark (one of the Originator Schools), for allowing us to use the photograph on the cover of the text, and to Chernice Rouse and Ismail Ali, pupils at the school, for agreeing to appear in the photograph.

Finally, our families, friends and colleagues – in the gender research community and beyond – have sustained us and encouraged us during the course of this work. We are especially grateful to them, and particularly to Emma, Nic and Simon, to Glyn, Ruth, Tom and Catherine, and to Peter.

# 1 Gender differentials within primary education

## Context and causes

Throughout the past decade of the twentieth century and into the early years of this century, the debate about boys' under-achievement and the gender gap has been a persistent theme in English education and beyond. In Australia (Kenway et al. 1998; Collins et al. 2000; Gilbert and Gilbert 2001), in the United States (Gurian 1998; Weaver-Hightower 2003), in mainland Europe (Kruse 1996; Sutherland 1999; Johannesson 2004; Van Houtte 2004), there have emerged concerns about how to 'rescue boys', to respond to boys' latent despondency and depression, or how to combat the apparent feminization of schooling (Biddulph 1998a; Hoff-Sommers 2000). Much of this debate, particularly in England, was contextualized within secondary schooling (Younger et al. 2005a), amidst concerns about the continuing gender gap particularly at the end of compulsory schooling (at age 16), and the failure of as many boys as girls to reach the benchmark grades (5 or more passes at least at C grade) in their GCSE examinations; in 2004, for example, 58.5 per cent of girls and 48.4 per cent of boys recorded this level of achievement (DfES 2004a).

In the primary sector, both in England and elsewhere, there has been less focus on the issue of 'under-achieving' boys. Indeed, pupils' attainment was not assessed in any standardized way across the nation before the implementation of the National Curriculum and the associated standard assessment tests and teacher assessments at 7 and 11 in the early 1990s, and even then the data from the initial years' tests were of dubious validity and reliability. Equally, texts and consultancies offering pedagogic and resource support to teachers (see, for example, Pickering 1997; Bleach 1998; Gardner et al. 1999; Noble and Bradford 2000; Noble et al. 2001) until recently focused almost entirely on the secondary sector, and the issue of boys' 'under-achievement' was conceptualized and analysed almost entirely from the perspective of older children.

## The changing focus on assessment in primary education

In one respect, this lack of focus on 'under-achieving' boys is not surprising, for there had been little emphasis on formal assessment in English primary schools throughout the 1970s and 1980s. National data was limited in scope, and differential variations – whether by social class, gender or ethnicity – tended to be hidden. The disillusionment with the rationale behind the tests (the 11+ examinations) which had determined entry to selective grammar schools in many parts of the country in the three decades immediately after the end of the Second World War, and the subsequent liberating emphasis of the Plowden Report (1967) on child-centredness, individualism, learning by discovery and an integrated topic approach to subject teaching, meant that there was little summative assessment of pupils' progress over each school year. Children received formative assessment and feedback on how they might improve pieces of work, and in many instances primary–secondary liaison meant that children in their final years of primary school completed some form of cognitive ability tests which informed their secondary teachers. But there was little sense of how pupils were performing within a local or regional context, and the competitive element within schools was not strong. Written reporting to parents was also minimal; although some primary schools were introducing pupils' records of achievement by the early 1990s, these gave little more, if as much information, as the reports of three decades earlier (see Figures 1.1 and 1.2).

| Arithmetic | Quite outstanding ability |
|---|---|
| Geography/History | Has produced some very good work |
| English | Very good |
| Reading | Now reads clearly and fluently |
| Writing | Good when he takes his time |
| PE | Most keen |
| Art | Fair |
| Music | Fair |
| Gardening | Good, shows interest |
| A good all-rounder; will go far; we all wish him success at the grammar school. | |

**Figure 1.1** Edward's Report, June 1959: Year 1 (top class)

Stephen has had a pleasing, hard working year; I have seen progress in all aspects of the curriculum. He perceives his abilities and weaknesses realistically and endeavours to put extra effort into more difficult tasks. He has gained confidence with mathematics and problem-solving. His handwriting has improved and consequently his work is presented in a tidier and more pleasing way. Stephen is aware that his spelling needs care.

**Figure 1.2**  Stephen's Record of Achievement, May 1992: Year 6

Although the emergence of Margaret Thatcher's New Right Conservative government in 1979 changed the tone of the educational debate, there were few fundamental changes in the ethos and workings of English primary schools until the passing of the 1988 Educational Reform Act. Then a cascade of changes transformed the scene. Fuelled by a reaction against the so-called progressivism of the Plowden Report, and citing falling standards of literacy and numeracy, weak classroom discipline and poorly motivated children, successive Secretaries of State for Education initiated a confrontational approach with the teaching profession which some have described as 'a reign of terror' during which 'primary teachers and their headteachers have had their confidence and self-esteem challenged at every turn' (Brighouse 1997: 106–7, quoted in Galton et al. 1999: 24). The emphasis on whole-class teaching methods, as opposed to groupwork and 'child-centred teaching that relied on impulse and inclination and a commitment to discovery learning in place of formal instruction' (Woodhead, as reported in *The Daily Telegraph* 'Inspector Attacks Woolly Teachers', 27 January 1995) was reiterated: 'Whole class teaching appears to provide the order, control, purpose and concentration which many critics believe are lacking in modern primary classrooms' (Alexander et al. 1992, para. 89). A secondary-focused, subject-dominated National Curriculum was imposed, to bring what was taught more firmly under control, and to limit the scope of integrated, inquiry-led approaches to teaching. In the process, primary school teachers lost control not only of content but also of process and pedagogy, and saw their professional autonomy diluted. Assessment requirements were defined at the ages of 7, 11 and 14 as well as at 16, so that 'within two years of the passing into law of the Education Reform Act there were new assessments in place at 7+ and trials underway at 11+' (Galton et al. 1999: 13).

The scale and impact of these changes cannot be underestimated. To Osborn et al.:

Primary education in England and Wales will never be the same again. The 1988 Education Reform Act was the most radical education legislation in half a century, and a decade of unremitting change followed it ... The expressed aim ... was, quite simply, to raise standards ... by raising expectations about pupil achievement and, through the imposition of a broad and balanced national curriculum for all pupils, to provide continuity and coherence in their learning experience. The introduction of the National Curriculum was complemented by provision for a standard and comprehensive assessment system ... designed not only to measure the performance of pupils ... but also to make it possible for market forces to operate by providing a currency of information which would fuel competition between schools.

(2000: 3, 6)

Alexander (2000) writes in similar vein:

At the end of the century, then, English primary education was firmly established as a distinct educational phase whose potential impact on Britain's educational and economic performance ... demanded the closest possible control by government and surveillance by its agencies. It was not so much the standing of primary education that had improved as its perceived strategic significance. Had it been otherwise, the debate about 'standards' would have focused on the quality of primary education overall, rather than – as actually happened – merely on pupils' test performance in literacy and numeracy.

(2000: 143)

In many respects, the 1997 election of New Labour did not impact strongly on primary education; rather than a re-evaluation, there was instead a consolidation and extension of the state's involvement in primary education, with literacy and numeracy targets for 11-year-olds enshrined within election pledges, and a subsequent involvement in pedagogy, in terms of the prescriptive template (three-part lessons, interactive whole-class teaching and plenaries) associated with the 'Literacy Hour' in 1998 (Wyse 2003) and a similar 'Numeracy Hour' in 1999. One of several adjustments of the primary National Curriculum content reduced the emphasis on the foundation subjects, and reinforced the primacy of English and mathematics, making it even more difficult to deliver the broad and balanced curriculum supposedly underpinning the National Curriculum. The emphasis on performance, on school's positioning within national, LEA and local league tables, was reinforced in the early years of the new century, within the context of school improvement, target-setting and data accumulation. In Brehony's words:

> It [the Labour government] has also fostered the adoption in the education service of new managerialism ... more specifically, in the primary phase, it has continued the trend begun by the Conservatives towards the elimination of its distinctive character ... the National Curriculum introduced by the Act envisaged a seamless experience from the age of 5 to 16. ... In this shift, from child-centred to society-centred education, an emphasis on learning was replaced by one on teaching.
>
> (2005: 30–1)

It might be argued that the publication of the *Excellence and Enjoyment* Primary Strategy (DfES 2003) was an attempt to redress the balance. Indeed, there were references to schools being encouraged to develop their own distinctive character, to teachers 'taking ownership of the curriculum to shape it and make it their own' (p. 4), to creativity and innovation (p. 31 ff.), to 'children's entitlement to a rich, broad and balanced set of learning experiences' (p. 27), to schools being enabled 'to continue to focus on raising standards while not being afraid to combine that with making learning fun ... to combine excellence in teaching with enjoyment in learning' (p. 4). Throughout the document, though, there was a continued emphasis on performance targets, testing and assessment, and the domination of the curriculum by teaching strategies associated with the Literacy and Numeracy Strategies. In a strong critique, Alexander argues that there was a marked 'ambiguity of intent' underlying the *Excellence and Enjoyment* Primary Strategy, summarized as 'a desire to be seen to be offering freedom while in reality maintaining control' (2004a: 15). This was evidenced in 'the reiterated appeal to experience and common-sense, ... the wilful amnesia in respect of the accumulated findings of published research on learning and teaching ... and the ignoring of findings from the government's own inspections' (2004a: 14). As in the policy documents of the previous decade, the emphasis in *Excellence and Enjoyment* continued to be placed on imposition, on political compliance, albeit perhaps more subtly disguised within the language of experience ('every teacher knows' ... 'in the best schools, teachers are already using') and what was known to be reasonable. There remained, in Alexander's words, little 'room for alternative professional judgement' and there was 'little evidence of government relaxing the iron grip of educational centralisation' (2004a:

17); imbued throughout with deeply patronizing language, ignoring the accumulation of knowledge from the past, and full of populist appeals to teachers' common sense, the Primary Strategy lacked a coherent case, argument and vision (2004a: 28). In similar vein, Brehony argued that 'the Strategy shows few signs of a serious desire to move away from standards in favour of creativity and a pupil-centred curriculum' (2005: 41).

The years since 1988 have seen both significant gains and losses in primary education, but it is the area of assessment which is central to our concerns here. In some respects, it is an exaggeration to suggest that little or no assessment took place in primary schools during the 1970s and 1980s, although 'testing in schools was at an all-time low' (Galton et al. 1999: 140) in 1976. Nonetheless, the 1978 Primary Survey (DES 1978), for example, commented on the match between ability and provision for some children in all areas of the curriculum, while highlighting teachers' under-expectation of other children who 'could have been attempting harder, more complex, more interesting, more challenging work' (Marjoram 1980: 29). Reading tests administered by the National Foundation for Educational Research (NFER) were quoted as indicating gradually improving standards through time (Thomas 1980), and there was a ready acceptance that effective assessment was at the heart of effective teaching, offering reliable and formative feedback to teachers and pupils alike. Indeed, the establishment of the Assessment of Performance Unit (1974), to identify and define standards and subsequently to measure and assess pupils' achievements against them, and the reintroduction of mass testing of pupils by LEAs, date from this period.

Throughout the 1970s and 1980s, though, there was little emphasis either on feedback to parents or on the relative performance of schools. Although parents were welcomed into primary schools as informal helpers and fund-raisers, it was also the case that in most primary schools they received little feedback on their children's progress, often limited to the occasional ten-minute consultation towards the end of the school year. Likewise, written reports on their children's progress had dropped out of currency in the years since the early 1960s; there was neither the ethos nor the expectation that these would be provided. The emergence of pupils' self-completed records of achievement in the late 1980s in some primary schools, did give teachers some scope to write a summative comment to parents, but these were extremely variable in their scope and information. The notion of league tables was equally foreign, 'unthinkable' to quote Galton et al. (1999: 135); indeed, the evidence points in a different direction, since Gipps and Goldstein (1983) reported a major reduction in the number of LEAs using English and mathematics attainment tests between 1960 and 1972, although intelligence testing remained a common practice.

At the same time, there was little emphasis on gender differentials between boys' and girls' attainments, simply because no national and few local databases existed. It is true that concerns were beginning to surface about gender differences in terms of teacher–pupil interaction in classrooms, with the suggestion that boys received disproportionate amounts of teachers' time and attention (Clarricoates 1980; Spender 1982; Stanworth 1987), but most of this research was situated in the secondary sector. Equally, although there was a growing focus on equal opportunities for girls, with the development of whole-school policies which addressed issues such as differential-option choice, the language of textbooks and classrooms, teacher strategies and teacher expectation (Whyte 1985; Arnot and Weiner 1987; Rudduck 1994), this too was almost entirely secondary focused. Indeed, the focus was much more on social class, and the impact of social class upon achievement, aspirations and expectations, than on gender differentials (Jackson 1964; Hargreaves 1967; Willis 1977; Tizard and Hughes 1984).

In both assessment and reporting there have been fundamental changes of approach since 1988. As we show in Chapter 2, there is now an avalanche of data available on the differential achievement of boys and girls in primary schools, which can be analysed at many different levels, to identify teacher-effect, school-effect and within value-added contexts. The publication of gender-specific data within league tables at national, regional and local levels is one outcome; detailed written reports to parents on their children's progress during the course of the academic year is another (see Figure 1.3). Target-setting for children, teachers and schools is yet another; support for schools identified as 'in serious weakness' or 'failing' is a further aspect of this.

It cannot be denied that the emphasis upon assessment, through tests, targets and performance tables, is a double-edged sword which can seriously distract primary school teachers from combining excellence in teaching with enjoyment in learning. There is a narrowness about National Curriculum assessments, particularly at Key Stage 2, an over-concentration on what can be assessed in the core subjects of English, mathematics and science by externally marked pencil and paper tests, and continuing doubts about the consistency, reliability and validity of the tests. Concerns have been expressed, too, about the minimalism encountered in some tests, particularly in English at Key Stage 2:

> We do all of this exciting stuff to stimulate creative writing, imagination, cross-links between subjects, and the like … emphasize that they need to write gripping and fast-moving

**Study Skills**: Abdul is working well within Year 4. He settles down to tasks well and he has developed much more of a 'have a go' attitude. Abdul's presentation of work has improved dramatically this year although occasionally he does still need reminding of this. Abdul is more keen to share his ideas now, with a small group; this is a skill that is developing in a class situation.

**Communication, Language and Literacy**: Abdul has worked extremely hard in literacy this year. His reading age has increased dramatically, and his written work has shown better vocabulary and a deepened imagination. Abdul still struggles with his spelling but is making more phonetical attempts, which is making his writing much easier to read. Abdul is developing his skills for speaking and listening but can still be shy in front of an audience ... Abdul has developed his handwriting well this year. Next steps: continue to work on spelling strategies; remember to include punctuation in longer written tasks.

**Numeracy**: Abdul has developed well in numeracy this year. He has developed his knowledge of the four operations and understands now when each operation needs to be used. Abdul can still sometimes get confused with multi-step problems. He still needs to develop his knowledge of the times tables, which will aid his mental maths. Abdul enjoys the visual side of maths such as fractions and symmetry and this is an area where he is developing well. Next steps: continued work on times tables; understand the link between multiplication facts and division problems.

**Knowledge and Understanding of the World**: Abdul has developed his vocabulary within this area and this has impacted on his work. He is able to make relevant predictions and conclusions in science. He has thoroughly enjoyed studying the Romans ...

**Creative Development**: Abdul is developing well the skill to perform in front of an audience and is beginning to self-evaluate his work. Abdul enjoys art although he can find this creative subject frustrating.

**Physical Development**: Abdul enjoys PE and is keen to participate in all activities. He is most comfortable in a team situation, where he boosts morale and team spirit.

**Personal, Social and Emotional Development**: Abdul listens well and in small situations he is able to discuss his feelings well. He still finds class discussions quite difficult to participate in.

**Class Teacher's General Comment**: Abdul has listened carefully to areas in which he needs to improve and has striven to succeed, with good results. Abdul is a happy caring boy who has a wide range of friends. He has put in 100% effort this year and I have been pleased with his progress.

**Figure 1.3**  Extract from Abdul's Record of Achievement, July 2005: Year 4

plots, create believable characters, create atmosphere, get in detail and humour ... and then the children are asked to write on this: [*shows copy of 2003 KS2 English levels 3-5 Writing Task which contains four pictures of children queuing to buy a new game, and two boys eventually buying the game, together with the accompanying instructions: Your task is to write a story based on the events in the storyboard above. You must decide how the story ends.*] ... We gave out the test paper, and they looked at us, through their boredom and dismay, and their expressions said it all ... What?! How on earth are we supposed to write imaginatively about this?!

(South London primary school headteacher)

At the same time, the use of this narrow assessment data to underpin and inform national, regional and local league tables continues to work against schools from socially and economically deprived areas, or schools which regularly admit pupils excluded from other schools, or those which have high levels of intake from refugee and asylum-seeking families. Such primary schools are often providing outstanding educational opportunities for underprivileged and disadvantaged children, yet the current relatively unsophisticated approach to value-added measures and league tables presents their work in an uncomplimentary and ill-conceived light. Indeed, in such a context, 'the uncritical use by the Labour government of the Conservative bivariate national assessment and examination data ... distorted the policy picture in ways that were detrimental to the disadvantaged' (Arnot and Miles 2005: 178). The emphasis upon booster lessons, catch-up materials and reading recovery programmes is well intentioned at one level, 'to use education as a prime lever to give poorer children improved life chances' (Ward 2005: 9) and 'to ensure that education helps in our drive for social justice' (Kelly 2005). It can nevertheless distract teachers and distort the curriculum to the extent that some children receive a minimalist and restricted primary education which becomes very narrowly focused on basic skills.

In other respects, however, this increased emphasis upon assessment must be welcomed: it enables children's individual learning needs to be better identified in a diagnostic sense and appropriate support and learning opportunities to be provided. It offers feedback on children's progress both to the children themselves and to their parents/carers, and crucially can open up possibilities and raise aspirations. It encourages a dialogue between teachers on children's achievement and learning, and about how common learning needs might be diagnosed, identified and accommodated in subsequent teaching. Crucially, assessment puts the focus centrally on learning: in Drummond's words, 'the process of assessing children's learning – by looking closely at it and striving to understand it – is the only certain safeguard against children's failure, the only guarantee of children's progress and development' (1993: 140).

Crucially, too, assessment has facilitated the identification of patterns and trends in national performance levels of boys and girls, of pupils from different ethnic groups, to some extent of pupils from different social classes. It has become more possible to recognize inequalities in the nature of educational provision within a locality, to focus on strengths as well as weaknesses within that educational provision, and assist the spread of good practice within communities of schools. Within the context of our own research, particularly within the Raising Boys' Achievement Project (Warrington et al. 2003; Younger et al. 2005b), the information from the emergent national databases has enabled us to recognize schools where the achievement levels of boys has challenged the notion of 'under-achieving boys', and – within case study contexts (see Chapter 3) – to identify those characteristics of curriculum, pedagogy, leadership, organization and socio-cultural strategies that have enabled boys to achieve better than might be expected.

We accept that there are clear dangers in the current high profile emphasis on league tables, tests and targets in English primary education, particularly when they are implemented and interpreted rigorously and without regard to context. Equally, though, the emphasis upon assessment and performance has improved our knowledge and understanding not only of the progress made by individuals and groups of children, but of the occurrence of educational inequality at different scales and dimensions within the primary sector in England. Both strengths and weaknesses in the educational system have been revealed, and sometimes patterns of inequity have come starkly into focus. Differential achievement of boys and girls within primary education is one of these inequalities, and it is to this that we now turn.

## Why boys' 'under-achievement'?

In Chapter 2 we outline the nature of the gender gap in English primary schools at Key Stages 1 and 2, while at the same time sounding notes of caution about too simplistic an interpretation of the data. It is undeniable, however, that – by the age of 11 – girls in many primary schools are performing better than boys, particularly in English, and that this pattern of differential achievement is sustained and exacerbated throughout secondary education (FitzGerald 2005; Phillips 2005; Smithers 2005). The debate about boys' 'under-achievement' has reached a frenzy in the early years of the twenty-first century, especially as policy-makers, researchers and teachers have sought an understanding about *why* boys apparently under-achieve. While much of this research has been articulated within secondary schooling, more recently a number of texts have emerged which have developed the arguments in the context of primary education (Skelton 2001; Skelton and Francis 2003a; Connolly 2004; Renold 2004a).

There are contributory factors which have been identified by other researchers: studies of participation and interaction in primary schools have suggested, for example, that some high-achieving boys contribute less actively and constructively to class discussion, and apply themselves less to academic work, as they progress through primary schools and construct their own image of masculinity which accords with family and peer role models (Holden and Wilson 2000; Myhill 2000). Other researchers have commented on differential gender interactions between pupils and teachers in the classroom, particularly as perceived by (some) boys (Burns and Myhill 2004). Teachers, of course, operate within their own notions of masculinity and femininity, and teachers' expectations of and pre-conceptions about certain boys can on occasions exacerbate laddishness. Certainly pupils' perceptions of teachers is that they have different expectations of boys and girls in terms of their behaviour, the quality of their written work, and the extent to which they punish and praise boys as against girls (Skelton 1996; Wing 1997; Younger et al. 1999; Francis 2000). In some schools, the behaviour of male teachers, in fraternizing with the macho boys and engaging in 'laddish' behaviour with the boys, serves only to reiterate and encourage some of the extremes of hegemonic masculinity. There has been emphasis, too, on girls' increased maturity and more effective learning strategies (Gipps 1996), with their emphasis on collaboration, talk and sharing (Askew and Ross 1988; Fennema 1996). A further group of explanations put the emphasis on teaching and learning, particularly in the context of reading and writing, since it is here where the under-achievement of boys is apparently greatest; indeed, this is our starting-point in the discussion which follows.

Before we begin this exploration, however, it is important to stress a note of caution, because not all explanations seem to us to have equal validity and strength. We express below some of our reservations about the emphasis upon biological differences between boys and girls in 'explaining' differential achievement, and position ourselves centrally within the social constructionist field. Equally, we are sceptical about explanations which suggest that boys under-achieve in primary schools because of the feminization of those schools, and the argument that the predominance of women teachers has led to primary schools favouring

PTO

girls and 'girls' learning styles' over those of boys (Biddulph 1998a). There is little evidence which suggests that men are more effective than women as teachers of boys; indeed, what evidence does exist suggests the converse (Thornton and Bricheno 2002), and our own extensive interviews with boys suggests strongly that it is personality, rapport and effectiveness which are far more important than gender in determining to them what constitutes a good teacher. We agree with Skelton, therefore when she maintains that:

> The assumption that raising the proportion of male teachers will provide boys with positive, work-oriented 'role models' is based on notions of gender which have long been challenged; that is, such strategies are underpinned by sex role socialisation theories whereby masculinity and femininity are located solely within male and female bodies respectively ... Current strategies to recruit more men into primary teaching are based on somewhat simplistic ideas of men as role models. The idea that a shift in the gender balance would tackle the 'feminized' nature of primary schooling is naïve.
>
> (2003a: 195–6, 207)

## Literacy issues

At one level, the nature of the gender gap at Key Stage 2 has inevitably directed the attention of many teachers and researchers to literacy issues (see Chapters 6 and 7). The introduction of the National Literacy Strategy (Beard 1999; Riley 2001) to primary schools in England and Wales was predicated on the notion that levels of literacy were too low in many schools and that there was too great an inconsistency in achievement and methodology between schools; in particular, boys' relative under-achievement in reading and writing was highlighted as a cause for concern (Millard 1997; Barrs and Pigeon 1998; Wood 2000). Boys' differing approaches to, and participation in, literacy activities have been identified within the context of the classroom. Maynard and Lowe (1999), for example, report that teachers they interviewed confirmed many of the stereotypes about boys' attitudes towards, and attainment in, writing. Thus, boys were characterized as less likely to enjoy writing activities than girls, as having a greater reluctance to write stories and to use figurative and descriptive language, as being less able to cope with the multiple demands of story writing. Similarly, Kanaris (1999), in a study of Australian primary school children's writing, has suggested that there are very real differences in the ways in which boys and girls use writing to construct meaning:

Girls generally write longer, more complex texts. They tend to use a wide range of both verbs and adjectives and develop their texts with more focus on description and elaboration. Boys' writing tends to be more 'event focused' and is much more egocentric ... [they are] less likely than girls to remove themselves from the centre of the action and tell their stories from the viewpoint of an observer.

(1999: 266)

As with writing, so with reading; there is a widespread belief that reading communities in schools have been more relevant to girls' needs than to boys' because of their focus on fiction and narrative, because of the emphasis on emotions and relationships, and because of their discouragement of certain kinds of literature (such as comics and non-fiction texts). Boys have been shown to develop more slowly as readers, to read less, to prefer non-fiction (Hall and Coles 1997; Barrs 1998; Moss 1999). In similar vein, Millard has argued that there is 'something aversive in the experience of reading in school that results in boredom and patterns of avoidance, attitudes that are particularly marked in boys' (1997: 31). Particularly she emphasizes the extent to which reading, at home and at school, is seen as a feminized activity, with female members of the family (and primary school teachers who are more likely to be female) providing the prime support for reading and the most common role models as readers (see Chapter 6). In such a context, the value and high status of reading may not be appreciated by many boys, and Millard reports the view that many boys felt that reading was simply 'a stage to go through', and that once they could read, many boys felt they no longer needed to do so (1997: 38).

This perception of the gendered nature of writing and reading in primary schools, and of girls' greater language facility, is vital to an understanding of why some boys perform less well than they might during primary schooling. Given the high status accorded to literacy in the primary school, and its dominant underpinning of so many teaching activities, it is hardly surprising that it is seen as a crucial factor in contributing to an understanding of the apparent under-achievement of some boys. Literacy issues cannot be divorced from the context within which they operate, however, and it is vitally important, in the search for 'explanations' for the lower levels of boys' achievements in English at Key Stage 2, to explore issues linked to the cultural settings of primary schools within the wider society in which they are located.

### Laddishness and notions of masculinity

In the parallel volume on raising achievement in secondary schools (Younger et al. 2005a), we argue that the main thrust of educational research on boys points in social constructionist directions, linking the relative under-achievement of some boys to the context and the environment in which they live, experience and move (Lingard and Douglas 1999; Connell 2000; Mills 2001; Arnot 2002; Skelton and Francis 2003a; Connolly 2004). In so doing, we acknowledge that there are some commentators who argue that causal explanations should be sought essentially in biological accounts. Such arguments are centred on essentialist approaches that maintain that gender difference is genetically determined and that differing characteristics are rooted in the extent of brain structure between girls and boys (Hoff-Sommers 2000; Gurian 2001), with links to boys' hormones, specifically testosterone, and the 'natural' development of boys (Biddulph 1998a; Sax 2005). Similarly, we are aware that there are those who argue for a biological construction of masculinity, citing studies which show behavioural sex differences at a very early age, before children are able to form any notions of socially constructed gender (Connellan et al. 2000; Kimura 2000; Baron-Cohen 2003; Archer, J. 2004; Sax 2005). Nonetheless, we hold to the belief that discussion of the relative importance of socialization and biology is unhelpful since it is extremely difficult to isolate the one from the other. Indeed, recent thinking in neuroscience suggests that neuronal connections are selectively strengthened as a result of experience, that certain forms of behaviour through time will cause the structure of the brain to develop in certain ways (Head 1999) and that differential social and cultural experiences will lead to differences in neural connections (Paechter 1998; Skelton and Francis 2003a).

A focus on social constructionist perspectives, then, leads us into a discussion of masculinity and laddishness. Research within the secondary school context has suggested that boys bring with them to school notions of masculinity which are frequently in direct conflict with the ethos of the school, and that boys often conform to the macho gender regime of the local community, which might place little value on authority, academic work and formal achievement (Mac an Ghaill 1994; Rudduck et al. 1996; Salisbury and Jackson 1996; Younger and Warrington 1996; Warrington and Younger 1999). Skelton has developed this theme within the primary context, identifying – through an ethnographic case study of an inner city primary school in a deprived socio-economic context – the ways in which primary school boys learn through various discourses to position girls and women negatively

(Skelton 1996). She describes how the difficulties experienced by the local community were manifested in the school itself through a form of hegemonic masculinity which was characterized by competition, intimidation and physical aggression. The resulting tensions between the culture of the school and the local community led to the school being viewed by the local populace as ineffective and out of touch with reality (Skelton 2001). In such contexts, images of laddish masculinity are promoted, associated with power, strength and assertiveness, whereby status and self-esteem are defined through the eyes of the peer group. The images of masculinity in this school 'were not those of sporting or academic achievers but ones of physically violent, compe- titive aggressors, [conveying] implicit messages about tough masculinity' (p. 194). Learning in such contexts is neither 'cool' nor acceptable, anti- social behaviour is valued rather than disowned, and appropriate male role models might more readily be linked to challenging and denying authority, rather than to achievement and to more conformist behaviour:

> The boys in the class were positioned by multiple discourses ... the tension created was that being a school pupil and being a lad demanded conflicting behaviours. While developing self-esteem might encourage conformity to classroom rules in the boys as school pupils, the opposite [lack of conformity] was expected of the boys as 'apprentice lads' ... For the teachers, the aim was to foster a sense of responsibility both academically and behaviou- rally in the boys (and girls) as school pupils, while for the boys the main concern was to establish their masculine identity and place in the male hierarchy.
>
> (Skelton 2001: 103–4, 105)

It is clear from their behaviour, attitude and assertiveness that some boys in primary schools do not lack self-esteem; their bravado and noise as they seek to define their masculinity, their attempts to impress, their willingness to challenge the school authority structure and overstep the line, are clearly evident in different school contexts.

Masculinity is a complex and multifaceted concept (Mac an Ghaill 1994; Connell 1995; Sewell 1998; Arnot et al. 1999; Martino and Pallotta-Chiarolli 2003), with different interpretations which vary through time and space, are fluid and flexible (Francis 2000), and culturally and historically dependent (Weaver-Hightower 2003). In many institutional contexts, there is frequently a dominant version of masculinity (Skelton 2001), usually some construction of hegemonic masculinity that embodies the public face of male power, and many boys strive to construct and mould themselves into this version of masculinity, to become 'a real man', 'a typical lad', 'one of the boys'. In many primary schools, skilful and knowledgeable participation in sport – particularly football – is often a major contributor to dominant versions of masculinity (West 1996). Swain (2000) has shown, for example, how discussions about football dominate the lives and interests of many boys and are exclusive of most girls, offering membership of an 'in-group', a communal sense of inclusion:

> The bonding value of football was seen as a key component of the boys' masculinity. It had an almost tribal appeal and was a chance to 'be with your mates', to form a collective group identity and culture of understandings, values and beliefs, rules and codes of conduct and behaviour: simply, it gave an opportunity to 'belong'.
>
> (2000: 101)

To many boys it is crucially important that they are accepted by other boys, that they are able to identify with and act in line with peer group norms, so that they are not seen as 'other' or different, but rather as belonging (Skelton 2001; Martino and Pallotta-Chiarolli 2003). Football is central in this sense of belonging; supporting the 'right' team, having the 'right' kit, knowing the 'right' terminology, being up-to-date with the latest e-mail team chat, all contribute to the acceptable badge of masculinity.

*All* boys *and* girls can play this game, if they are so inclined, and spend time learning the jargon and the text; not all manage to do so with credibility, however, and others have no inclination to do so. Not all boys and girls can gain admission to the 'club' when the demands are defined in terms of physical skill and competence, for it is not a sense simply of supporting, but of actual physical involvement. Thus, physicality and athleticism become crucial; physical resources of coordination, speed, fitness and strength become dominant (Swain 2003). Skill and competence convey even more credibility and standing, bringing status and desirability, and peer group leadership. In Swain's words:

> Football acts as a model for boys, and they use the game as a way of constructing, negotiating and performing their masculinity, ... the games of playground football are viewed as a series of ritualized and fantasized performances ... a series of set-piece, highly visible, ritualized and stylized exhibitions, an open stage for boys to perform their masculinities.
>
> (2000: 103)

In some primary schools, this aspect of masculinity is embraced, with special privileges for those involved in school football, and male teachers engaging proactively with boys in informal playground games to 'break down barriers' and to 'establish a sense of togetherness with the boys'. Often girls are excluded and difference is emphasized (Skelton 2001).

This close association between images of masculinity and sport can, of course, work positively if the 'key footballers' are also academic achievers, who set a tone in the classroom which is work- and achievement-orientated. If their aspirations, and those of their parents/carers, are in line with those of the school, these boys can be key players in schools, offering positive role models and exerting a strong positive influence on the levels of engagement of other boys with school life. If not, however, and the boys are on the margins of school life and exhibit clear anti-school traits, they can exert a strong negative influence on the levels of engagement of other boys with school life. Equally, a definition of masculinity in this way through sport excludes those boys and girls who lack interest and/or skill in the physical activity, although some girls gain kudos and social standing through their association with skilful boys or through their own extensive knowledge and vociferous support of the 'right' team. More often, though, there is a process of subordination and marginalization for those on the periphery of engagement.

Such acceptance within the peer group is often dependent on an act, negotiating a particular identity, incorporating aspects of laddishness of behaviour and risk-taking, and a certain bravado and noisy demonstration of masculinity. Such behaviour, of course, can be expressed through outlets other than sport: through disruptive behaviour and attention-seeking in class (Beckett 2001; Skelton 2001), through cultural interests such as fashion, music, television programmes, computer expertise (Swain 2003), through having 'fit' (i.e. physically attractive) girl friends (Connolly 1995; Renold 2000, 2003, 2004a), through being tough and carrying out acts of daring and bravado (Swain 2003), through humour, language and dress. Boys in such contexts can become disaffected, continually disciplined, stereotyped: 'they were more likely to be drawn into fights and to develop "hardened" identities which then meant they were more likely to be noticed by teachers and disciplined for being aggressive' (Reay 2003). While such expressions of laddishness may on occasions run counter to the expectations of the home, such behaviour is seen as a reasonable cost by boys if it allows them to protect their macho image, and enables them to ensure their acceptance as part of the chosen social group. It is often an imperative if boys are to avoid peer group ostracism. The effect of peer group pressure upon image and

PTO

attitude can thus be a crucial factor affecting motivation and commit-ment to work (Tinklin et al. 2001).

To gain a good reputation in the eyes of the peer group, to be sought after, particularly by girls, boys need to be assertive and noticed by teachers and peers. In this context, the challenging and aggressive behaviour of some boys not only leads to their rejection of academic work, but is part of a complex performance (Butler 1990), an 'integral part of learning to do masculinity' (Gilbert and Gilbert 2001: 7), associated with a public acknowledgement and working out of masculinity which in itself contributes to potential under-achievement (Bohan 1997). Gaining membership of this group, fulfilling the entrance criteria, sustaining the group norms over time, is like 'passing an examination' (Martino and Pallotta-Chiarolli 2003). There are thus 'badges of masculinity' (Majors 2001) which can generate conflicts with authority structures, which in turn can create communication barriers, prevent some boys from developing positive gender identities and often generate strong counter-cultures to learning and 'a laisser-faire stance towards school which was an admirable characteristic of the "cool" culture of emerging adolescent masculinity' (Wood 2003). While some boys have the self-confidence, assurance and resilience to carry labels such as 'keener' (Wood 2003), 'geek' and 'boff', others deliberately cultivate disengagement to avoid such negative images.

### Why some boys under-achieve: laddishness as a self-protection strategy

We have discussed elsewhere (Younger et al. 2005a) how this culture of laddishness becomes manifest in anti-work attitudes and strategies, which contribute towards what Diane Reay has called 'protest mascu-linities' (Reay 2003: 163). While we have reservations, as we discuss in Chapter 3, about the all-embracing nature of notions of laddishness, there are two specific aspects which need some exploration in the context of boys' apparent under-achievement. One aspect is linked to image, as 'real boys' strive to avoid anything associated with the feminine, for fear that it might attract the label of 'homosexual'. The other aspect is the adoption of specific strategies that reduce the possibility of failure and the consequent loss of status and esteem in the group context.

It is evident from a number of studies over the past decade (Mac an Ghaill 1994; Salisbury and Jackson 1996; Kehily and Nayak 1997; Martino and Meyenn 2001; Mills 2001; Frosh et al. 2002; Martino and Pallotta-Chiarolli 2003) that homosexuality has been stigmatized within youth cultures and within schools. Boys who are identified as different – through their clothing, their voice, their mannerisms and gestures, their interests, their friendship networks – have often been exposed to homophobic abuse, most consistently from other boys (Epstein and Johnson 1998; Gilbert and Gilbert 1998; Beckett 2001; Martino and Pallotta-Chiarolli 2003). To many boys, whether heterosexual or homosexual, being labelled as 'gay' is their greatest fear, carrying with it possibilities of marginalization, abuse, shame and bullying. In Mills' words, 'homophobia ... produces a terror that ensures boys' and men's complicity in the perpetuation of societal violence' (2001: 72). Much of this work has been located in secondary schools, where the implicit homophobic culture has sometimes meant that boys have had to work hard to gain and display their badges of masculinity: displaying feelings and emotion, appreciating poetry, being involved in dance, developing caring relationships with girls which are not explicitly sexual, have all been high-risk activities for boys, carrying connotations of possible 'gayness'. This fear of homosexuality has a negative impact on boys' sense of self and their social relations with other boys and men but also with girls and women (Beckett 2001). Thus, being a 'real' boy entails adopting an oppositional position and a distancing from all that is feminine (Martino 1999; Frosh et al. 2002).

In the primary sector, such behaviour and attitudes may be less explicit, but the fear of being labelled as gay is real, nonetheless; indeed, Swain's (2003) study of junior school masculinities discovered boys' widespread use of the term 'gay' and 'poofter' as forms of inter-personal abuse in a wide variety of contexts. Some boys are really uncomfortable with this need to position themselves as 'real boys'. Thus Harry, a quiet, mature boy in an inner city primary school, with a friendship network consisting largely of girls, speaks of his fears about his imminent transfer to a single-sex secondary school:

> It was my mum's first choice, but I just don't like it there ... it's an all boys' school. It's going to be less sensitive there; sometimes boys are a bit rough and not sensitive; I'm dreading it.

Some of the most important work in this context over the last decade has been carried out by Emma Renold (2000, 2001, 2003, 2004a, 2004b). She has shown, for example, how primary school boys define their hegemonic masculinity through girlfriends and sport, and she documents how 'homophobic performances and misogyny seem to offer a way of producing "heterosexual coherence", which in turn signified a coherent masculine identity' (2000: 323). In a later study, Renold illustrates how boys who failed to cultivate their own masculinity were positioned as subordinate 'others' within a hegemonic masculine matrix that equated 'other', or 'non-macho' identifications with the feminine, and with qualities such as weakness, passivity and immaturity. Such behaviour, she argues, 'throws into doubt a boy's heterosexuality, thereby creating the potential for their behaviour and practices to be "homosexualized"' (2001: 376). Such boys were teased, excluded and humiliated for choosing not to invest in and project dominant and hegemonic forms of 'age-appropriate' (hetero) masculinity, and provoked feminized (e.g. 'sissy' and 'girl') and (homo)sexualized (e.g. 'gay', 'bender') name-calling. Interestingly, though, 'girls who crossed border crossings in their behaviours and attitudes were never the subject of derogatory homosexualized name-calling' (Renold 2004: 149a). Reporting on similar work in Australia, Jordan (1995) has argued that some primary school boys adopt a definition of masculinity as avoiding whatever is done by girls, to distance themselves from the feminine, in terms of literacy and language subjects, communication and emotional expression and academic work. She argues that the 'fighting boys' who resist the school's demands have appropriated the role of hero in the warrior narratives of little boys' fantasy games, casting the 'good boys' who conform to the requirements of the school as 'wimps' and 'sissies'.

This aspect of hegemonic masculinity means that, even in primary schools, feminized characteristics are often derided and aggressively countered, and boys adopt explicit and sometimes extreme versions of masculinity. In many schools, this is expressed in terms of adopting an anti-work stance, not striving to excel in anything other than sport, because working hard, being cooperative, quiet and engaged in school work are perceived by many boys as part of being a girl, as a feminine activity (Walkerdine 1989; Mac an Ghaill 1994; Epstein et al. 1998; Skelton 2001; Jackson 2003): 'being academically oriented, for a boy, is often devalued and denigrated because of its equation with femininity' (Renold 2001: 375). Not only this, but the explicit link with possible homosexuality is clear:

> Not only were heterosexist practices connected to specific kinds of school performance, but ... students could clearly articulate the positioning of workers and achievers as gay.
>
> (Frank et al. 2003: 122)

> If boys want to avoid the verbal and physical abuse attached to being labelled as 'feminine' or 'queer', they must avoid academic work, or at least they must appear to avoid academic work.
>
> (Jackson 2002: 40)

Jackson's words bring us to the second aspect of the debate about the impact of laddishness on boys' 'under-achievement'. Research in primary schools over the past decade, and particularly the many interviews we have carried out with boys, have made it clear to us that many boys use laddish strategies to safeguard their own position within the peer group, and to protect against failure and subsequent loss of esteem within the group. Thus, in Skelton and Francis's words,

> due to their construction of masculinity as competitive, boys who are clearly not 'winning' in terms of school achievement very quickly find other ways to demonstrate their successful masculinity (for example, by being the 'hardest', 'cheekiest to teachers' or 'anti-heroes in the classroom').
>
> (2003b: 6)

These images and strategies might be exhibited in terms of disruptive and off-task behaviour, apparent or real lack of effort in terms of classwork and homework, or a resistance to the whole ethos of the school.

Carolyn Jackson (2002, 2003) has developed this line of thinking persuasively within the context of self-worth theory, drawing on the work of motivation theorists such as Dweck (1999) and Covington (1998) who suggest that 'self-worth protection or self-handicapping strategies may be provoked by situations that provide a threat to one's self-worth' (Jackson 2002: 42). Thus, some boys have quickly realized that they are unable to be successful in the kinds of academic demands which schools make of them, and have decided not to enter the academic competition at all. As a consequence, they develop subtle strategies, cloaked in laddishness to avoid this possibility of failure, adopting what Hey et al. describe as a 'can't win, won't win and don't want to play stance ... a not trying, self-sabotaging position complicit with anti-learning' (2000).

Equally, however, this avoidance of academic work can itself be a front, in that some boys only avoid the *appearance* of engaging in academic work (Epstein et al. 1998), and adopt stances which conceal their interest or involvement, in order to preserve status within the peer group. Thus, boys have often spoken, in one-to-one interviews, of having to *pretend* not to be interested or involved in their work in order to preserve their status and protect their macho image. In such contexts, there is of course the possibility of achievement without effort, but: 'It also provides a convenient excuse if success is not forthcoming – failure without effort does not necessarily indicate a lack of ability, but success without effort indicates true genius' (Jackson 2002: 46). This is a complex issue, but it is nonetheless clear that the possibility of failure can lead to the generation of self-protection strategies. These strategies might also be a consequence of pupils' lack of self-esteem as learners, linked to their repeated failures to achieve, and the adoption of such behaviour, itself an integral element of laddishness, further militates against some boys achieving their potential.

## Conclusion

We have attempted in this chapter to contextualize the changing role of assessment within English primary schools over the past 40 years, focusing on the informality and unevenness of assessment practices in the immediate post-Plowden years, and contrasting this with the growing scale and intensity of assessment in the years since 1988. We have signalled our unease with certain aspects of this emphasis upon testing, targets and league tables, while acknowledging that the accumulation of data on a national scale has enabled us to identify inequalities and unevenness of provision and achievement at local and regional level, particularly in the contexts of gender, social class and ethnicity. However imperfect the data, policy-makers, headteachers, governors and teachers have been enabled, more effectively than before, to identify strengths and weaknesses within the system, and to address the needs of individual children.

Turning to the apparent gender differentials that exist, we have reviewed the scope of the concerns about boys' 'under-achievement' and the different perspectives which have evolved as we have sought to try to understand this phenomenon. We recognize that this debate may be transformed in the future as we continue to develop our understanding of neuro-scientific approaches to learning. Overall, however, in these discussions, we identify closely with social constructionist explanations, acknowledging that issues associated and laddishness are central to our understanding of boys' 'under-achievement'. Equally though, we recognize that the debate is more nuanced and sophisticated than this, as we show in Chapter 3: a multiplicity of masculinities and femininities exist, and some are more dominant and acceptable in some contexts than in others. To acknowledge the importance of image in impacting upon students' attitudes to work and behaviour, and to recognize the centrality of laddishness and 'ladettishness' in constructing an understanding of students' behaviours, aspirations and achievements, is not to proffer or accept a counsel of doom, but to establish a framework within which schools can construct appropriate responses and strategies, which make the transformation of aspirations and achievement acceptable to the students concerned.

# 2 The achievement debate

Over the past decade, surveys and National Curriculum assessments have shown consistently that, by the age of seven, girls perform better than boys in reading, writing and spelling. The 1997 Standard Assessment Test (SAT) results at Key Stages 1 to 3 (i.e. at ages 7, 11 and 14) ... provide *evidence of the underachievement of boys* in both primary schools and in the early years of secondary school.

(Evans et al. 1998: 1; our italics)

Early SATs data suggest that gender patterns are being shaped at an early age – girls at Key Stages 1 and 2 appear to be achieving higher performances than boys, particularly in English: more boys are scoring at the extremes of the grading system particularly at Mathematics and Science, and *are underachieving in English at ages 7 and 11.*

(Arnot et al. 1996: xii; our italics)

The statistical gap in the performance of boys in relation to girls in national tests only accounts for the *existence of the underachieving boy*: from this perspective there are no under-achieving girls.

(Jones and Myhill 2004a: 552; our italics)

As we have seen in Chapter 1, the discourse about 'under-achievement' and 'the gender gap' have become a part of the globalized educational agenda, at least in many parts of 'the developed North', in the past two decades. Unsurprisingly, discussions about the relative performance of boys and girls, and the apparent 'under-achievement' of boys, have preoccupied educational administrators, academics and school leaders in many secondary schools in the United Kingdom (Younger et al. 2005a). As standardized testing spread into Key Stages 1 and 2, however, with the subsequent publication of league tables and national profiles of results in English, mathematics and science, so this concern began to permeate through to the primary sector, with a renewed focus on gender. Not only did established gender differences exist in behaviour, learning styles and play preferences by Year 1 of primary schooling (Whitebread 1996; Francis 1997; Wood 2000; Skelton 2001; Warrington et al. 2003); emerging data from National Curriculum tests suggested that differences in achievement also existed.

These differences in the achievement of very young children, assessed in Key Stage 1 at the age of 7, were quite narrowly defined. Over the ten year period, 1995-2004, both national test data and teacher assessments of pupils (Table 2.1) revealed a consistent trend in mathematics and science, with the percentages of both girls and boys achieving the benchmark of level 2 or above slowly rising through time, and a small gender gap in girls' favour, of around 3-4 percentage points, being consistently sustained. In English, a similar pattern was discernible, although the gender gap in achievement tended to be larger, averaging at 8.9 percentage points, and was more pronounced in writing (10.1 percentage points average) than in speaking and listening (6.9 percentage points average) or in reading (8.5 percentage points). As in mathematics and science, however, the increased percentage of pupils achieving the benchmark level 2 reflects a continuing improvement through time.

**Table 2.1**  Percentage of girls and boys achieving level 2 (+) in the National Curriculum Key Stage 1 Teacher Assessments, 1995–2004

|  | 1995 | 1996 | 1997 | 1998 | 1999 | 2000 | 2001 | 2002 | 2003 | 2004 |
|---|---|---|---|---|---|---|---|---|---|---|
| **English** | | | | | | | | | | |
| girls | 86 | 84 | 85 | 86 | 87 | 88 | 89 | 89 | 89 | 89 |
| boys | 76 | 74 | 75 | 76 | 78 | 80 | 80 | 82 | 81 | 81 |
| **Speaking/ listening** | | | | | | | | | | |
| girls | 88 | 85 | 86 | 87 | 88 | 89 | 90 | 90 | 90 | 90 |
| boys | 81 | 78 | 79 | 80 | 81 | 83 | 83 | 84 | 83 | 84 |
| **Reading** | | | | | | | | | | |
| girls | 84 | 83 | 85 | 85 | 86 | 88 | 88 | 88 | 89 | 89 |
| boys | 74 | 74 | 75 | 76 | 77 | 80 | 81 | 81 | 81 | 81 |
| **Writing** | | | | | | | | | | |
| girls | 83 | 82 | 83 | 84 | 85 | 86 | 88 | 89 | 87 | 88 |
| boys | 72 | 71 | 72 | 74 | 74 | 77 | 79 | 79 | 78 | 78 |
| **Mathematics** | | | | | | | | | | |
| girls | 80 | 84 | 85 | 87 | 88 | 90 | 89 | 90 | 90 | 91 |
| boys | 76 | 80 | 82 | 83 | 85 | 86 | 88 | 87 | 87 | 88 |
| **Science** | | | | | | | | | | |
| girls | 86 | 85 | 87 | 87 | 88 | 89 | 90 | 90 | 91 | 91 |
| boys | 83 | 83 | 84 | 85 | 85 | 86 | 88 | 88 | 88 | 88 |

*Source*: DfES, Autumn Packages, 1999–2004

An analysis of the pattern of achievement recorded in the end of Key Stage 2 tests reveals similar trends. Although some of the early outcomes of National Curriculum tests must be treated with caution, partly because of the nature of the tests themselves and partly because testing was not prescribed for all schools until 1997, there are clear trends in the performance levels of girls and boys in more recent years (Figures 2.1 and 2.2). Thus:

- The gender gap in English has stabilized at around 10 percentage points since 2000, with around 80 per cent of girls and 70 per cent of boys within the cohort regularly achieving level 4 or above in the National Curriculum tests.
- Girls' and boys' performance levels in mathematics have been remarkably consistent since 2000, with a negligible gender gap.
- Similarly, there has been a sustained pattern of performance in science, with little or no gender differentiation, although science outcomes generally have been markedly higher than in mathematics (86 per cent in science compared to 74 per cent in mathematics in 2004).
- These patterns of achievement are replicated at higher levels (level 5 or above) in English and science (Figure 2.3), but in mathematics more boys than girls normally achieve at level 5 attainment (29 per cent compared to 25 per cent).

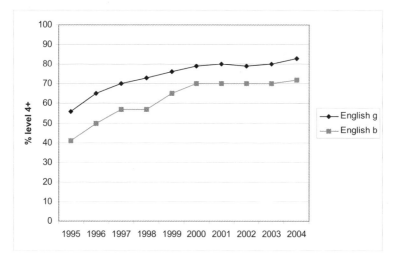

**Figure 2.1** Percentages of girls and boys achieving level 4 (+) in the National Curriculum Key Stage 2 English Tests, 1995–2004
*Source*: DfES, Autumn Packages, 1990–2004

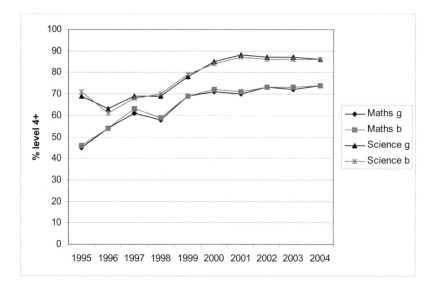

**Figure 2.2**   Percentages of girls and boys achieving level 4 (+) in the National Curriculum Key Stage 2 Mathematics and Science Tests, 1995–2004

*Source*: DfES, Autumn Packages (1999–2004)

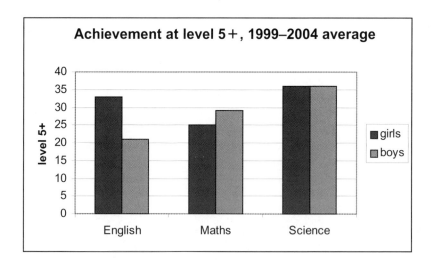

**Figure 2.3**   Percentages of girls and boys achieving level 5 (+) in the National Curriculum Key Stage 2 Tests, 1999–2004: five-year rolling average

*Source*: Autumn Packages (1999–2004)

It is thus the nature and persistence of the gap between the levels of girls' and boys' performances in English that largely account for the overall difference in the performance levels of girls and boys in the Key Stage 2 National Curriculum tests. Closer analysis of the English data through time highlights the scale of the disparity: not only is there a wider gender differential between girls and boys in writing than in reading (see Figure 2.4), but these differentials have been more or less static, at around 6 per cent for reading and 15 per cent for writing. Significantly, though, the data also reveal lower levels of girls' *and* boys' performance in writing (71 per cent of girls and 56 per cent of boys achieved level 4 or above in writing in 2004) than in reading (where 87 per cent of girls and 79 per cent of boys achieved level 4 or above). These differences were confirmed in the international survey of reading standards of 10-year-olds carried out in 2001:

> In common with all other countries participating in PIRLS (Progress in International Reading Literacy Study), the perfor-mance of girls was significantly better than boys ... the difference in mean achievement of boys and girls in England was 22 scale points, compared to an international difference of 20 points.
>
> (Twist et al. 2003: 24)

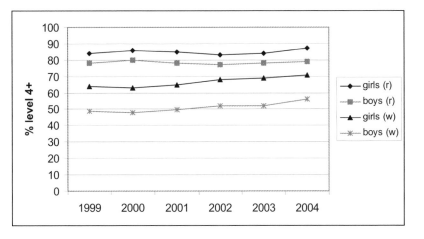

**Figure 2.4** Percentages of girls and boys achieving level 4 (+) in the National Curriculum Key Stage 2 Tests in Reading and Writing, 1999–2004

*Source*: DfES, Autumn Packages (1999–2004)

Indeed, the gender differential in England was greater than in 22 other countries which took part in the study, and was only smaller than in eight participating countries. Equally, however, in terms of absolute attainment internationally, measured through overall scores of average reading achievement, boys in England had the third highest score, and girls in England the second highest score.

## Dimensions of the gender gap at Key Stages 1 and 2: increasing complexity

An analysis of levels of performance within English at Key Stages 1 and 2 reveals an increasing complexity, however, and warns against the dangers of too simplistic an approach. In certain local education authority areas (LEAs), the percentage of boys and/or girls achieving at least level 4 in their National Curriculum English tests in 2004 is well below the national average of 72 per cent of boys and 83 per cent of girls (Figure 2.5). Predictably, there is also a group of local education authorities where the performances of boys and/or girls are above the national average (Figure 2.6). In many respects, the LEAs represented in Figures 2.5 and 2.6 are not surprising: local authorities where populations have greater affluence and disposable incomes, higher socio-economic status, lower levels of unemployment and lower social deprivation indices are more likely to be represented in Figure 2.6 than in Figure 2.5. Equally, the LEAs identified on Figure 2.5 tend to be concentrated in inner urban environments, more associated with socio-economic deprivation and longer-term unemployment. It is worth noting, however, that there is still a marked gender dimension to be considered here; boys' performance levels show a greater disparity around the mean, with more LEAs recording levels which are either above or below the national mean, than do girls' levels.

Figures 2.7 and 2.8 take the analysis one stage further, by focusing on the scale of the gender gap in English Key Stage 2 results in 2004. It is immediately clear from these maps that we need to take great care when discussing the concept of the gender gap, for both maps reveal that a gender gap can exist as a result of quite different outcomes. Thus in Figure 2.7, which identifies LEAs where the gender gap is at least 3 percentage points above the national average, there are LEAs such as Darlington, Gateshead, Poole and Dorset where the large gender gap is a result of girls' levels of performance being well above the national average, while the level of boys' performances is close to the national average. Equally, however, Figure 2.7 also identifies similar LEAs, such as Middlesbrough, Rochdale, Reading and Cornwall, where a similar gender

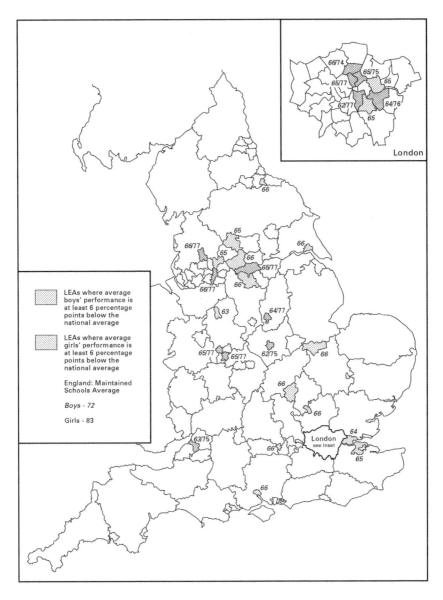

**Figures 2.5** Key Stage 2 National Curriculum English Tests, 2004. Local Education Authorities with lowest percentage of pupils achieving level 4 (+)

*Source*: National Curriculum Assessments at Key Stage 2 for 11 Year Olds in England, 2004 www.dfes.gov.uk/rsgateway/DB/SFR/s000542, accessed 28 April 2005.

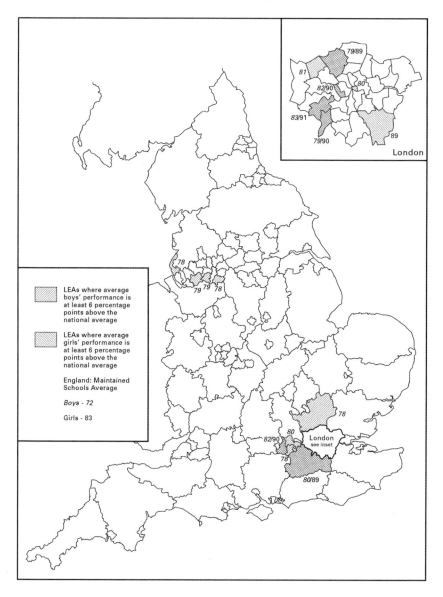

**Figure 2.6** Key Stage 2 National Curriculum English Tests, 2004. Local Education Authorities with highest percentage of pupils achieving level 4 (+)

*Source*: National Curriculum Assessments at Key Stage 2 for 11 Year Olds in England, 2004 www.dfes.gov.uk/rsgateway/DB/SFR/s000542, accessed 28 April 2005.

gap exists for quite different reasons: here, the gender gap reflects levels of boys' performances which are well below the national average, while girls' perform close to the national average. A similar gender gap can exist, therefore, in broadly similar local education authorities, but for quite different reasons, suggesting that the impact of school and LEA policies are equally as important in impacting upon pupils' performances as the socio-economic contexts in which the LEAs are located. Figure 2.8, which pinpoints three groups of LEAs where the gender gap is at least 2 percentage points below the national average, reiterates the need for caution when discussing this notion of the gender gap. Although LEAs such as Stockport, Haringey and Hartlepool have the same 8 percentage points difference between the performance of girls and boys in Key Stage 2 English in 2004, their data reflect quite different outcomes: in LEAs like Stockport, a gender gap below the national average reflects a level of performance from both girls and boys which is significantly above the national average (86 per cent of girls, 78 per cent of boys), while in LEAs such as Haringey, the levels of performance of both girls and boys are well below the national average (74 per cent of girls, 66 per cent of boys), and in LEAs such as Hartlepool, levels of performance are close to the national average (82 per cent of girls, 74 per cent of boys). While elements of this regional analysis are hardly surprising, given the nature of statistics, it does warn us yet again against making simplistic generalizations about the gender gap, without proper vigilance and contextualization.

A more sophisticated interrogation of the pattern of achievement and of the nature of the gender gap leads us to a focus on the intersections between gender and ethnicity. At Key Stage 1, an analysis based on pupils' ethnicities reveals that the gender gap did not vary significantly from national patterns (Table 2.2); except for the very small number of traveller and gypsy/roma children (less than 0.002 per cent of the population), the gender gap for all ethnic groups was close to the national average in both reading and writing, and in mathematics. This conceals significant variations in the levels of boys' and girls' achievements *between* ethnic groups, however, particularly between Chinese and Indian children, on the one hand, and Pakistani, Bangladeshi and Black pupils on the other.

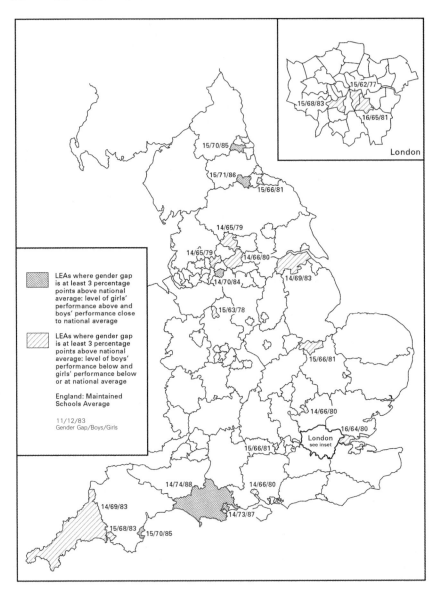

**Figure 2.7** Key Stage 2 National Curriculum English Tests, 2004. Local Education Authorities with greatest gender gap in terms of percentage of pupils achieving level 4 (+)

*Source*: National Curriculum Assessments at Key Stage 2 for 11 Year Olds in England, 2004 www.dfes.gov.uk/rsgateway/DB/SFR/s000542, accessed 28 April 2005.

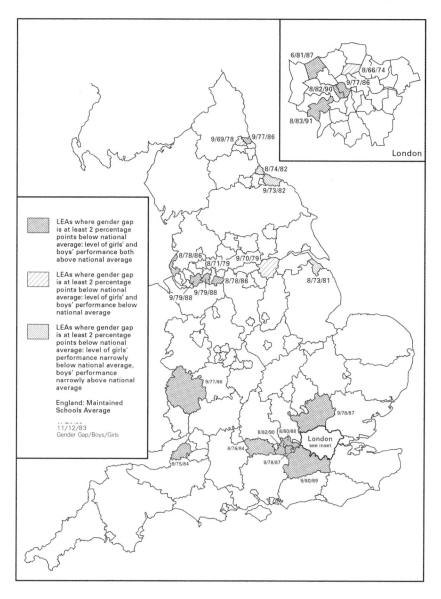

**Figure 2.8** Key Stage 2 National Curriculum English Tests, 2004. Local Education Authorities with lowest gender gap in terms of percentage of pupils achieving level 4 (+)

*Source*: National Curriculum Assessments at Key Stage 2 for 11 Year Olds in England, 2004 www.dfes.gov.uk/rsgateway/DB/SFR/s000542 accessed 28 April 2005.

**Table 2.2** Percentage pupils achieving at Key Stage 1, Level 2 and above, 2004, by ethnicity and gender

|  | Reading | | Writing | | Mathematics | |
|---|---|---|---|---|---|---|
|  | boys | girls | boys | girls | boys | girls |
| White | 81 | 90 | 77 | 88 | 90 | 92 |
| White British | 82 | 90 | 77 | 88 | 90 | 92 |
| Irish | 82 | 90 | 78 | 88 | 90 | 93 |
| Traveller of Irish Heritage | 25 | 38 | 22 | 38 | 51 | 49 |
| Gypsy/Roma | 36 | 53 | 32 | 54 | 50 | 67 |
| Any other | 77 | 84 | 72 | 83 | 88 | 90 |
| Mixed | 81 | 89 | 76 | 88 | 89 | 92 |
| Asian | 78 | 85 | 73 | 83 | 85 | 88 |
| Indian | 86 | 92 | 81 | 91 | 91 | 93 |
| Pakistani | 73 | 81 | 68 | 79 | 82 | 84 |
| Bangladeshi | 72 | 81 | 68 | 80 | 82 | 85 |
| Any other | 80 | 86 | 76 | 85 | 89 | 90 |
| Black | 75 | 84 | 68 | 81 | 82 | 86 |
| Black Caribbean | 76 | 86 | 69 | 82 | 83 | 88 |
| Black African | 74 | 82 | 68 | 79 | 81 | 86 |
| Any other | 76 | 86 | 69 | 83 | 84 | 87 |
| Chinese | 87 | 92 | 85 | 92 | 95 | 96 |
| Other | 72 | 78 | 66 | 77 | 85 | 85 |
| All pupils | 81 | 89 | 78 | 88 | 88 | 91 |

Source: www.dfes.gov.uk/rsgateway/DB/SFR/s000564/SFR08-2005v2.pdf (last accessed 20 April 2005)

These variations are exacerbated when performance levels are analysed at Key Stage 2 (Table 2.3). Once again, however, it is not marked differences from the national gender gap that attract the attention, but the differences in the achievement levels *between* ethnic groups. Thus, in English tests in 2004, although the gender gap between Chinese girls and boys reflected the national average of 11 percentage points, a higher proportion of Chinese girls (87 per cent) and boys (76 per cent) achieved level 4 or above at Key Stage 2; similar higher than average performance levels were recorded by Chinese pupils in mathematics and science. The same pattern of higher than average performance was evident also in all three subjects among Indian pupils, although the fact that a higher proportion of Indian boys (79 per cent) achieved level 4 or above in English than boys in any other ethnic group, meant that the gender gap was narrower than the national average. At the other extreme, pupils of Pakistani, Bangladeshi, Black African and Black Caribbean ethnicities performed less well, with significantly lower proportions reaching the Key Stage 2/level 4 benchmark than the national average, not only in English, but in each core subject. While the gender gap was occasionally different from the national average in some instances (for example, with Black Caribbean pupils where the performances of boys were markedly depressed in each subject), the main concern is with the high proportion of pupils who performed below the 'expected' levels. There is strong resonance here with Gillborn and Mirza's work on educational inequality, race and gender (Gillborn and Mirza 2000) and with more recent work by Archer and Francis (2005), and with the view that ethnicity differences are as significant, if not more so, than gender in explanatory frameworks which consider differential achievements between and within groups of boys and girls.

**Table 2.3** Percentage pupils achieving at Key Stage 2, level 4 and above, 2004, by ethnicity and gender

|  | English | | Mathematics | | Science | |
|---|---|---|---|---|---|---|
|  | boys | girls | boys | girls | boys | girls |
| White | 72 | 84 | 75 | 74 | 87 | 87 |
| White British | 73 | 84 | 75 | 74 | 87 | 87 |
| Irish | 77 | 87 | 79 | 78 | 88 | 88 |
| Traveller of Irish Heritage | 17 | 30 | 23 | 23 | 36 | 40 |
| Gypsy/Roma | 22 | 38 | 24 | 27 | 42 | 48 |
| Any other | 70 | 80 | 74 | 72 | 83 | 83 |
| Mixed | 74 | 85 | 73 | 74 | 86 | 87 |
| Asian | 68 | 79 | 70 | 69 | 79 | 79 |
| Indian | 79 | 87 | 80 | 79 | 87 | 87 |
| Pakistani | 61 | 74 | 62 | 60 | 72 | 73 |
| Bangladeshi | 66 | 77 | 68 | 65 | 77 | 77 |
| Any other | 70 | 81 | 77 | 77 | 82 | 82 |
| Black | 62 | 77 | 61 | 65 | 75 | 79 |
| Black Caribbean | 61 | 79 | 58 | 64 | 75 | 81 |
| Black African | 63 | 76 | 62 | 65 | 74 | 76 |
| Any other | 64 | 78 | 63 | 65 | 77 | 82 |
| Chinese | 76 | 87 | 89 | 90 | 88 | 90 |
| Other | 61 | 71 | 70 | 69 | 75 | 76 |
| All pupils | 72 | 83 | 74 | 73 | 85 | 86 |

*Source*: www.dfes.gov.uk/rsgateway/DB/SFR/s000564/SFR08-2005v2.pdf (last accessed 20 April 2005)

One final aspect of this discussion of achievement and the gender gap needs mention, and this relates to the performances of boys and girls who are eligible for free school meals. Data on affluence and deprivation, on class and welfare, are not accessible at the level of the individual child or individual schools, and although various government ministers have suggested a direct link between under-achievement, class and deprivation (Blunkett 2000), the only analysis available relies upon the surrogate data of eligibility to free school meals (DfES 2005a). When the data is scrutinized at this level, however, stark differences emerge. In 2004, at Key Stage 1, the gender gap was exacerbated, notably in reading and writing, because boys entitled to free school meals (FSM) not only performed significantly less well than other boys but also relatively less well than girls eligible to free school meals (Table 2.4). Indeed, while fewer girls eligible for FSM achieved level 2 or above in reading and writing compared to other girls (percentage points difference 16/17), the disparity for boys eligible for FSM was around 21/22 percentage points. Similar outcomes were evident at Key Stage 2 (Table 2.5) for English, where not only were achievement levels of pupils eligible for FSMs lower, but the gender gap was wider (15 percentage points) because of the relatively poorer performance of boys eligible for free school meals.

The multifaceted nature of this discussion alerts us, then, to the need we have highlighted elsewhere (Younger et al. 2005a) for sensitivity and caution when discussing the notion of the gender gap. Particularly, it is important to avoid what Gorard (2000) has labelled as the 'politician's error', confusing percentage point differences and percentage changes. Thus, a change in the percentage of boys achieving the

**Table 2.4** Percentage pupils achieving at Key Stage 1, level 2 and above, 2004, by free school meals and gender

|  | Reading | | Writing | | Mathematics | |
|---|---|---|---|---|---|---|
|  | boys | girls | boys | girls | boys | girls |
| Non-Free School Meals eligibility (81% of population) | 85 | 92 | 80 | 91 | 91 | 94 |
| Free School Meals eligibility (19% of population) | 64 | 76 | 58 | 74 | 78 | 82 |
| All pupils | 81 | 89 | 78 | 88 | 88 | 91 |

*Source*: www.dfes.gov.uk/rsgateway/DB/SFR/s000564/SFR08-2005v2.pdf (last accessed 20 April 2005)

**Table 2.5**  Percentage pupils achieving at Key Stage 2, level 4 and above, 2004, by free school meals and gender

|  | English | | Mathematics | | Science | |
|---|---|---|---|---|---|---|
|  | boys | girls | boys | girls | boys | girls |
| Non-Free School Meals eligibility (82% of population) | 76 | 86 | 78 | 77 | 89 | 89 |
| Free School Meals eligibility (18% of population) | 51 | 66 | 55 | 55 | 71 | 71 |
| All pupils | 72 | 83 | 74 | 73 | 85 | 86 |

Source: www.dfes.gov.uk/rsgateway/DB/SFR/s000564/SFR08-2005v2.pdf (last accessed 20 April 2005)

benchmark grades in English (level 4 or above) at Key Stage 2, for example, from 65 per cent in 1999 to 72 per cent in 2004 (Figure 2.1), is an increase of 7 percentage points, but a 10.8 per cent positive change in the level of boys' performances; similarly, the percentage points change for girls is also 7 percentage points (in 1999, 76 per cent of girls achieved the benchmark level, whereas, in 2004, 83 per cent of girls did so), but the percentage change is 9.2 per cent. In similar vein, Hammersley (2001) points out that there are a number of methodological issues which we must consider if we are to avoid some of the misconceptions which confuse the debate. In the primary context, for example, there are issues in some schools associated with the number of pupils who have been disapplied,[1] and the number of pupils assessed only through teacher assessment because of absence for the test. Particularly in the primary context, there is the difficulty – if not the impossibility – of making year-on-year comparisons of trends of performance because of the small scale of the cohort, making statistical comparisons unreliable.

## 'Under-achievement'

There is an interesting presumption in much of the literature, as we show in the quotations which introduce this chapter, that differential achievement between girls and boys – and the subsequent gender gap – is indicative of under-achievement of boys. As we have already illustrated, however, achievement patterns differ markedly, according to local authorities, ethnicity and eligibility for free school meals, so the actual under-achievement scene is much more complex than this, and gender is only one component. Equally, we have suggested that a gender gap might differ from the national average as a result of a number of factors, and need not in any way be synonymous with 'under-achievement'. Some of the LEAs in England identified in Figure 2.7, for example, had a gender gap at Key Stage 2 (in English, in 2004) which was *above* the national average because more girls achieved level 4 or above while boys in those areas performed at around the national average; this hardly indicates under-achievement *per se*. Similarly, some of the LEAs in Figure 2.8 exhibited a lower than average gender gap, but this reflected the fact that both girls' and boys' performance levels were *below* the national average, and might indicate 'under-achievement'. Any link between a gender gap and patterns of achievement and under-achievement is far more complex than might be casually assumed, therefore.

This complexity highlights the need to reflect on different perspectives on 'under-achievement', and to re-examine ways in which the concept is used in different contexts. Indeed, the whole notion of 'under-achievement' causes considerable difficulty; West and Pennell (2003: 4), for example, claim that the term is widely used but rarely clearly defined, and that 'under-achievement' is a concept about which there is no consensus, having different connotations to different individuals. Plewis (1991) makes the distinction between sociological interpretations of under-achievement, which tend to relate to a group whose mean achievement falls below that of a selected reference group, and psychological interpretations, which place more emphasis on under-achievement at an individual basis, measured as the discrepancy between a test for individual intelligence, such as IQ tests and cognitive ability tests, and individual performances in educational tests such as national curriculum tests. In the psychological sense, then, applied to the simplistic gender discourse, it is the individual child (usually a boy) who under-achieves when his apparent potential (often assumed to be measured in Key Stage 1 tests) is not matched by subsequent performance in Key Stage 2 tests. In the sociological context, under-achievement is associated with a group, again normally of boys, whose under-achievement is defined in terms of the relativity of their performance *vis-à-vis* girls. It is this view which is enshrined in the quotations at the beginning of this chapter; performance and achievement are compared against another group, rather than against individual potential. This distinction is particularly relevant within the context of discussions about the gender gap, because too often our use of 'under-achievement' is ill-defined and hinders understanding. We need, as Smith (2003) argues, to re-examine what we mean by 'under-achievement', what 'under-achievement' is in relation to, and how we might reliably identify those who under-achieve.

Equally, there are occasions when 'under-achievement' is confused with low achievement. Indeed, one of the issues in the early stages of our own work on the 'Raising Boys' Achievement' project was to clarify with project schools the reasons why they were identifying some boys as members of focus groups for interview; while some of these boys *were* clearly under-achieving, in terms of the work they were producing as against their own potential as defined by benchmark tests, others were performing at a low level compared to their peer group but at an acceptable level when compared against their own prior achievements. This scenario is not unusual; Jones and Myhill, for example, record similar findings:

> It emerged that the term 'underachievement' was proving problematic because, frequently, those selected as under-achievers were low achievers, including some pupils with special educational needs. For these teachers the terms under-achievement referred to low levels of performance, not to children whose performance was lower than they might have expected.
>
> (2004b: 551)

It is crucial in any discussion, therefore, that we avoid this tendency to treat 'under-achievement' and 'low achievement' as synonymous (Smith 2002). In the secondary context, for example, we identified highly able boys and girls, who had indeed been achieving at a relatively high level, but were 'under-achieving' (in the psychological interpretation) against their prior attainment, although they were frequently not perceived as such; their under-performance remained hidden (Warrington and Younger 1999). There is a perception issue here, of course, which can engender complacency, particularly in schools in affluent locations where children achieve at high levels in national tests.

These perceptions of ability and achievement can also reinforce some of the gender stereotypes we highlight in Chapter 3. Jones and Myhill (2004a), for example, suggest that teachers' constructions of under-achievement often differ according to gender, with under-achieving girls perceived as lacking understanding and confidence while conforming to the school ethos. Under-achieving boys, in contrast, are more likely to be defined in terms of their challenging behaviour and the frustrations they express in trying to accommodate to the school's ethos. As a result, Jones and Myhill argue, girls are far more likely to be described as high achievers than boys, and boys are twice as likely to be described as under-achievers than girls. This relates back again to the recognition – or rather the lack of recognition – of under-achievement, and the performance of some girls at school. Increasingly, it is argued

(Warrington and Younger 2000; Arnot and Gubb 2001; Jones and Myhill 2004b) that teachers frequently do not recognize disengaged and off-task girls in classrooms, or focus upon girls' changing attitudes to learning as they progress through school. Although girls are sometimes disruptive, disinterested and detached in the classroom, and indeed closer to the conventional image of under-achieving boys (Osler et al. 2002; Jackson 2003, 2004), their *under-achievement* may not be recognized because their achievement levels are frequently higher than those of similar boys and because their disengagement in academic work is more subtle and less explicit. Here, then, is under-achievement which is less visible (Younger et al. 2005a), with the under-achieving girl remaining 'a shadowy vague figure' (Jones and Myhill 2004b: 560).

## The 'value-added' debate

The increasing emphasis on performance and accountability in the English education system, with the introduction of the National Curriculum, national testing at Key Stages 1 to 4 and the publication of annual league tables of school results, reinforced the need for a more sophisticated debate on notions of 'achievement and under-achievement'. Initial data sets, at national and local authority levels, failed to depict anything other than crude measures of performance, and in most cases merely replicated broader social and economic data. The development of value-added measures (Fitz-Gibbon 1996; DfES 2002, 2004a, 2004b, 2005b) was one attempt to bring an increasing sophistication of analysis into the system, to enable students' progress and attainments through time to be defined. Thus, in the primary sector in England, it is now claimed that 'value-added' comparisons can be made between an individual pupil's performance in the National Curriculum tests at Key Stage 1 and their subsequent performance at the end of Key Stage 2, and eventually related, within their secondary education, to their performance in GCSE/GNVQ examinations:

> We have developed a way of measuring the progress that individual pupils have made between taking assessment tests when they are generally aged 7 and in Year 2 (KS1) and assessment tests when they are generally aged 11 and in Year 6 (KS2). We call this the value added measure. Value added measures are intended to allow fairer comparisons between schools with different pupil intakes. For example, school A might show high percentages of pupils achieving Level 4 and above, while school B shows lower percentages. But in value

added terms, the pupils at school B may have made more progress than other pupils who were performing at the same level at KS1, and therefore have a higher value added 'score' than school A.

(DfES 2005b: 1)

Additionally, primary schools are also enabled, through Autumn Package data (DfES 2004a, 2005b) to compare the performance of their own cohort of boys and girls at Key Stage 2 with the 'the median Key Stage 2 equivalent performance of other pupils in other schools, with the same or similar prior attainment at KS1'. Thus, it is claimed, the progress of similar students in different schools can be compared throughout their primary schooling, specifically at the end of each Key Stage, and indeed, schools are encouraged to use the Autumn Package data to compare their own 'performance' against similar schools.

Value-added measures such as these, reinforced by school-specific PANDAS (Performance and Assessment Reports), by LAs' own analyses and by commercially marketed predictive measures such as the NFER cognitive ability tests (CAT), (Thorndike et al. 1986) and the information system for the middle years (MidYIS) developed by the University of Durham, have provided schools, parents and governing bodies with a mass of data which enable them, if they are so disposed, to reflect in detail about the performance of individual children and cohorts of pupils through time, and to make comparisons between their own school and others in the locality and elsewhere. There are implicit dangers in this approach, as we discuss later, but it cannot be disputed that, interpreted with care, the use of value-added data can offer valuable perspectives on achievement levels and identify aspects of under-achievement that might exist within a school, in whatever contexts.

A national value-added analysis, carried out in 2002 (National Statistical Bulletin/DfES 2003) revealed interesting gender-based perspectives on achievement and under-achievement (Table 2.6).[2] This analysis was based upon the results of approximately 644,100 pupils (51 per cent boys, 49 per cent girls) whose 1998 Key Stage 1 results were matched to their 2002 Key Stage 2 results, to identify the progress they had made during the four years of their Key Stage 2 primary schooling. Although this data set does not include all pupils, but only those who achieved at the 'expected' level (i.e. level 2c) or above at Key Stage 1, the analysis does confirm some of the patterns *and* some of the complexities identified earlier in this chapter. Thus, for *these* pupils, this analysis reiterates the superior performance of girls in all ethnic groups in English, particularly in writing. Equally, however, the data show that in all ethnic groups except Chinese, more boys than girls progressed in mathematics and science. As with the national picture for all boys and girls, the lowest levels of progress (except in science) was made by Black Other, Black Caribbean and Black African boys, and there was a stark disparity for both girls and boys in all ethnic groups in their performance levels for reading and writing, with the closest correlation being achieved by Pakistani and Bangladeshi girls (Table 2.6).

This national value-added analysis highlights other dimensions of the gender and achievement debate, however, which often receive less emphasis. There is, for example, the relative poor performance in writing of pupils in the majority ethnic group, white girls as well as white boys. Not only did fewer white boys make the expected level of progress during Key Stage 2 (only 36 per cent), but this was true too, for the white girls (with only 47 per cent of those who achieved level 2c also achieving level 4 at the end of Key Stage 2). Interestingly, too, there was not a gender gap, within this value-added analysis, between the performance of white girls and white boys in reading; nonetheless, higher proportions of Bangladeshi and Black Other girls, and Chinese girls and boys, achieved the expected level in reading at Key Stage 2. It is worth reiterating, too, that fewer girls achieved expected levels at Key Stage 2, across virtually all ethnic groups, in mathematics and science, than is revealed in a comparison of national statistics for all boys and girls. Interesting subtleties emerge, then, when we examine patterns of achievement in

**Table 2.6** Progression of pupils from level 2c at Key Stage 1, 1998, to the expected level (or above) at Key Stage 2, 2002, by gender and ethnicity

| | Percentage of pupils achieving at or above the expected level at KS 2 | | | | | | | | | |
| | English | | Mathematics | | Science | | Reading | | Writing | |
| Ethnicity | Girls | Boys | Girls | Boys | Girls | Boys | Girls | Boys | Girls | Boys |
| --- | --- | --- | --- | --- | --- | --- | --- | --- | --- | --- |
| White | 70 | 66 | 59 | 70 | 85 | 90 | 78 | 78 | 47 | 36 |
| Indian | 75 | 71 | 69 | 79 | 86 | 90 | 76 | 78 | 64 | 51 |
| Pakistani | 67 | 66 | 58 | 71 | 77 | 84 | 68 | 72 | 60 | 48 |
| Bangladeshi | 84 | 74 | 67 | 78 | 85 | 88 | 82 | 78 | 75 | 57 |
| Black Caribbean | 67 | 54 | 52 | 57 | 81 | 84 | 73 | 66 | 53 | 36 |
| Black African | 73 | 65 | 61 | 66 | 81 | 82 | 77 | 71 | 58 | 45 |
| Black Other | 73 | 60 | 56 | 61 | 85 | 88 | 80 | 73 | 54 | 33 |
| Chinese | 90 | 79 | 89 | 94 | 97 | 92 | 92 | 85 | 76 | 60 |

*Source*: National Statistical Bulletin/DfES (2003).
(www.dfes.gov.uk/rsgateway/DB/SBu/b000402/pupil_progress_final.pdf (last accessed 2 May 2005)

ethnicity and gender terms which are defined in such national value-added data sets. As we discuss in Chapter 3, these patterns again challenge the homogeneity of 'boys' and 'girls', and the notion that we can make valid generalizations about 'boys' and 'girls'. Such discussions alert us, too, to the dangers of assuming that all girls, even those who achieve at 'expected' levels at Key Stage 1, continue to achieve at Key Stage 2 and beyond.

The increasing sophistication of methods of value-added analysis, however, must not conceal some of the inherent problems associated with their development and use. Although commentaries accompanying value-added analyses warn against simplistic predictions, the dangers of extrapolating from small samples and comparing from year-to-year, and using predictions as a guarantee of future performance (University of Durham 2003; DfES 2004a), the nature and promotion of such analyses tend to imply that it is possible, within broad guidelines, to anticipate a given future level of performance for students who have a prior level of potential. Indeed, the very language of the National Curriculum tests in England is predicated on such assumptions:

> The national levels have been designed so that most pupils will progress approximately one level every two years. The expected level at each Key Stage describes the level achieved by the typical pupil. The expected levels are a Level 2c at Key Stage 1, a level 4 at Key Stage 2 and levels 5 or 6 at Key Stage 3.
>
> (DfES 2004b)

This approach assumes, though, that it *is* realistic to expect most students to achieve a steady and sustained rate of progress through their schooling, and that such progress can be accurately measured through formal tests, so that 'under-achieving' pupils can be identified against their potential, as demonstrated in previous assessments. There are a number of dubious issues with such a notion, however, and limitations on the credibility of aspects of value-added data (Goldstein 2001; Gray et al. 2003). Such an approach places heavy reliance on students' performance on a limited number of specific occasions (when they are assessed on National Curriculum tests or sit psychometric tests), it assumes reliability and validity of assessment techniques and gender-fair tests (Gipps and Murphy 1994; Black and Wiliam 1998; James 1998), and it can over-play the impact of pupils' prior educational experiences (such as the quality of their educational experiences in nursery or infants' school) on their subsequent rates of progress and their achievements.

Within the primary context, Tymms and Dean (2004) have been particularly critical of the worth of value-added data, particularly as published within the context of primary school league tables. They argue:

> The small size of many primary schools will result in wild fluctuations in the official statistics from year-to-year ... the quality of end of Key Stage 1 data, (particularly) internal marking and the possibility of differences between infant schools and all through primary schools make the validity of comparisons between the different schools questionable ... value-added scores do not take account of pupil turnover and the fact that, for many schools, a high proportion of their pupils were not on their school roll for all of the preceding 4 years, (and) the results do not compare like with like.
>
> (2004: 1)

They conclude that, 'although value-added information is an essential tool for professionals, the publishing of value-added indicators in their current form is misleading and should be discontinued' (2004: 1). To be fair, current thinking within DfES recognizes some of these short-comings, and there are attempts to develop a more sophisticated and reliable 'contextual value-added' methodology for the KS1 to KS2 transition, to be piloted in 2006, to 'take account of not only prior achievement but also a number of other pupil and school characteristics associated with performance differences but outside a school's control' (DfES 2005c). These include not only factors such as gender, ethnicity, special educational needs, level of free school meals, and EAL (English as an additional language) status, but wider-ranging considerations such as pupils' ages within the school year, a postcode measure of affluence and deprivation, mobility and looked-after-children status.

This approach to contextual value-added data may well address some of the criticisms voiced about the use of value-added data in the primary sector, although our own experiences in working with primary schools on the RBA Project suggests strongly that value-added analyses are often afforded a status and a degree of objectivity beyond their merits, and are frequently used without discernment and appropriate caution. Equally, there is the possibility that highly valued pupil aptitudes and skills, such as problem-solving, collaboration and decision-making, creativity and imagination, are downplayed and under-valued within such a tightly constrained ethos. In such contexts, both the differing aspects and the true extent of pupils' potential may be under-estimated, and decision-makers can become fixed on notions of ability which can lead schools to set targets which are too low and which can result in pupils being offered an educational diet (in terms of sets, learning experiences and even schools) that offer insufficiently challenging demands to the students. Then, value-added measures can lead to what is effectively under-prediction, which in turn generates low expectations and low achievement levels, which may in turn be unrecognized under-achievement!

## Reflections on the achievement debate

The debate about the gender gap and under-achievement in English primary schools is complex and multifaceted. The contextualization of the debate within the government's agenda to raise standards, particularly of literacy and numeracy, meant that the debate inevitably assumed a political complexion (Alexander 2004b). Early attempts to develop and publish national league tables, comparing schools' performances, were rudimentary and imperfect (Gray et al. 1999; Goldstein 2001). Support materials, in the form of booster materials and 'catch-up' curricular materials, homework clubs and twilight and Saturday morning clubs, reinforced an increasing obsession with the benchmark grades, particularly at Key Stage 2, and a risk of re-creating the GCSE A*–C economy (Gillborn and Youdell 2000) of the secondary sector.

Indeed, in many schools, a clear outcome was that resources, energy and effort were directed to a small number of borderline students, usually containing a high proportion of boys, who were neither secure in their chances of obtaining these benchmark grades, or perceived as beyond hope. As we indicate elsewhere (Younger et al. 2005a), there was much in English education at the turn of the century, in the primary sector as well as in the secondary sector, to suggest that this understandable preoccupation of schools with the proportion of boys and girls achieving the benchmark grades, was distorting educational provision and equality for all. The fixation with league table position and the subsequent effect upon school reputation, student numbers and levels of resourcing, was leading schools to adopt what Gillborn and Youdell called 'a form of *educational triage*, a means of rationing support so that some pupils are targeted for additional time and energy' (2000: 134).

At the same time, underpinning the National Curriculum and measures of value-added, and central to the DfES Autumn Package (DfES 2004a) is the assumption that there is an expected rate of progress which most children will make in a Key Stage of their education (for example from level 2 to levels 4 across Key Stage 2). Such a view implies that ability is inherent, that it is fixed, that it can be measured accurately and that 'in measuring ability one is somehow getting at an underlying characteristic which explains or predicts an individual's performance in another activity such as reading (or) general educational attainment'

(Kershner 2003: 45). Test results, whether at Key Stage 1 or Key Stage 2, thus come to be seen as offering a measure of future potential for learning and achievement, based on the implicit assumption that intelligence is stable and fixed, and a good predictor of educational success and potential.

There are a number of dangers with such an assumption, particularly related to expectations, aspirations and self-fulfilling prophecies. Hart et al. (2004), in their powerful and illuminating discussion of teaching practices and discourses which are free from such determinist beliefs about ability, identify the very real dangers intrinsic in an unthinking approach to the notion of inherent ability: of a restricted notion of human educability, of fixed and identifiable ability labels which are absolute and predict future progress, of the minimalism of expectations of students' potential, of creating a sense of powerlessness in teachers, schools and indeed parents. In essence, it presents many teachers with an enormous dilemma, since:

> The new emphases on target-setting and value-added measures of achievement have made it increasingly difficult for teachers who reject the fixed view of measurable ability to hold on to their principles, since they are continually being required to act as if they subscribe to it.
>
> (2004: 9)

The outcome can be a curtailing of opportunity and aspiration:

> such a view of ability, ironically, can lead to a situation where particular groups of students, notably perhaps those from some working-class backgrounds, those on free school meals, those from some minority ethnic cultures, under-achieve simply because too little is demanded of them.
>
> (Younger et al. 2005a: 43)

Given these powerful and countervailing arguments, it might be argued that the current emphasis on end-of-Key-Stage assessment, and particularly on value-added measurements, should be downgraded. Indeed, such a view is currently widespread: Smithers (2003) reported, for example, that 'an alliance of local authority chief education officers, school governors and headteachers has called for a review of primary school league tables in England, to make national tests less high stakes' and the resulting data more reliable and meaningful. We have considerable sympathy with such a view, particularly within the explicit context of the primary school league tables, not only because of issues linked to assessment but because of the distorting effects which such a testing regime has on the curriculum in many primary schools.

Nonetheless, it has to be recognized that the renewed emphasis on assessment in primary schools, through end-of-Key-Stage tests and teacher assessments, has sharpened the focus on much primary practice and thinking, and consequently on teaching and learning. As we make clear in Chapter 1, issues to do with educational opportunity and raising aspirations, and patterns of inequality based on social class, gender and ethnicity, were less transparent when assessment practices were less formalized and their outcomes less accessible to outside scrutiny.

This returns us to the central focus of the first part of this chapter: any discussion of the gender gap and of 'under-achievement' is a complex issue, and it is dangerous to arrive at simplistic generalizations without contextualization. Indeed, our work has led us to the belief that it is not the gender gap *per se* which is the main issue at all in English primary schools, especially since it does not exist to any significant extent in boys' and girls' achievements in two of the core subjects. It is important, too, that we do not lose sight of the fact that the achievement levels of girls and boys in primary schools in England consistently have risen through the past decade (Table 2.1, Figure 2.1). Even if there has been some recent plateauing of performance levels, the PIRLS data have confirmed that children in England, both girls *and* boys, 'are on average among the most able readers in the world at the age of ten' (Twist et al. 2003: 7). As in the secondary sector, there has been too little celebration of the achievements of girls and boys through primary schooling, and of their teachers. In a context where the overall trend of performance, for successive national cohorts of girls and boys, has been upward, the emphasis on 'boys' under-achievement' is misplaced.

Crucially, however, this renewed focus on assessment has allowed us to recognize, with some assurance, which specific groups of children, girls as well as boys, consistently do less well than others, year-on-year. Thus we identify:

- Black Caribbean[3] pupils where the performances of boys were markedly depressed in each of the core subjects at Key Stage 2.
- Pakistani and Bangladeshi pupils' achievements in English where the performances of boys *and* girls was well below national levels.
- The high levels of performance of Chinese and Indian pupils where the performances of girls and boys were above the national average, but that in such a way that – for Chinese heritage pupils – the gender gap in English at Key Stage 2 mirrored the national average, while for Indian heritage pupils, the gender gap was below the national average.

- In value-added terms, the relative poor performance in writing of pupils in the majority ethnic group, white girls as well as white boys.
- The glaring differences in achievement, at both Key Stages 1 and 2, between children in receipt of free school meals and those who were not.
- Marked regional and LA differences which reflect starkly different socio-economic characteristics within school catchment areas.

While it *is* true that a gender gap continues within the English primary sector, and that in absolute numerical terms there are a significant number of boys nationally who achieve less well than girls of apparently comparable ability, we must conclude that it is the variations in absolute achievement levels between schools, communities and regions, which is at the heart of our concerns with differential achievement across primary schools.

## Notes

1 Schools must provide a broad and balanced curriculum for all pupils, but may disapply pupils from the National Curriculum if they have statements of special educational needs, or if the curriculum does not allow pupils sufficient flexibility to pursue their talents and aspirations.
2 Table 2.6 must be treated with caution, however, for it does not identify what proportion of any ethnic group achieved level 2C at Key Stage 1. We may be dealing, for example, with very small percentages of pupils in any one ethnic group in this analysis.
3 We use 'Black Caribbean' pupils, 'Pakistani and Bangladeshi' pupils, 'Chinese' and 'Indian' pupils, as a form of shorthand to describe pupils of Black Caribbean, Pakistani and Bangladeshi, Chinese and Indian heritage.

# 3  Raising boys' achievements

## Inclusivity rather than exclusivity

> The success of a moral panic relies not on its ability to reflect complicated nuanced effects but in its ability to oversimplify highly complex situations, forecast danger and attribute blame.
>
> (Titus 2004: 158)

The concept of 'moral panic' (Young 1971; Cohen 1972) is one which repeatedly has been applied to the issue of boys' 'under-achievement' in the past decade. It has conveyed connotations of danger and extreme anxiety, a sense of crisis which has threatened the fabric of society, a warning that one sector of the school population is becoming marginalized, disenfranchised and discontented. The alleged gender gap in achievement has been problematized, gender policies in schools have been rewritten to give more prominence to boys' needs (Yates 1997) and equal opportunity initiatives for girls have virtually disappeared (Myers 2000) in the rush to rescue the apparently increasing number of lost boys. Rather than celebrating the achievements of girls, it is as though their very successes are threatening to boys and to men, and to their grip on political, economic and social power (Kenway 1995; Weiner et al. 1997; Warrington and Younger 1999; Younger et al. 2005a).

In this context, researchers working on the issue of raising boys' achievements in the early years of the twenty-first century have needed to be very clear about their own motives, and about how to situate their work. Indeed, when in June 2000 we were invited by the British government's Department for Education and Skills to direct a project on *boys' under-achievement* (subsequently retitled Raising Boys' Achievement), we were faced with a number of dilemmas. What exactly was the significance of a gender gap, where it existed, in many schools? Could we identify strategies and policies which might address boys' under-achievement, however defined, without disadvantaging girls? How far would we be compromised by working on a DfES-sponsored project on such a contentious issue? How could we reconcile our central engagement with this work with our own clear empathy towards a feminist agenda?

As we state elsewhere, these dilemmas certainly focused the mind, and, as we worked on the project, they 'have led us into a process of continual clarification and redefinition of the scope of the work we subsequently engaged in with schools' (Younger et al. 2005a: 60). Throughout, we have tried to bring together the various strands of our own work and that of others to inform the debate from a theoretical and a practical perspective. We have located the debate centrally within an inclusive context, having in mind the fundamental rights of *all* boys and *all* girls. We have acknowledged, as Titus (2004) indicates, that the issue is highly complex and nuanced, and needs more than short-term and quick-fix solutions. Complex and multifaceted issues need integrated, clearly articulated and systematically evaluated solutions that embrace and permeate every aspect of a school's life and organization.

## The Raising Boys' Achievement Project: the underpinning theoretical position

### Achievement for all

Throughout the past decade, our work on the 'boys' agenda' has been situated within a theoretical position that has acknowledged inclusivity rather than exclusivity. In an initial study of one school, we wrote that 'our intention is to provide some initial insights ... through an intensive study of how the changing relationship between girls and boys is experienced', arguing that the study of gender relations in education must take account of the position of *both* sexes and focus upon the educational experience of girls *and* boys together (Younger and Warrington 1996: 300). In a subsequent paper, we acknowledged that any research on the influence of gender on achievement will inevitably present a partial picture: 'we recognize that there are other factors, such as ethnicity, social class and parental educational levels, which are equally, if not more, important in determining differential levels of achievement in schools' (Younger et al. 1999: 327). As our analysis of the complexities of the gender gap makes clear (Chapter 2), there are specific groups of children who consistently do less well than others, year-on-year, and for whom the current primary education system in England is less enabling. It is these pupils we have been concerned with as we have sought to explore, develop, refine and evaluate intervention strategies and approaches, together with school policies, culture and ethos, which help students achieve. This recognition of the intersection of ethnicity, gender and class (Archer and Yamashita 2003; Ali 2003; Archer, L. 2004) is central to the theoretical position which we have adopted in the RBA Project, evidenced in the schools we have worked with and the different types of strategies we have tried to develop, and explicit in our attempt to argue that contemporary gendered power relations are more complicated and contradictory than suggested by the new orthodoxy that girls are doing better than boys (Reay 2001; Skelton 2001; Skelton and Francis 2003a; Renold 2004a).

## A concern with boys *and* girls

As part of this concern with inclusivity rather than exclusivity, we have focused not only upon the learning needs of boys but also of girls. We have argued elsewhere that it is imperative, in examining boys' relative under-achievement, 'not to lose sight of the equal opportunities debate as it relates to girls' (Younger et al. 2005a: 58), believing strongly that 'girls and women are still disadvantaged within the wider patriarchal society, and that, despite their achievements, the odds are still often stacked against girls in school as well as outside it' (Warrington and Younger 2000: 495). There is considerable research evidence about girls who, for whatever reason, are at risk during their years of schooling (Osler et al. 2002; Lloyd 2005), although currently much of this is located within the secondary sector. Fieldwork observations during the RBA project suggest that the experiences of girls in primary schools, however, are not dissimilar to those of girls in secondary schools. It is not unusual for girls' learning to suffer as a result of the disruption of boys; girls in classrooms are often intimidated by the aggressive language and behaviour of some boys. Reay, for example, describes how the behaviour of boys towards girls meant that

> as a direct result, the 'nice girls' began to use the classroom space differently, taking circuitous routes in order to keep as far away from these boys as possible ... [they] did not challenge the boys but rather developed avoidance strategies which further circum-scribed their practices.
>
> (2001: 159)

At the same time, girls' characteristic behaviours offer a dilemma for some teachers. Girls not unusually offer behaviour which is closer to the teachers' ideal, being perceived as responsible, passive, cooperative, diligent, hard-working, well-behaved, polite and neat (Clarricoates 1989; Wing 1997; Platten 1999; Skelton 2001; Skelton and Francis 2003a; Johannesson 2004: Jones and Myhill 2004a, 2004b). Thus, to Francis:

> Gender role maintenance eventuates in a dichotomous and oppositional construction of gender in the primary school:

femininity is constructed as sensible, selfless, mature and facilitating; and masculinity is constructed as silly, selfish, immature and demanding ... Such a position is taken up as an integral part of female school culture, gaining shared approval from other girls and facilitating bonding. It theoretically pleases the female teacher as it conforms to her declared wishes (i.e. obedience, conscientiousness, etc.).

(1997: 181)

Equally, though, there is a tendency for some teachers to downplay the value of these qualities in girls, suggesting that many girls lack self-expression and self-confidence, that they are too anxious to please the teacher rather than exploring independence in learning, suggesting that it is less positively challenging and exciting (and conversely, more boring) to teach girls (Stanworth 1981; Walkerdine 1990; Francis 1997). This dilemma becomes exacerbated when girls behave differently to teachers' expectations, when some girls mirror boys; when Reay's 'spice girls' exhibited more assertive and less compliant behaviour, for example, this was seen by adults as inappropriate and counter-productive to learning (Reay 2001); similarly, Arnot and Gubb's (2001) 'stroppy girls' and 'intractable girls' were seen as negative influences in the classroom. Those girls who do challenge and reject the conventional view of what it is to be a girl, who do strive for more independence, assertiveness and self-expression, are often devalued and seen as bad influences in the classroom (Connolly 1998; Reay 2001; Skelton and Francis 2003a).

These concerns and contradictions about teachers' expectations of girls in primary schools would be sufficient to justify our determination not to minimize girls' learning and social needs while developing work within the Raising Boys' Achievement (RBA) Project. There are other issues, however, which mean that the needs of girls are equally pressing. In Reay's work on gender discourses, girls' cultures and femininities in the primary classroom, for example, she argues that:

Despite widely differentiated practices, all the girls at various times acted in ways which bolstered boys' power at the expense of their own. While peer group discourses constructed girls as harder working, more mature and more socially skilled, still the boys and a significant number of the girls adhered to the view that it is better being a boy ... in this particular primary school, girls and boys still learned many of the old lessons of gender relations which work against gender equity.

(2001: 153)

Similarly, Skelton (2001) argues that the day-to-day practices of primary schools reinforce rather than dispel traditional forms of gender identity, and that there is little evidence that equal opportunity strategies based on the presentation of alternative, non-sexist images of masculinity and femininity have been effective. There is also the view that girls who under-achieve still seem to be invisible in many primary school classrooms, vague figures in their teachers' eyes, with a *lack* of potential and confidence compared to the *unfilled* potential of many under-achieving boys (Jones and Myhill 2004a). Thus, in the words of Johannesson: 'If they [girls] are uninterested in the school subject matter, they remain silent and are, therefore, more likely than boys to be forgotten because the boys are more likely to show disruptive behaviour' (2004: 35).

Throughout the Raising Boys' Achievement Project, then, while most of the empirical focus has been on boys, we have been resolute in taking a position which has not minimized or negated the very real needs of girls in primary schools. While wishing to celebrate the relative achievements of girls, we have avoided an essentialist rhetoric which presumes that *all* girls are high achievers. Central to the theoretical position we have assumed is the belief that in many primary schools girls continue to face gender-specific problems and disadvantages, that some 'girls continue to be devalued, and to devalue themselves' (Skelton and Francis 2003b: 11), and that we need, as Bell (2004) argues, to pay greater attention to the monitoring of withdrawn, quiet, 'less visible' girls, whose quietness may hide severe problems.

## Diversity and variety

Situating the Raising Boys' Achievement Project within an inclusive context has meant, third, that we have been alert to promoting notions of diversity and variety, rather than assuming that white middle-class masculinity is hegemonic and the ideal, and that there is one traditional femininity to which all girls subscribe. Despite extensive research over the past decade, the notion persists that 'real' masculinity is defined in terms of attributes such as physical strength, individuality and self-reliance, assertiveness and rationality, competitiveness and emotional neutrality. These gender stereotypes tend to persist in many of the discussions of how to respond to issues of boys' under-achievement in primary as well as in secondary schools, and we have been anxious not to let such stereotypes go unchallenged. As early as 1996, Skelton was warning against assuming standardized and uniform interpretations of masculinity and femininity across all schools:

There is a differential attachment to masculinity which exists between and within schools ... it is essentialist and reductionist to assume that *all* schools operate within identical constraints, are always consistent, relate similarly to external pressures and do, thereby, engage with male power and constructions of masculinity in the same way.

(Skelton 1996: 185)

Similarly, Reay has maintained that

performing gender is not straightforward [although] the seduction of binaries such as male:female, boy:girl, often prevents us from seeing the full range of diversity and differentiation existing within one gender as well as between categories of male and female.

(2001: 163)

A multiplicity of femininities and masculinities can exist within primary classrooms (Swain 2000; Beckett 2001; Connolly 2003; Renold 2004a); what is dominant in one context might not be dominant in another, and what is hegemonic might vary through time in the same place.

We have been concerned, then, to develop intervention strategies, aimed to raise achievement, that recognize the diverse constructions of masculinity and femininity, and acknowledge what the complexity of 'performing gender' involves for many children. This has been of critical interest for us, particularly in the context of socio-cultural issues, because at times we have challenged boys to re-evaluate what it is to be a boy (Chapter 5), requiring them and their teachers, to re-examine their own notions, values and beliefs. This has not always been easy, particularly in the context of laddishness and avoidance of the feminine which we outlined in Chapter 1. The fear of being labelled as 'other', as a 'sissy' (Thorne 1993) or a 'poofter' (Swain 2000), carries high social and emotional costs; it can incur banishment or subordination (Connolly 1996; Skelton 2001), exposing boys to 'gender-jabs and gender-ridicule' (Renold 2004a: 87). Equally, there is a cost carried by those girls who reject the more popular and dominant ways of being a girl, and preserve difference through their alternative dress and fashion, their different interests and their rejection of boys and the male gaze. Whether 'tomboys' (Thorne 1993), 'nice girls' (Reay 2001), or 'square girls' and 'top girls' (Renold 2004a), these girls act in ways which carry risk to image and esteem within the peer group. It is worth noting, however, that Millard claims that the risk is greater for boys than for girls: boys who act like girls are considered to be more deviant than girls who take on the characteristics of boys, and such boys will remain excluded and outside the group longer than such girls (Millard 1997). There is a diversity within ethnicity, too, to which we must not be blind: Mirza (1992) has written, for example, of the dangers of stereotyping black girls by characterizing them as loud, confident, overtly sexual, working class, while Ali challenges the perception of Asian girls as 'passive, quiet and shy, and (thereby) fulfilling a different kind of stereotypical requirement of "Others"' (Ali 2003: 274).

This diversity of gender constructions, and the need to avoid stereotypes which often embody unhelpful generalizations, have focused our attentions on approaches to teaching and learning, in socio-cultural aspects (Chapters 5 and 6), in literacy (Chapters 6 and 7) and in pedagogy (Chapter 8), which have acknowledged difference and individuality. As in the secondary schools with which we worked, we have been concerned to offer intervention strategies which are relevant to teachers of boys and girls who define their sexuality differently from the 'mainstream': 'gentle caring boys as well as macho, football-loving boys; those boys who prefer music, dance, poetry; more sensitive, caring boys who find their comfort zone in the company of girls and women' (Younger et al. 2005a: 62), girls who associate more with sport, with risk-taking, with rule-breaking and assertiveness. Throughout our work with schools, therefore, we have recognized the diversity of 'boys' and 'girls', in terms of class, ethnicity and sexual orientation and the need to disaggregate the data. In so doing, we have attempted to ensure that interventions identified and developed to support the learning of boys and girls in schools have not discriminated against children who behave differently from expected norms. We have not assumed that strategies developed in one context are necessarily appropriate and transferable to others.

In discussing diversity among boys and girls, of course, we need to acknowledge, as we suggested in the previous chapter, that the issue of under-achievement does not affect all boys, nor that all girls are immune from under-achievement; to take such a position is naïve in the extreme. Indeed, in some primary schools, the levels of boys' achievement, in English as well as in mathematics and science, match those of girls. It is well documented that some boys can preserve their image and creditability within their peer group through apparently effortless achievement (Jackson 2002). Both Pollard (1987) and Renold (2004a) describe how some boys adopt strategies linked to humour, minimize their own achievements, engage in mildly reluctant cooperation and laddish performances in the playground and out-of-school to protect their position (Skelton 1996), while at the same time enabling them to participate willingly and eagerly in classroom learning. There are links here with Connell's concept of layering (1995) and the contradictions within masculinity which boys need to negotiate and manage if they are to retain their membership of the hegemonic group while at the same time pursuing academic success.

Equally, we need to remain aware that there are an increasing number of disengaged girls who *do* under-achieve; these exhibit characteristics similar to the picture that teachers painted of under-achieving boys 'being in various degrees confrontational, disruptive and challenging of the school ethos' (Jones and Myhill 2004a: 541). Significantly, perhaps, Jones and Myhill suggest that recognition that such a group of girls existed was more likely to come from the children than the teachers, with teachers seemingly unaware of how these girls' behaviour had changed as they got older. This reinforces our belief that it is essential that we acknowledge explicitly 'the privilege which advantages some boys over others, and over some girls, and to recognize that this usually reflects, at least in the United Kingdom, social class factors' (Epstein et al. 1998). We need, in Gilbert and Gilbert's words (2001: 1), 'to substitute a more complex and inclusive set of stories about boys at school' with the emphasis on diversity and difference' (Younger et al. 2005a: 63).

## Contrasting attitudes

The emphasis on the variety of gender constructions was strongly reinforced by the research conducted within the RBA Project on pupils' attitudes towards their schooling. Drawing upon a survey of 1310 pupils in Year 5 (pupils aged 9–10) across the range of the primary schools involved in the project, the main concern of this aspect of the research was to explore the extent to which there was a 'gender gap' in their attitudes and responses to school (Gray and McLellan 2005). Pupils completed a questionnaire (based on that discussed in Thomas et al. 2000, and MacBeath and Mortimore 2001), which contained 30 items, relating to pupils' engagement with school, behaviour, self-esteem and relationships with peers; pupils were asked to tick one response from a choice of four ('always', 'most of the time', 'sometimes', and 'never'). At one level, the analysis of the survey's outcomes tends to reinforce gender differences: Gray and McLellan report that on 19 items, the responses given by girls were considerably more positive than those of boys, with girls much more likely, for example, to 'like going to school', to think the 'work [was] very good', and to report that they 'behaved well at school'; by contrast, there was only one item where the boys' responses were more positive than those of girls, although it should be noted that on one-third of the questionnaire items the responses of the two sexes did not differ at statistically significant levels. A factor analysis of the attitude questionnaire showed that girls were more positive in terms of their 'engagement with school' and 'pupil behaviour' but that boys had higher 'self-esteem'. There were no differences between the two sexes in terms of 'relationships with peers'.

Subsequent cluster analysis of the data revealed a more sophisticated patterning of the responses, however, and identified the existence of five groups of pupils: (1) 'the socially engaged but disaffected'; (2) 'the committed but lacking self-esteem'; (3) 'the enthusiastic and confident'; (4) 'the moderately interested but easily bored'; and (5) 'the alienated'. At one level, the gendered nature of some of these groupings was apparent: the first and fifth clusters were dominated by boys, with more than three boys in each cluster for every two girls; cluster 3, meanwhile, was heavily dominated by girls with almost three girls for every two boys (Table 3.1). Some of these groupings are identifiable in previous literature (Boaler 1997; Sukhnandan et al. 2000; Warrington and Younger 2000), but there is also the need to be cautious. The emergence, for example, of a group of girls who were strong on 'self-esteem' (cluster 3) needs to be recognized, as this is the converse of some conventional wisdom (Skelton and Francis 2003a). Equally, some of the groupings were less gendered than others, and the analysis also indicated that gender-based differences were, to some extent, matters of degree; 'alienated' boys can be identified, for example, but they made up only 14 per cent of the sample, and there were more boys in every other single category; conversely, while there *are* significantly more boys than who were socially engaged but disaffected (cluster 1) or moderately interested but easily bored (cluster 4), over 35 per cent of girls also fell into these two categories, so the potential number of girls who might subsequently under-achieve because of boredom or disaffection is high. There is evidence, too, that in a substantial minority of the case study schools, one or two groupings of boys and/or girls tended to dominate, suggesting that different primary schools may face pupils with different dispositions towards schooling, bringing different challenges; while Gray and McLellan's work was not in a position to address the question of the schools' role in creating gendered identities, it underlines the need for a range of strategies aimed simultaneously at changing key elements of *all* pupils' experiences while responding sensitively to specific gender-related aspects.

This evidence helps us to go beyond the simplistic generalizations which persist in much of the debate about boys' under-achievement. Indeed, Gray and McLellan (2005) conclude that the evidence suggests that simply taking a narrowly gendered approach to school improvement, based on some of the prevailing stereotypes, may not be the best way of addressing some of the complexities surrounding gender in primary schools. These stereotypes nevertheless, are clearly apparent in

**Table 3.1**  Incidence of cluster types broken down by sex

| Cluster | All (%) | Boys (%) | Girls (%) | No. of boys in cluster for every girl |
|---|---|---|---|---|
| Socially engaged but disaffected (cluster 1) | 25 | 31 | 18 | 1.72 |
| Committed but lacking self-esteem (cluster 2) | 22 | 19 | 26 | 0.73 |
| Enthusiastic and confident (cluster 3) | 23 | 16 | 30 | 0.53 |
| Moderately interested but easily bored (cluster 4) | 19 | 20 | 17 | 1.18 |
| Alienated (cluster 5) | 12 | 14 | 9 | 1.56 |

*Source*: Gray and McLellan (2005)

some of the intervention strategies advocated by 'new groups of (predominantly male) gender consultants with an interest in performance agendas' (Arnot and Miles 2005: 175).

## From male repair to gender relational approaches

The literature on 'boys under-achievement' is in danger of being overwhelmed by the plethora of texts, teaching packages, websites and sources of consultancy advice which offer information and guidance to teachers on how to motivate, teach more effectively and raise the achievement of boys. While much of this has been secondary orientated (Hannan 1997, 1999; Bleach 1998; Gardner et al. 1999; Noble and Bradford 2000; Noble et al. 2001), it has been widely assumed that many of the strategies and practices have applicability, regardless of the age of the boys concerned. Conventionally, then, boys are supposed to prefer learning through practical, active ways, which include problem-solving, a variety of short, sharply focused activities and which place emphasis on competition rather than on collaboration (Hey et al. 2000), since competition is conventionally seen as a more effective motivational spur for boys than for girls (Head 1996; Boaler 1997). Within this context, it is not surprising that many teachers see gender differences in pupils' attitudes and their dispositions towards learning; 'boys work well, [teachers] said, when instructions are clear and explicit and the work is paced in short, sharp bursts, whereas girls tend to enjoy longer open-ended tasks and dislike unfinished work' (Wood 2003: 373). Similarly,

Jones and Myhill, reporting on a study which identified more than twice as many negative comments from teachers about boys (54 negative comments) as about girls (22 comments), noted this 'tendency for teachers to repeat many of the commonly-cited gender stereotypes that often go unchallenged as accepted social wisdom ... boys are seen as having poor handwriting and presentation skills, are not keen readers, cannot sit still, are disruptive and need clear guidance' (Jones and Myhill 2004b: 553). Much of this has become embraced within custom, apparent good judgement and common sense, and as such has gained increased credibility through DfES publications and websites (DfES/NPDT 2003; DfES/London Challenge 2004). Thus the Raising Boys' Achievement Toolkit, produced by the DfES's National Healthy Schools Standards project (DfES/NHSS 2004), claims to address

> the current gender gap in pupil performance and is intended to support self-review – to help schools identify their priorities and to recommend the kinds of tried-and-tested strategies that *will* help raise achievement. Above all, the booklet is intended to provide help and support in a very practical way.
>
> (DfES gender and achievement website: our italics)

Similarly, the Breakthrough Project (DfES/NPDT 2003), offers exemplification to teachers, in terms of over 100 explicit strategies in areas such as leadership and environment, teaching and learning methods, mentoring and targeted interventions, to enable them to implement programmes of work which have been '*tried, tested and implemented effectively* in many successful secondary schools' (DfES/NPDT 2003: 5: our italics) and which will help teachers make 'rapid, systematic and sustainable improvements' in boys' achievements (DfES/NPDT 2003: 16).

These approaches tend to be rooted within a theoretical position that advocates men's rights approaches, on the basis that boys think, act and behave in the same way, and which maintains that schools are failing boys because the schools themselves are feminized and feminizing, and employ teaching styles and classroom management practices and approaches to learning which are favoured by girls (Skelton 2001). There are direct links here with recuperative masculinity policies, with 'a "male-repair" agenda which seeks to confirm commonality and identity among men' (Younger et al. 2005a: 67), to identify rites of passage for boys on their journey to becoming 'real men' and to give boys a sense of pride, status and well-being in their own manhood (Majors 2001). In this context, boy-friendly teaching strategies are accompanied by boy-friendly subject matter, boy-friendly reading schemes, an emphasis on computer technology, enabling boys to feel more valued by giving them a high profile within the school (Skelton 2001). At the core of these male-repair programmes, advocated extensively in the United Kingdom by consultants such as Hannan (1997, 1999) and in Australia by Browne and Fletcher (1995) and Biddulph (1998b),

> is the idea that boys are the victims of feminism ... the gender gap a consequence of girls' success and the feminisation of schooling ... such programmes are aimed at enabling boys to affirm themselves as males and to define themselves positively in relation to education and schooling.
>
> (Skelton 2001: 54)

We do acknowledge that it is important that boys develop positive self-esteem and that they should be comfortable with themselves and their own sexuality, but there are aspects of the 'recuperative masculinity approach' that are difficult to reconcile with the theoretical position which we believe should underpin the debate on raising boys' achievement. Our concerns with valuing diversity and different expressions of sexuality among boys suggests that it is difficult to talk about 'boy-friendly' strategies *per se*; indeed, research suggests that many boys remain involved, motivated and on target to achieve to their potential, and seek only to disguise their achievements in some way. Equally, the increasing multiculturalism and ethnic diversity within British society make the definition of 'boy' a particularly hazardous and unsafe task. Likewise, our concern with achievement for all, and recognizing under-achievement as a condition which girls are exposed to as well as boys, shifts the focus of the debate for us away from a male-repair agenda. Implicit within this approach, too, is the notion that girls do not need active or stimulating teaching, and are compliant and undemanding within the classroom, learning whatever the diet offered to them (Francis 2000; Younger et al. 2005a: 68). A further concern we have with this 'male-repair' agenda is the suggestion, implicit within much of the literature that advocates it, that raising boys' achievements is simply a matter of implementing a number of 'quick-fix' solutions in a tight and mechanistic way. Indeed, the Breakthrough Project (DfES/NPDT 2003) required participating schools to monitor on a monthly basis the strategies they had implemented to raise boys' achievements, and refine and redirect the strategies on a regular basis in the light of the outcomes. We have serious reservations about whether fundamental issues associated with boys' under-achievement effectively can be addressed in this way, and such short-termism reinforces our view that this is an over-simplistic approach.

We remain unconvinced, then, that the 'recuperative masculinity' approach allows schools to properly address issues of boys' under-achievement within a sustainable and inclusive context. Evidence from primary school research suggests that these approaches serve rather to reinforce dominant versions of hegemonic masculinity and reinforce male stereotypes (Reay 2001; Renold 2001; Skelton 2001; Skelton and Francis 2003a). Equally, despite the remarkable degree of confidence in the assertions of both the DfES-sponsored projects we cited earlier, as our italicized emphases suggest, we have yet to see evidence that suggests that such strategies do transform boys' achievements, even in the short term yet alone the longer term, and would suggest that such confidence is not yet justified by the outcomes. Rather, we agree with Wood when she argues that 'quick-fix, or "boys-only" solutions are an inadequate response to complex problems' (2003: 366).

In the Raising Boys' Achievement Project, then, we have tried to develop an alternative approach that acknowledges the diversity of boys, recognizes the problems some girls face and focuses on achievement for all within an inclusive context. In so doing, we have drawn to some degree on the experiences and insights of pro-feminist work (MASA 1996; Salisbury and Jackson 1996), but we recognize too that interven-tion strategies, if they are to be most effective, need to be credible and accessible to teachers, and to avoid dangers of counter-productivity (Skelton 2001, 2003b). Central to this alternative approach is the notion that gender is fluid rather than fixed, that notions of stereotyping about boys and girls need challenge more than acceptance, that teachers should not expect nor encourage children to behave differently because of their gender. With Skelton and Francis, and the other contributors to their book on *Boys and Girls in the Primary Classroom* (Skelton and Francis 2003a), we have attempted to develop strategies 'based on the notion that children develop and understand their gender identity as relational' (p. 15), reflecting that 'there is a co-dependence between femininities and masculinities which means that neither can be fully understood in isolation from the other' (Reay 2001: 154).

Fundamental to this approach has been our engagement with headteachers and with teachers to identify intervention strategies that have had the potential to transform boys' and girls' achievements within this gender-relational context (Chapter 4). This has led us to focus initially on the socio-cultural context, to consider how boys are beginning to develop concepts of masculinity that might be in direct conflict with the ethos of the school, and to identify ways in which schools are challenging this through approaches which encourage them to be as fully involved in all aspects of school life as possible. This has been an exciting and rewarding experience, focusing on the very real achievements of some teachers in some schools in enabling boys and girls to retain an involvement in their schooling rather than becoming alienated, and to support them in achieving despite the odds (Chapter 5). In Chapter 1, we identified the performance of some boys in literacy as a key aspect of under-achievement, and thus as a second area of concern we have directed attention to developing strategies which have targeted reading and contributed to the development of pupils' self-esteem as learners (Chapter 6). A further aspect of literacy is explored in Chapter 7, in terms of engaging boys in writing through talk and drama, and developing an integrated approach to literacy, with a focus on the process of becoming a writer, rather than on the technical aspects of learning to write. Finally, we explore more explicit issues to do with pedagogy, focusing on boys' and girls' perspectives of successful learners, and reviewing the potential of work on preferred learning styles (Chapter 8).

## Conclusion

In the Raising Boys' Achievement Project, as in other research we have carried out with schools, our aim has been to work with teachers to develop research-based knowledge about the ways in which gender – and the working out of gender by boys and by girls – affects schooling and the quality of learning opportunities for both girls and boys. We have been motivated by the desire to make an effective and realistic contribution to the debate about boys' and girls' achievements in primary schools, which resonates with the experiences of teachers, parents and students, but which appreciates difference between and within boys and girls, and acknowledges that schools need support to implement effective interventions which recognize diversity and the fluidity of gender.

As we have outlined in this chapter, we have marked reservations about the short-term, tightly targeted strategies associated with recuperative masculinity approaches, and suggest that they have limited value in bringing about longer-term transformation in achievement levels and in gender constructions. At the same time, it will be clear from our discussion of the nature and causes of the differentials in achievement between some boys and some girls in primary schools in England (Chapter 1) that we have a closer empathy with pro-feminist lines of enquiry. We feel, however, that there is a rhetoric/reality divide in much of the current pro-feminist work, particularly when it is expressed in terms of curriculum initiatives and teacher-led classroom strategies (Skelton 2001), and many of our discussions with primary school teachers suggest that the approaches are seen to be too high-risk to be effective in realizing their aims. The intervention strategies we have adopted on the RBA Project, therefore, have tried to incorporate the spirit and purpose of much pro-feminist work, but within a framework in which teachers have felt comfortable and confident. Thus, we have attempted to develop the project's work 'within a gender equity context, to emphasize issues of inclusivity, to develop work in schools within a gender-relational context, incorporating notions of difference and agency, and placing the emphasis on boys *and* girls' (Younger et al. 2005a: 71). Throughout, our concerns have been rooted in a desire to facilitate the academic and social achievement for all students, to offer equal opportunity for all pupils, wherever they live.

# 4 'Working together is invaluable'

## A collaborative approach

> The value of pursuing research of this kind within an established group cannot be understated. Sharing good practice, offering support, keeping to timescales and drawing up realistic action plans were all done with a dedicated and committed professionalism to the project and to one another.
>
> (Primary school headteacher, RBA project)

Ailwood (2003: 29) has suggested that 'as theory has become more focused and more complex, it has also become rather more difficult to translate into policy terms', and that an important strategic step in influencing policy is to attempt to move 'nuanced discussion of gender into school sites'. Thus, while the principal focus of the RBA project was on monitoring, refining and transferring strategies which appeared to be successful in raising achievement, this was undertaken within a context of discussion, engagement with schools and staff and a two-way process of learning and evaluating. We were not simply concerned to trial strategies for a short time before moving on to the next school or the next project, but to establish relationships and to develop rapport and trust between members of the project team and staff in schools, to listen as well as to put forward ideas. We believed that raising achievement could not be effected through strategies put into place on a short-term, isolated or *ad hoc* basis, but required a commitment to establishing approaches which were both sensitive to the context of the school, and which had been carefully planned and thought through.

The research design of the RBA project foresaw a four-year project with an initial pilot stage lasting for the first year, a two-year main intervention stage and a final extension year. This chapter explains that research design and process, together with an evaluation based on our own reflections and conversations with headteachers and deputy headteachers, and on the observations of the five other researchers involved directly in working with the primary schools at various stages. At the end of the main intervention stage of the project, link researchers explicitly sought comments from the schools on the research process, and at the penultimate project conference, one-to-one interviews were conducted by researchers who had not been involved in the primary project. The final project conference at the end of the extension stage also included a workshop which gave schools the opportunity to reflect and talk about their experiences of being part of the project. The chapter begins, however, with a brief overview of the execution and key outcomes of the pilot stage of the project, since this sets the scene for discussion relating to the later stages.

## The pilot stage

The pilot stage was mainly concerned with the identification of strategies that looked promising in terms of raising boys' achievement without detracting from achievement levels among girls. It involved both project directors and the research associate working with four primary schools, identified following discussion with the DfES and local education authority officers, together with a literature and website search. These were schools which, through time, had shown a commitment to raising achievement and had narrowed the gender gap at Key Stage 2 (see Warrington et al. 2003, for further details). The schools, located in a deprived urban area of the West Midlands, in an affluent village in rural Cambridgeshire, in an inner London borough with a high proportion of ethnic minority students and in a former mill town in West Yorkshire, were selected so as to represent a geographical spread, and to reflect contrasting socio-economic characteristics.

The high profile given by media and government to the 'problem' of boys' under-achievement had undoubtedly led during the 1990s to a large number of initiatives designed to improve the attainment of boys (see Chapter 1). However, it was also apparent as the project began that few of these initiatives had been systematically evaluated over a period of time. It was also evident that some schools were suffering from 'initiative overload', taking on all kinds of ideas at once in order to improve boys' attainment. Thus, our intention of isolating particular strategies was more difficult than we had imagined, since we found at the pilot stage and again later as we entered the main phase of the project, that schools tended to employ a 'basket' of strategies, taking on several improvement initiatives simultaneously. Sometimes the basket contained explicit, clearly articulated strategies, but more often it contained approaches that had become such an implicit part of the culture of a particular school, that the school found it difficult to acknowledge that it was doing anything special. It was only through spending time analysing with headteachers and staff what their priorities and approaches were that we were able to unpick both common threads and different approaches.

Common to all four schools was a clearly defined whole-school ethos which emphasized a sense of membership of the school among pupils, teachers and support staff, and this sense of membership was extended to parents, who were also encouraged to feel a valued part of the school:

> The whole expectation thing goes across the board. We share it with the parents. We tell them we expect your child to succeed and you've got to support us. Then I know it's reinforced at home. When I first came, the attitudes of the Year 6 boys were unbelievable, and one of the first things I did was meet with their parents when they were in trouble and set the parameters, and say, you've got to know that your child and I are working together for them to achieve.
>
> (Headteacher, West Yorkshire Pilot School)

Once their children joined the school, parents were encouraged to drop in and talk about their worries, and a number of visits to the school by the researcher showed that this was a reality and not merely rhetoric. These schools also prioritized the individual child: as this Acting Headteacher of the West Yorkshire school explained:

> Here it's very much that the children come absolutely first in everything. I haven't worked in a school like this one where so many extra things are put on for the children during social times, where their social and emotional welfare is actually top of the list, higher than their academic ... it doesn't mean that we don't value the academic, it means that you can't have the academic if they're not happy. They don't learn as well if they're not happy, if they're not warm, if they don't feel trusted, if they're not given responsibilities.

The sense of being part of a team, together with the promotion of a culture of success among the pupils, a sense of agency which carried responsibility and choice, a sense of security and a focus on the individual child, were the hallmarks of all four schools, and were articulated by the boys and girls we interviewed:

> It's a really nice school, all the teachers are nice and all the children are nice. They care for us and help people who are not as advanced as others. It's really good here.
>
> (Year 5 girl, South London school)

Our school is the best because the teachers are all excellent and we have perfect staff ... We're all a team, actually, in the whole school, so we work together.

(Year 6 boy, West Midlands school)

In addition to establishing the kind of *schools* we were seeking to work with us in the second stage of the project, the pilot stage in both primary and secondary schools also enabled us to clarify the kinds of *approaches* that schools were undertaking in successfully raising achievement. Whole-school organization provided a fundamental under-pinning to two main approaches in the primary schools we worked with. First were socio-cultural strategies, which were concerned to focus on engagement, positive attitudes and self-esteem for learning, and so to challenge images of laddish masculinity which conflicted with the ethos of the school. Second were pedagogic strategies, within which were two strands, one focusing upon literacy and the other on classroom dynamics and teaching and learning styles.

## The intervention stage

Having therefore identified both the kinds of schools and the types of approaches we were interested in analysing in further depth, we began the main intervention stage of the project. This envisaged the organization of eight 'triads' – groups of three schools each with a lead school and two partners (24 schools in total). The idea of forming collaborative 'triads' as a structure for school improvement in the second stage came from a project involving secondary schools in one local authority area (Rudduck et al. 2000, 2003), where two or three 'cluster' schools were linked to a 'host' school within relatively easy travelling distance. In the RBA project, the host schools were termed 'Originator' (lead) schools and each was linked to two 'Partner' schools (Figure 4.1).

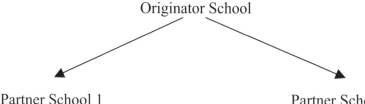

**Figure 4.1**  The triad structure

The eight Originator Schools were selected in a more formal way than those in the pilot stage, being identified according to certain criteria in relation to achievement in National Curriculum tests at Key Stage 2. In addition to an explicit concern with the issue of 'boys' under-achievement' within an inclusive context, we sought (1) evidence that the gender gap in English (which we had identified as the crucial core subject in this context) at Key Stage 2 was narrowing through time (over the period 1996–2000), as a result of improvements in the levels of boys' performance; and (2) a continuing improvement – or at the very least stability – in the levels of girls' performances. Schools where the gender gap had narrowed because of a fall in girls' performances were not considered.

Originator Schools were thus identified where differences between the average points score of boys and girls in Key Stage 2 English test results were narrowing through time, but within the context of a rising trajectory of results for both boys and girls (Table 4.1). Achievement points scores allowed the performance of all pupils to be considered, rather than focusing simply on those pupils achieving a certain level of performance. As in the secondary context (Younger et al. 2005a: 65–6), schools were selected where this narrowing of the trend lines between girls' and boys' performances reflected boys' improving at a greater rate than girls, but in both cases trends through time indicated improvements over most of the time period 1996–2000. We acknowledged that, given schools' individual circumstances and particularly the small sample size in many primary schools, average points scores might dip in one particular year, and we accepted a one-year tolerance within the year-on-year sustained pattern of improvement. Thus, in the example shown in Table 4.1, although the gap between the level of achievements of boys and girls was higher in 1999 than in 1998, the trajectory of achievement of both sets of results increased through time, and the gender gap overall narrowed from 1.52 points to 0.82 points.

**Table 4.1** Sample Originator School: comparison of boys' and girls' mean points scores in English, 1996–2000

|  | 1996 | 1997 | 1998 | 1999 | 2000 | National 2000 |
|---|---|---|---|---|---|---|
| Boys | 24.57 | 25.10 | 25.74 | 25.83 | 27.10 | 25.70 |
| Girls | 26.09 | 26.40 | 26.61 | 26.95 | 27.92 | 27.40 |
| Gender gap | 1.52 | 1.30 | 0.87 | 1.12 | 0.82 | |
| Ratio boy/girl | 0.94 | 0.95 | 0.97 | 0.96 | 0.97 | 0.94 |

Note: For information on the calculations involved in constructing points scores, see: http://www.dfes.gov.uk/performancetables/primary_05/p.4shtml

Following the statistical analysis of data and scrutiny of inspection reports, telephone interviews with possible schools sought to establish that they were schools which espoused the kind of ethos discussed above, and which in addition had put into effect certain measures which had contributed towards the raising of achievement in the preceding four years. While these measures were not gender-specific, all the schools had given some particular attention to raising boys' achievements, and had been effective in improving the profile of boys in their schools. It was not easy to find schools that met the criteria we had set, and the resulting geographical distribution of schools was therefore not as broad as we had hoped, though two of the four pilot schools did meet the criteria. In the final selection two Originators were located in Inner London (one in East and one in South London), one was in suburban Outer London, one in a south coast town, two in relatively rural areas of East Anglia, one in an urban area of the West Midlands and the other in a former mill town in West Yorkshire. These did, however, in line with our emphasis on inclusivity, ensure that a mix of socio-economic character-istics was represented, as will be evident in subsequent chapters. The two Partner Schools invited to work with each Originator School were situated in the same local education authority area and were broadly similar in socio-economic context, but were schools where there was a more marked gender gap in achievement.

In some respects, the triad model was not dissimilar to the Beacon Schools initiative, established by the British government in 1998 and operating until 2005. This identified high-performing schools across England for the purpose of developing partnerships between these and neighbouring schools, so that successful practice could be spread, and standards in pupil attainment raised in the partner schools. Beacon Schools were provided with significant financial inputs so that they could offer advice in the form of in-service training and consultancy, mentoring, seminars, and so on (DfES 2005d). The main differences between the two models were, first, that Originator Schools were chosen on the basis of a narrowing of the gender gap rather than on high attainment *per se.* Second, the Beacon School model originally envisaged a relationship between two schools rather than three (though, as Rudd et al. (2004) discuss, a network model was to develop later). More significantly, the Beacon School model allowed a large degree of freedom in choice of partners, forms of dissemination and focus, and Rudd et al. (2004) in their five-year evaluation of that initiative, report that there was little evidence of groups of schools working around common themes. In the RBA Triad model, on the other hand, Partner Schools were selected by the project team in consultation with the Originator Schools, to work together on the single topic of raising boys' achievement. Some funding was made available by the project for supply teacher cover while school representatives were involved in triad meetings and conferences, but schools otherwise received no extra resources. A final point of difference was that, although the Triad model was hierarchical in structure, we envisaged from its inception that there would be a three-way flow of ideas, rather than the top-down dissemination model which characterized the Beacon School model in its early days (Rudd et al. 2004).

The aim of the triad structure was for a representative of each school (in four triads these were headteachers, in two they were deputy heads and in two there were two heads and one deputy), working with a member of the research team (the 'link researcher'), to define the core of an intervention strategy and to attempt to transfer it, with contextual specific modifications, into the Partner Schools. As time passed, it was envisaged that this process would help to sharpen the focus and effectiveness of the strategy, and further improve achievement in the Originator Schools, as well as impacting on achievement in the Partner Schools.

### The triad model in practice

Such was the original research design, but all research within the social world is an iterative process, responding to unexpected circumstances and evolving through the relationships which develop between the various participants (Warrington 1997). Thus, only in one primary triad did the original model work out: that is, an Originator School was able to pinpoint a strategy which had led to a raising of boys' achievement within that school; this was transferred to two Partner Schools, and the Originator School maintained a lead throughout the lifetime of the project. In a second triad, a strategy did come from the Originator School and was taken on by the two Partner Schools, but one of the Partners quickly assumed the role of leader. This was because the headteacher of the Originator School was reluctant to give full consideration to the work of the project until a school inspection was completed, while staff at the lead Partner School were very keen to get the strategy up and running. It is important to stress, however, that in both of these triads there was a process of discussion and negotiation within the triads: from the beginning, it was crucially important to select strategies which would fit comfortably within the ethos and culture of each school, and so there was never any question of a strategy being imposed by the Originator on the Partner Schools. As one of the Partner School representatives in the first triad commented, mutual respect was successfully nurtured and there was never any tension because equality was established within working relationships.

In the other six triads the original research design foundered in the first instance because, as in the pilot stage, while all the Originator Schools had put into effect certain measures to raise achievement, none had focused on just one form of intervention strategy. Success in narrowing the gender gap was attributed to an all-embracing culture of achievement, rather than to a specific strategy, and, although the process of unpicking the essence of the approach had already been completed in the Originator Schools which had been part of the pilot, it took far more time than had been imagined for each link researcher to gather evidence and to reflect, with the school heads and deputies, on what was actually happening in both in the other Originators and in the Partner Schools. This process of reflection, which took place in one-to-one conversations with schools and at triad meetings, was not only necessary from the perspective of the project, but was useful for the school. As one headteacher put it:

> We were able to reflect upon the focus, the culture of our schools, in a way you couldn't do alone. ... I think it was the ability to analyse what you do in your school and to make your practice more rigorous which was so important.

It was therefore the case that the chosen strategy in six of the primary school triads was a result of much more extended discussion between the three schools and the link researcher. In five of the triads, the agreed strategy was a variation on something which was already happening in the relevant Originator School, taking it in new directions. As link teachers from two Originator Schools explained:

> Each school had a different context and needed to take from the shared experiences what was relevant for them.

> The initial idea was to analyse what we were doing as a school so that the others could try some of our strategies to see if that raised boys' achievement in their schools. When we listed all the strategies we'd put in place – because it had been an issue for us for about five or six years – there were some things which obviously the other two schools could put in place. But then what we ended up doing was thinking almost afresh: we looked at the strategies we'd been using and then we came up with some new strategies because we were also keen to further improve our boys' achievement. So we picked from what the other schools were doing as well.

A second reason for divergence from the original model was that, although the original research design envisaged a hierarchical structure, with ideas being transferred from Originator to Partner Schools in the first instance, such a structure was strongly resisted by most of the primary schools once the triads were set up. Perhaps in resistance to the competitive, performance-driven culture initiated by Conservative governments of the 1980s and 1990s, and continued by New Labour (see, for example, Arnot and Miles 2005, and Walford 2005), the primary school heads and deputy heads we brought together argued for a more collaborative structure of working. Even where the Originator School was acknowledged as initiator, this was quickly set aside:

> There was a lead school to begin with, but once we were actually in the project, it was equal.

> We were an Originator School but in the triad we worked very much equally and no one school took the lead.

Such a pattern of working reflects the experiences of the Beacon School initiative, where the labelling of Beacon Schools as 'expert' initially caused difficulties in establishing collaborative partnerships. Here, too, the early models of dissemination and consultancy evolved into the creation of networks of mutual support, premised on the notion of reciprocal learning and capacity building (Rudd et al. 2004).

However, while the schools themselves used the language of equality and collaboration, it was clear to the link researchers, as suggested above, that some schools did in fact take a lead. While none of the schools asserted a position of superiority or overt leadership, in most triads one school effectively took on the role of leader: in three cases this was the Originator School, in two cases it was a Partner, and in a further two cases two schools drove the project, with a weaker second Partner. From the perspectives of the researchers, only in one triad was there really no obvious leadership, with schools working independently within a broadly agreed approach.

It was important to allow these various models to evolve in their own way: trying to drive the triads in a particular direction would have been counter-productive. Even though in some triads there was less collaborative sharing than we had hoped, participants in all triads worked well together for the most part, attending triad meetings and conferences, and apparently benefiting from these experiences. Commenting on his experiences of the conferences, one delegate expressed the view that:

What has been very beneficial is that we've come together at places like this, and you hear what everybody else is doing. There's a consensus of views and argument and discussion. Now I haven't had this for years, and I've realized now how absolutely valuable it is and how much I enjoy it.

## Working together in triads

While the project was concerned with measurable achievement in quantitative terms, much of the research fell within a qualitative sphere, commensurate within the social sciences generally of a shift from a focus on quantitative research to the practice of qualitative methods as valid means of interpreting and explaining the social world. In other words, there has been a pronounced shift from the notion that research can be objectively planned and executed to one that recognizes the centrality of researcher and researched as complex human beings. Thus, the qualitative aspects of the research were underpinned by a feminist methodology (Roberts 1981; McDowell 1992; Moss 2002) that tried to take into account the positionality of the various members of the research team, to be reflexive, and to be aware of the inter-subjectivity of the research process.

As mentioned above, each triad was assigned a member of the research team as link researcher. One of the project directors, as well as overseeing the primary part of the RBA project, also took on the role of link researcher with one triad, while a full-time research associate worked with another. A university colleague with expertise in literacy was responsible for two triads focusing in that area (as well as working with one special school – see Chapter 8), and two seconded teachers were employed as link researchers in the other triads. In addition, a research assistant took on the further development of initiatives in two triads in the extension year of the project. The link researchers had shared ethnicity and gender, but had different levels of experience and expertise, with some of the team having more experience of the day-to-day activities of schools, and others having greater knowledge of research methodology. Clearly these differences had an impact on the organizational structure, on the choice of strategy and on the data collected from individual triads. Such impacts are inevitable, but regular meetings of the research team ensured that, as far as possible, a common approach to data collection and analysis was adopted, with full discussion of the research instruments used at different stages. In addition, the various skills within research team complemented each other, and so the team was strengthened through the diversity of expertise within it. Cross-project liaison was also facilitated through inputs from the research associate who worked with both primary and secondary schools and the faculty colleague who took responsibility for work with special schools across the project. The co-director responsible for the secondary schools in the project also worked closely with the primary research team. Project conferences, which brought together all participating schools with members of the research team, were held annually.

The development of strong working relationships between link researchers and their schools was, we believe, one important aspect of the project's success. In a climate of critical inspections from the Office for Standards in Education (Ofsted), where teachers have experienced an assault on their sense of professionalism (Jeffrey and Woods 1996) and where accountability has been extended from schools to individual teachers (Elkins and Elliott 2004), some teachers have not surprisingly become defensive and suspicious of 'outsiders'. It was therefore essential from the outset for link researchers to establish good rapport with the project representatives within each school and to built up trust. Thus, while the number of visits made by each researcher to the schools was very time-consuming, the development of these strong links cannot be under-estimated. Some real friendships were made during the course of the four years, and there was some genuine sadness among some of the participants at the final conference that the project had ended. And while it could be argued that the development of such strong relationships could impinge upon the research, compromising the 'objectivity' of the researcher and preventing her from standing back far enough, we felt that in a situation where we were genuinely trying to establish collaborative links with our schools, any possible costs were far outweighed by the benefits to the project as a whole.

It is perhaps significant that none of the 24 schools dropped out during the two years of the intervention stage of the project. This was due in part to the schools' belief in a worthwhile project, but also we feel, to the establishment of those contexts of trust between schools and link researchers. Our own role as project directors was also important, since we ourselves were very 'hands-on' in approach, visiting as many schools as possible, attending a number of triad meetings and being involved as link researchers.

Interviews with school representatives showed that the relationships with the link researchers were highly valued for a variety of reasons. Not only did link researchers contribute in a practical sense, for example, through organizing triad meetings, but they also kept the meetings focused and helped to move the project forward. Link researchers challenged the schools to think in different ways, assisted them in overcoming problems and analysing what was happening, and helped them draw up realistic action plans. In addition, although some schools collected data independently, the link researchers were responsible for collecting comparable data across the triads. An inside knowledge of schools and an understanding of what was realistic within the constraints of time were particularly appreciated by the schools working with the seconded teachers. In general, the link researcher relationships worked very well, as two school representatives describe:

> I certainly think that the person who worked with our triad made it. It was fantastic working with her. She made all our schools feel as if what we were doing was fantastic, but it was so interesting to learn from her as well. It's difficult to say triad because this was a foursome really. Obviously she was 'leading' but the fact that we were all involved in it made us feel equal partners I think.

> The role of the link researcher to oversee development, to administer and collate data and to provide the bigger picture, as well as keeping the project focused when it went off at tangents, was essential.

As Rudd et al.'s (2004) assessment of the Beacon School initiative pointed out, staff must get on at a personal level if partnerships are to work, and some of the Beacon School partnerships foundered due to personality differences. In the RBA project, a level of tension between members of one triad contributed to the fact that the three schools ended up working on quite different strategies, albeit within a specific theme. Such tensions came to the surface occasionally through criticisms by teacher representatives in the Originator School about various aspects of the project, and were expressed in interview by a Partner School member of the triad:

> There's a bit of a personality thing ... some people you get on well with and some people you don't. And if you're only in a group of three schools it can be difficult. Some people are better at handling constructive criticism. I don't think our triad was particularly effective but you know we did sort of keep each other going.

This was the exception, however, and even the representative from the second Partner School in the same triad saw things differently: 'I think we did all get on so well, and we were superbly led by [link researcher], and that made the whole experience very interesting.'

Several interviewees from across the triads stressed the importance of compatible personalities for effective working. Some had known each other well before working together on the project, and felt that this was an important factor in contributing to good triad relationships. Most, though, had had little contact with those they were brought together with, but apart from the triad mentioned above, there were no difficulties, even in those triads where there was a mix of headteachers and deputies:

> As a team of three plus [link researcher], we immediately got on very well personally. It was a very easy group to work with, so therefore we felt that there were very open views about what we should do – and we did toy with lots of potential areas of research.

The triad structure proved important at the beginning of the project when groups were deciding what to do and why it was worth doing, and discussing the monitoring and data collection needed to enable evidence to be drawn out. At this stage, participants particularly valued the reassurance from other members of the group that they were on the right track. Triad meetings in particular provided a spur to action, and helped schools to keep a focus on the project in a context of other new initiatives and pressures on time:

> Working as a triad kept the research going ... it didn't let it get overtaken by other things that were happening in school. You set a timescale to have jobs done by and because you'd set them as a triad you kept to them because you'd have to be reporting back to each other. So it did keep the research moving along at a fair pace.

> I think being part of a group made us stick with the project. My past experience of things is that it's easy with the pressure of life and initiatives to have to let go of things. And you know, we could well have let go of this project if we hadn't been in it together. I think that's crucial to seeing it through.

Towards the end of the project the group was also important in endorsing a sense of achievement, as 'everything fell into place'.

Participants felt that the three-school model was a good one, providing a balance between what was manageable, while still being owned by all in the group. One interviewee felt that the project was much more reflective than is often the case with a research project, since the involvement of four people led to a more rigorous analysis and testing of ideas than was sometimes the case. The group structure

- Sharing of ideas with other professionals and taking on good practice – generating ideas through doing things together.
- Mutual support through the sharing of common concerns with people they trusted.
- Professional development and a broadening of outlook.
- An opportunity to work with different/new schools than one would normally have contact with, and to visit other schools and see them in action.
- Being able to focus very closely on a specific issue – looking critically and professionally at a crucial aspect of current practice and analysing the effects of particular strategies in detail.
- The confidence to risk ideas within a supportive context and to test new approaches that might not previously have been considered.
- A re-focusing on learning in a context where many new initiatives are based on delivery of the curriculum rather than on improving learning.
- Dedicated time to stand back, reflect and analyse, which isn't always possible for heads and deputies involved in the day-to-day running of their schools.
- School development.

The project has enabled the school to move forward. So that's brilliant, in terms of being more rigorous about how we engage boys in the life of the school. We thought we were rigorous before but we weren't.

(Partner School headteacher)

**Figure 4.2**  Benefits gained from triad membership

provided a forum where, as one participant put it, 'simplistic assertions' could not be made. A number of specific benefits were seen to derive from being part of a triad, as listed in Figure 4.2.

Apart from some criticisms within one triad, as already noted, participants felt strongly that the triad model had worked well. As one of the independent researchers who interviewed some of the school representatives noted:

There was undoubtedly a real sense of enthusiasm for the project – virtually unqualified satisfaction, commitment and, indeed, gratitude at having been included. All were extremely appreciative of the skills and tact of their link researchers.

Some of the interviewees mentioned ways in which the triad experience could have been more productive, but the only common factor here was a desire for increased (funded) time for staff to visit other schools and to have more meeting time rather than relying on telephone or email communication. Time was, however, one of the factors which prevented some schools from developing their strategy to the extent they would have wished. Outside factors such as building work, staff illness, the movement of participants to new posts and, in one case, problems of staff retention, all impacted upon the smooth running of the project. In some instances a whole term was lost as schools prepared for, and underwent, an Ofsted inspection.

There were other frustrations for the research team. While interviewees talked about the way in which the triad meetings focused their attention on the project, this was not always the experience of the link researchers! In one triad in particular, where the school participants knew each other before the project began, the researcher commented that the sense of familiarity resulted in a very relaxed approach to the project: deadlines were often not met and visits sometimes lacked organization. There were clearly gender dynamics evident in this triad, with three established male headteachers and a younger, female researcher, who sometimes found it difficult to keep the meetings focused.

### Transferring the strategies

Although with very few exceptions the dynamics of relationships within the triads and between triads and link researchers worked well, and defined strategies were identified, this does not mean that the process of transfer, as envisaged in the research design, was straightforward. In the first instance, as already discussed, in most cases the process did not involve transferring a strategy from an Originator to two Partner Schools, since most strategies evolved through extensive discussion between all members of a triad. Thus, unlike in the secondary part of the project, where the model was one of strategy *transfer* (Younger et al. 2005b), among the primary triads it was, in most instances, one of strategy *implementation*.

Key to this process of implementation in particular schools was the role of each triad member since, as Fielding et al. (2005) point out, the transfer of good practice is a social process, sustained by relationships and trust; it is a personal and inter-personal process that has to engage with teacher and institutional identity. Among the factors which Fielding et al. identify is the role of the headteacher, who affects transfer by 'setting the tone' of the school, by distributing leadership, by building networks and by coordinating or facilitating the practice of transfer. As these authors point out, simply initiating partnership was not enough; rather, there was a need for consistent communication of the same message.

It was clearly evident that strategies were most effective, and became fully embedded within the ethos of the school, where headteachers were totally committed to the project and where they or their deputies were effective in enthusing relevant staff in putting the strategies in place. As Table 4.2 shows, this turned out to be the case in 18 of the 24 participating primary schools. In the other six, it is probably true to say that the process of implementation went less well than we might have hoped. Interestingly, as Table 4.2 shows, in four of the schools where the strategy did not become fully embedded in the intervention stage, the school representative on the project was a male headteacher. In each of these cases, although the heads were evidently enthusiastic about the strategy, and took the initiative in putting it in place, there was insufficient support from some members of staff to ensure that it became fully implemented and embedded. In the other two cases, the female deputy heads were unable to obtain sufficient backing from their (male) headteachers to ensure full implementation of the chosen strategy. In one case the head *was* a strong and effective leader, but did not accept that the strategy would be helpful to his school; in the other, the project lacked the wholehearted support of the head. In all these instances there was a lack of power, either of well-established headteachers over staff, or of deputy headteachers in the face of more powerful headteachers; a sense of teamwork, with everyone pulling in the same direction, was not evident in these schools. Thus, while the project representatives of all of these schools expressed enthusiasm for the project, the research team itself was disappointed over some of the limitations encountered in its implementation.

The role of the headteacher therefore – either directly, or through effective participatory or distributed leadership (Harris 2003; Hammersley-Fletcher and Brundrett 2004) – was almost certainly the most important factor in ensuring that strategies became fully implemented. These were headteachers who, despite the constraints brought about by the introduction of market disciplines and the attendant bureaucracy of accountability and transparency (McEwan et al. 2002), were able to realize in their practice what they saw as their core leadership values. These were 'purposeful leaders' (Mortimore et al. 1988), 'invitational leaders' (Stoll and Fink 1999), and 'reciprocal leaders' (Beck 1999), who had strongly held philosophies and who were held in trust and respect by staff working in their schools. Indeed, in most of the Originator, and some of the Partner Schools, leadership within the schools was described in inspection reports as 'excellent' or 'outstanding'. They were headteachers who would certainly meet the description of successful headteachers as identified by Day:

**Table 4.2** School representatives and embeddedness of strategies

| Triad | Originator or Partner | Position of school representative | Gender of school representative | Strategy fully embedded? |
|---|---|---|---|---|
| 1 | Originator | Headteacher | Male | Yes |
|   | Partner | Deputy headteacher | Female | Yes |
|   | Partner | Deputy headteacher | Female | Yes |
| 2 | Originator | Headteacher | Female | Yes |
|   | Partner | Headteacher | Female | Yes |
|   | Partner | Headteacher | Male | Yes |
| 3 | Originator | Deputy headteacher | Female | Yes |
|   | Partner | Deputy headteacher | Female | Yes |
|   | Partner | Deputy headteacher | Male | Yes |
| 4 | Originator | Deputy headteacher | Male | Yes |
|   | Partner | Headteacher | Female | Yes |
|   | Partner | Headteacher | Female | Yes |
| 5 | Originator | Headteacher | Male | Yes |
|   | Partner | Headteacher | Female | Yes |
|   | Partner | Headteacher | Female | Yes |
| 6 | Originator | Deputy headteacher | Female | Yes |
|   | Partner | Deputy headteacher | Male | Yes |
|   | Partner | Deputy headteacher | Female | No |
| 7 | Originator | Headteacher | Female | Yes |
|   | Partner | Headteacher | Male | No |
|   | Partner | Deputy headteacher | Female | No |
| 8 | Originator | Headteacher | Male | No |
|   | Partner | Headteacher | Male | No |
|   | Partner | Headteacher | Male | No |

These headteachers had a passion for their schools, a passion for their pupils and a passionate belief that who they were and how they led all made a difference to the lives of staff, pupils, parents and the community.

(2004: 427)

Much of the literature in this area describes such a leadership style as 'transformational', a model of leadership focused on people and relationships, and requiring an approach that seeks to transform feelings, attitudes and beliefs (Hopkins 2001). Transformational leadership provides opportunities for others to lead (Southworth 1998), it helps teachers to cross the thresholds of their classrooms (MacBeath et al. 1998), it breaks down barriers between 'leaders' and 'followers', with a strong emphasis on teamwork and participation in decision-making (Day et al. 2000). Transformational leaders

> [h]ave been shown to be reflective, caring and highly principled people who emphasise the human dimension of the management enterprise. They place a high premium upon personal values and are more concerned with cultural rather than structural change.
>
> (Day et al. 2000: 176)

Alongside the qualities of transformational leadership, Hopkins (2001) argues that 'instructional leadership', which has a more specific orientation towards student learning, is also required for authentic school improvement. And, indeed, this was the case with the head-teachers of the outstanding schools in the project, who, while emphasizing teamwork and democratic decision-making, were not afraid to exert their authority in managing teachers in their delivery of the curriculum.

While the role of the headteachers was crucial to the success of the project in each school, it is also worth noting that in most instances a representative of the local education authority played an important role, either directly or indirectly, in the design and transfer of strategies. In four triads, the particular strategies chosen emanated from training initially provided by the local education authority. Thus, learning styles, target-setting, paired reading and some citizenship initiatives were all ideas that originated from local authority training days, although here the local authority itself played no direct role in the transfer of the strategy within the project. In one triad, however, schools worked quite closely with local education authority advisors in developing drama initiatives and then disseminating them more widely across the authority as the project helped to finesse the approach (see Chapter 7). In two other instances, a local education authority advisor became very interested in literacy initiatives and strongly supported the development of the project's work and its transfer to new schools in the extension stage of the project (see Chapter 6). Thus, while the participation of the local education authority was by no means necessary for the successful identification or development of the strategies – indeed, in one triad it played no part whatsoever – there were instances where its role was a valuable one in transferring ideas further afield.

## The extension stage

The aim of the final extension year was two-fold. One aim was to take further the idea of transferability and to transfer established strategies into new schools, while the other was to explore issues of sustainability. With the exception of triad 8, which had been unsuccessful in terms of fully embedding the strategies (Table 4.2), triads can be assigned to three groups in the final year of the project. In group 1 (triads 5 and 7), there was continuing active involvement of a link researcher to further embed and develop the strategies. As a result, the two schools in triad 7 where the strategies had been less securely developed at the end of the intervention stage, saw them become much more fully embedded. In both of these triads, new data were collected and new insights gained. The second group (triads 3 and 6) more fully encapsulated the model that had been planned, with a link researcher working with some of the schools in each triad to take the strategy in new directions and to bring in further schools. The third group (triads 1, 2 and 4) was left with no researcher involvement in the final year, but a triad meeting in each at the end of that year established that strategies were still firmly in place and had been extended in different ways. In fact, it was encouraging to find that some schools had taken ideas from listening to colleagues at the wider project conferences and were trying some of the other strategies in their schools.

While the extension into new schools was less than had been hoped, and not as extensive as in the secondary phase of the project, this can partly be explained by the move through promotion or retirement of the link person in one school in each of five triads, and sick leave of link people in schools in two other triads. In triad 2, a promising link was made with a new school, only for the school to withdraw before the completion of the extension project because of competing pressures. Nevertheless there was some successful transfer to new schools, as discussed in Chapters 6 and 8, and some valuable insights were gained.

## Amassing the evidence

The role of the link researchers at each stage in the project was to document the process of transfer and to collect data to provide evidence of the effectiveness of each strategy. At the beginning and end of the intervention stage, certain methods were used which were common to all schools (Table 4.3); these allowed comparisons across schools. In addition, other methods were chosen during each stage of the project which were determined by the context of the triad and the specific strategy being implemented. These included interviews with teachers,

**Table 4.3**  Methods of data collection common to all schools

| Method | Timing | Purpose |
| --- | --- | --- |
| Semi-structured interview with headteacher | Beginning of intervention stage | To provide background information about school and establish school's approach to raising achievement. |
| Gathering documentation (school prospectuses, Ofsted reports) | Beginning of intervention stage | To provide background information |
| Semi-structured focus group interviews with three groups of under-achieving boys | Beginning and end of intervention stage | To provide data on boys' attitudes and views on gender and achievement before and after the intervention strategy |
| Attitude survey of whole year groups | Cohort 1 – end of Year 6 Cohort 2 – beginning of Year 5 and end of Year 6 | To compare Y6 pupils who had not experienced the intervention strategy with those who had; to compare one cohort of pupils before and after the intervention strategy |

visual methods (inviting pupils to respond to photographs), classroom observations, questionnaires to staff, students and parents, and analysis of pupils' writing. Further details are provided in relevant chapters.

However, while earlier discussion in this chapter has focused on the relationships between the various adults involved in the project, not to be under-estimated is the power of the pupil voice. As Davies (2005) suggests, a new respect for children is evident within much educational research, recognizing the value of collaboration with children as research participants. Wood (2003) has shown, for example, how pupils' perspectives on under-achievement are more informative about the impact of schooling on behaviour and achievement than those of their teachers, so that taking pupils' views into account leads to a much broader view of the complex, intersecting factors engendering under-achievement. Thus, in the RBA project, focus group and individual interviews with pupils were a central aspect of data collection in every school, enabling pupils' perspectives to be heard on how the strategies impacted upon their learning and on their attitudes towards the learning process through time. In all the primary schools the impact of each strategy was assessed through a focus group of 8–12 boys who were interviewed, either individually or in groups of two or three, on several occasions throughout the project. The boys were chosen by their teachers as under-achieving in that they were not reaching the levels expected of them in National Curriculum tests, given their prior achievement; nor were they making sufficient effort to develop or extend their skills or apply themselves in situations where they were expected to succeed:

> There are children in this school, and some of them are boys, who I would say are under-achieving, who are bright and able but who are not performing, not achieving the quality they're capable of, that you would expect of their ability. Partly you could say that's because we have very high expectations and are not prepared to say, that's good enough.
>
>                        (Headteacher, South London school)

Detailed case studies were built up for each boy, including attainment through time; where appropriate, writing samples were analysed, and classroom observations focused on these pupils. The individual attention received by these boys each time the researcher visited the school became something they looked forward to, so that it has to be recognized that link researchers were playing something of an informal mentoring role. This could, of course, itself have had positive impacts on their achievement at the end of Year 6, regardless of the strategies put in place through the project, and in this sense outcomes could be seen as biased. The rewards of developing such relationships with the boys, however, both from their perspectives and that of the researchers outweighed any disadvantages. Our key focus in data collection on the boys themselves provided a rich vein of evidence, as the following chapters demonstrate.

While the government had commissioned research on boys, in line with our gender equity philosophy (see Chapter 3), we did interview some girls. These interviews took place at the pilot stage, and in three Partner Schools where we felt some concern that there might be too much attention on boys, and wanted to reassure ourselves that girls were not being disadvantaged. The focus on pupils themselves was not simply in order to obtain evidence, although such a practice is, as Davies (2005) suggests, now widespread. What is less common, as Wood (2003) points out, is to take pupils' voices into account in policies to improve teaching, learning and achievement. This has been a key focus in the work of Jean Rudduck (see, for example, Rudduck et al. 1996; Rudduck and Flutter 2000, 2004), who argues strongly for serious consideration of what pupils say about their experience of being a learner in school and for finding ways of involving them more closely in decisions that affect their lives (Rudduck and Flutter 2004). A stronger focus on pupil participation, these authors argue, can enhance progress in learning: this was the whole purpose of the RBA project.

## Conclusion

This chapter has demonstrated three key principles that have guided our research. First, it has shown a commitment to *process* as well as *outcome:* how we came to the conclusions concerning the various strategies was as important to us as the actual findings themselves. Closely allied to this was an emphasis on *relationships* – between representatives from triad schools, between triads and link researchers, between representatives across triads, between members of the research team and between researchers and the subjects of their research. The importance of time to establish trust and productive working relationships was crucial to the success of the project. Finally the emphasis was on the *pupils* themselves, which involved not just listening to them but engaging with them, being interested in them and helping to ensure that their perspectives were valued and taken into consideration in the schools' own evaluations of project initiatives. Together, these three principles situate our research as part of a process which has promoted and extended critical discourse among teachers and researchers, 'opening up channels for debate and consideration of a range of solutions to classroom problems' (Atkinson 2000: 322). The purpose of educational research, as Atkinson argues, is not merely to provide answers but to inform discussion.

# 5 'Here we really believe in ourselves'

## Tackling socio-cultural issues

### The socio-cultural context

As already discussed in Chapter 1, it has become apparent through the extensive research we have undertaken exploring the parameters of boys' under-achievement, that many of the issues associated with under-achievement are related to tensions between the culture of the school and images of masculinity held in the local community and wider society. In our earlier work with secondary schools, we found again and again the negative influence on learning of laddish behaviour, of boys 'acting the clown' in order to impress their friends, of boys pretending not to be interested in, or involved in their work in order to preserve their status and protect their macho image (see, for example, Warrington et al. 2000). Francis notes similar findings, asserting that 'Loud, physical and sometimes aggressive and/or disruptive behaviour is an integral expression of many boys' construction of masculinity ... and is likely to impede their achievement' (2000: 120). Similarly, Skelton and Francis (2003a) note that boys' construction of masculinity as competitive, macho and 'laddish' results in their gradual alienation from school as they seek to position themselves as 'hard' and 'cool'.

As Chapter 1 points out, these kinds of issues are relevant, not just for secondary schools, but also for primary schools where children have very clear views of the expectations held for their own gender (Wing 1997). This is perhaps most evident in the playground, where young children are actively involved in constructing their own gender identities (Connolly 2003), with boys seeking to construct a form of masculinity through which they can acquire popularity and status within their peer groups (Swain 2003, 2004). As Swain points out, there are constant pressures on individuals to perform and behave to expected group norms, and they do this, he argues, through drawing upon an array of social, cultural, physical, intellectual and economic resources available to them at any one time. They may employ the strategy of being sporty and athletic, since sport has become a major signifier of masculinity in many schools, with football being by far the most valorized game among boys' peer groups (Swain 2000). Other strategies discussed by Swain involve acting tough and/or hard, for example, by fighting or publicly denying adult authority; using humour and wit, sometimes as a confrontational device against teachers; wearing fashionable clothes and trainers; and possessing culturally acclaimed knowledge, for example, being able to talk knowledgeably about the latest computer game. One of the problems seems to be that, as Jordan (1995) notes from her research in Australian primary schools, the pressures for gender conformity, even at an early age, are much stronger on boys than on girls. Furthermore, boys tend to experience contradictions between the cultural messages associated with hegemonic masculinities and those teaching practices conducive to optimal learning in primary schools (Hey et al. 2000).

However, every setting will have a hierarchy of masculinities, and will generally have its own dominant or hegemonic form of masculinity (Swain 2003), and thus there are different gender regimes operating in different places. As Skelton suggests, 'the form of hegemonic masculinity developed by a school is not "fixed" and is likely to vary from school to school' (1996: 194). She argues, therefore, that in trying to understand the form of hegemonic masculinity expressed in a particular primary school, it is important to consider the nature of social relations within the local community, taking into account the roles of class and ethnicity in shaping masculinities (O'Donnell and Sharpe 2000). In Skelton's (1996) study, undertaken in a deprived, working-class area with high levels of male unemployment and crime, hegemonic masculinity within the primary school was characterized by competition, intimidation and physical aggression – as it was in the local community. It is thus necessary to recognize that in *some* places there are considerable tensions between the culture of the school and the local community, so that pupils, rather than aspiring to secure the approval of teachers for conformity and good behaviour, seek to gain the recognition of other boys and adults in the school through their potential as a 'lad' (Skelton 2001). Although, as Reay (2003) comments, the majority of boys relate perfectly well to their female teachers and girls, in working-class schools a number of boys experience a tension between ensuring their masculinity is kept intact and maintaining academic success. As they move on to secondary school these are the boys who are likely to fall into Mac an Ghaill's (1994) category of 'macho lads', who view the school as a system of hostile authority and meaningless work demands. They are likely to obtain high self-esteem, not through academic achievement, but through involvement in crime, not getting caught, constantly challenging behaviour, drink and drugs, and so on (Skelton 2001). It is on two triads in predominantly working-class environments, where these kinds of issues were at the forefront, that this chapter focuses.

## Confronting the issues

In such contexts, Francis and Skelton (2003) point out, the adoption of a gender-relational perspective on the development of masculinity and femininity means that teachers need to *actively* intervene, first, recognizing their own preconceptions of gender, as well as those children bring with them into the classroom, and then developing strategies to challenge prevailing images. Thus, although not always explicitly acknowledged as such, successful strategies in tackling boys' under-achievement in primary (and secondary) schools, especially those in challenging circumstances, are those which are concerned with what we term 'socio-cultural' approaches. These kinds of approaches attempt to change images of laddish masculinity held by the peer group or perhaps the family and community, and to develop an ethos which helps to eradicate the 'it's not cool to learn' attitude among boys.

In many instances, socio-cultural approaches underpin, and form an integral and foundational aspect of, other strategies to raise boys' achievement. In this respect we broadly agree with authors such as Jackson (1998), Francis (2000) and Skelton (2001), who argue that many of the practical strategies to combat under-achievement can only make a superficial difference if they do not also address the more negative aspects of heterosexual masculinity and the perpetuation of a laddish gender culture. This is a real challenge, since in some instances schools unwittingly reinforce the laddish behaviour of the boys. For example, male bonding between boys and male teachers, as well as strategies that emphasize competition rather than cooperation, can, as Kenway et al. (1998) point out, reinforce laddishness and hegemonic forms of masculinity. Skelton (2001) discusses this in the context of male teachers in primary schools, where on occasions laddish behaviour, and fraternization with pupils rather than colleagues, can be particularly exclusionary for girls. Despite the evidence over several years of a number of feminists, that schools are gendered locales, many schools would not even acknowledge their role in perpetuating the gender divisions within society.

As already suggested, different challenges might arise in different areas. For example, one of the challenges in the schools we worked with in an area of inner London was to engage white working-class boys who came from families where no-one was employed in the formal labour market, and to convince them that they could make choices about their future. Strategies that appear to be working, then, are those that are embedded in the social and cultural fabric of the schools and communities in which they are set. What is important is that schools respond to the specific aspects of masculinity that both impede the learning of particular groups of boys, and may also have detrimental effects on girls' learning. This does not imply an acceptance of a deficit view of these young people's homes, but it does mean, as Skelton found in her 1996 study, attempting, in some instances, to create a clear demarcation between school and outside behaviour, and operating on a very different basis from that of the 'outside' community by imposing rule boundaries between school and community.

In some schools it may be only a small number of boys who, in the later stages of primary schooling, conform to a self-image that prevents success at school, but frequently such boys are very influential within the peer group and the school, and present a continual challenge. Furthermore, because some of these boys act as key leaders, influencing others within their cohort, this can have a wider impact on achievement. Where these boys espouse an anti-work ethos, it is important to minimize their influence by incorporating them within the mainstream of the school with the aim of establishing:

- a sense of pupil membership of the school and a sense of belonging;
- a sense of pupil responsibility and choice;
- feelings of physical and emotional security for pupils in the school;
- a sense of esteem and self-worth based on being a learner.

## Triad involvement in socio-cultural strategies

Within the RBA Project, socio-cultural strategies had a high profile during the pilot and intervention stages of the Project. There is a variety of ways in which socio-cultural strategies can be put into effect: this chapter discusses two triads which put into place such strategies through a whole-school, organizational approach, while the following chapter incorporates the work of a triad engaged in a socio-cultural strategy through a pedagogic framework. The first triad on which this chapter focuses was located in a predominantly working-class urban catchment area in the West Midlands. In the Originator School, a large junior school, 14 per cent of pupils had a first language other than English, compared with 11 per cent in Partner School 1 and 26 per cent in Partner School 2. The proportion of children eligible for free school meals in the Originator School was slightly above the national average, whereas both Partner

Schools had significant proportions of pupils in this category (just over 30 per cent, compared with the national average of 18.3 per cent). Both Partner Schools also had above average proportions of pupils identified as having special educational needs and parental expectations were said to be low. Partner School 2 had significant problems of teacher recruitment. Performance at Key Stage 2 in the Originator School had consistently exceeded the national average in all three core subjects (Figure 5.1), and there had been a steady increase in boys' performance. There were exceptionally high levels of achievement in science, with a narrow gender gap in both science and mathematics, although the gender gap in English was more variable, linked to variations in girls' attainment. Although there had been overall improvement in results in both Partner Schools, performance in National Curriculum tests in all core subjects at Key Stage 2 was well below the average for similar schools.

The second of the triads engaged in a whole-school approach was situated in a deprived inner London borough, south of the River Thames, with all three schools serving large local authority housing estates. In the Originator School, over 60 per cent of pupils were eligible for free school meals and almost half did not have English as their first language. Nevertheless, National Curriculum test results showed improving levels of achievement, with boys outperforming girls in the core subjects overall (Figure 5.2). The percentage of boys gaining level 4 in Key Stage 2 English rose from 48 per cent in 1996 to 89 per cent in 2000, and in the years 1997–2001, the performance of girls and boys in all core subjects at Key Stage 2 exceeded the national average by 1.2 points, while the

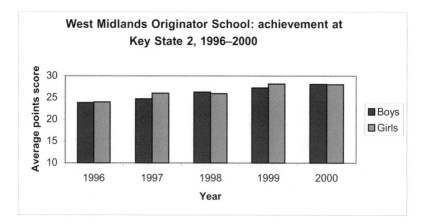

**Figure 5.1**  Key Stage 2 results, West Midlands Originator School (all core subjects)

*Note*: for information on calculation of average points scores, see: http://www.dfes.gov.uk/performancetables/primary_04/p4.shtml

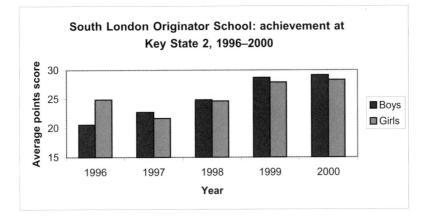

**Figure 5.2** Key Stage 2 results: South London Originator School (all core subjects)

*Note:* for information on calculation of average points scores, see: http://www.dfes.gov.uk/performancetables/primary_04/p4.shtml

average gender gap in Key Stage 2 English over the past five years has been only 0.1 point in favour of girls, compared to a national average of 1.6 points. At the start of the Project, the two Partner Schools also had above average proportions of children eligible for free school meals and relatively high proportions of children whose first language was not English. Like the Originator School, both Partner Schools performed well in National Curriculum tests, with results in core subjects at Key Stage 2 generally well above the national average for schools in similar circumstances. Results were more fluctuating in the Partner Schools, however, and Partner School 2 had a more significant gender gap in favour of girls across the five years.

The rationale behind a whole-school approach to tackling socio-cultural issues is to encourage all boys to be as fully involved in all aspects of school life as possible, in the belief that engendering involvement means that they are then less likely to turn away and feel alienated from learning. If the school is able to overcome the 'it's not cool to learn' attitude among groups of boys, and thus to challenge forms of hegemonic masculinity, then boys will be more likely to engage in learning. Many under-achieving boys, particularly those from the deprived socio-economic contexts in which these schools were situated, gain self-esteem through conforming to peer expectations in terms of consumption, or through prowess in sport, but at the same time lack self-esteem in learning, seeing academic achievement not as something to be aspired to, but associated with being a 'geek' and contrary to peer group norms. Knowing they can excel at something in school boosts self-confidence, which in turn is likely to impact positively on achievement in other areas.

It was clear from interviews with the headteachers of the Originator Schools in both triads that the kind of ethos engendered in their schools was fundamental to their success. The headteacher of the South London Originator School emphasized a 'strong positive ethos' where each child was made to feel valued and special, and where learning was both exciting and rigorous. Children were helped to understand that they had choices in their lives and self-discipline underpinned all the school was trying to achieve. They were also given a great deal of responsibility, and gained confidence as a result. In the West Midlands Originator School there had also been the development of a positive whole-school culture, seen as key to raising expectations of both staff and children. There was a culture of equality and teamwork, endeavouring to promote an ethos of learning as acceptable within a physical environment designed to stimulate feelings of pride and self-esteem among the children. In all of the schools there was an awareness of the need to tackle the behaviour of particular groups of boys. An initial meeting with the three headteachers forming the inner London triad, for example, revealed that all felt they were up against societal pressures which conflicted with the school ethos: they talked about the challenges of establishing their schools as secure, supportive environments, in which pupils could experience a consistent approach to behaviour, the need to value, but also offer alternatives to popular culture, the difficulties posed by the attractions of alcohol and drugs, and the pressure on boys to like football. They talked about primary school boys being naturally keen and enthusiastic, but often forced by peer group pressure to 'be something they're not'. The headteachers of both Originator Schools in South London and the West Midlands acknowledged that one of their first challenges on becoming Heads was to change the culture of aggressive behaviour among older boys in their schools, transforming the ethos from a macho intimidating one. Both of the Partner Schools in the West Midlands were concerned about high proportions of boys who were disruptive and disengaged.

Once the precise focus of the strategy had been agreed in both triads, it was decided that in each school a group of between 8 and 12 boys would be tracked by researchers through their final two years of primary schooling (Years 5 and 6) to try and assess the impact of the various initiatives, both on their engagement with school and learning, and on their academic achievement. These boys were interviewed on average on five occasions, either singly or in groups of two or three, and details of their progress were obtained from their class teachers. All the boys (except in the South London Originator School) were selected by the schools as under-achievers, in the sense that all were felt to be academically capable of doing better, but that attitude, lack of engagement or poor behaviour impeded learning. The boys were from mixed backgrounds: in the South London triad, 8 of the 26 under-achieving boys from the three schools were from white, working-class homes, and 18 were of Black African or Black Caribbean origin. As Chapter 2 shows, such boys are less likely to do well at school.

It was possible to discern from our discussions with teachers that the boys deemed to be under-achieving were often either key leaders among their peer group, distracting other children, or they were boys who were easily led and distracted by the key leaders. They were frequently described as bright, or as having plenty of academic potential, but were not prepared to put an effort into their school work. Often they were particularly reluctant to put pen to paper:

> He's a classic under-achieving boy – quite bright but he sees little value in school work – he's more interested in hair styles, trainers and self-image.

> He influences other children far too easily and has a tendency to play the clown.

> He is in the highest literacy and numeracy groups but is easily distracted and finds it difficult to sustain work throughout a period. He sometimes finds listening to others difficult because he is keen to develop his own point of view.

The focus group was different in the South London Originator School because strategies to tackle boys' under-achievement had been in place for a number of years, and the headteacher believed that under-achievement was not an issue by the time the children reached Year 5. The focus group boys here therefore consisted of boys from unsettled home backgrounds, six of whom were described as 'low achievers' and six of whom were felt to be achieving 'against the odds'.

## Getting the boys on board through citizenship initiatives

Following the recommendations of the Crick Report (Crick 1998), citizenship has become part of a non-statutory framework for personal, social and health education (PSHE) in primary schools, and this provided the backdrop for the set of intervention strategies adopted by the West Midlands Triad. Linked to work in PSHE, school councils were seen as the focus for strategies which aimed to establish a sense of pupil membership and responsibility, as well as empowering children to have a voice and to make choices about what happened at school. A whole range of approaches (see Table 5.1) fell broadly under the aegis of citizenship education, 'which includes the provision for pastoral and personal development of students and thus relates to both pedagogy and school ethos and culture' (Crick et al. 2005: 8). These initiatives were evaluated through pupil and teacher interviews, through observation and in some cases through measuring attitude change. It is not the intention here to spend a great deal of time describing in detail each of these activities since, as already suggested, they were chosen to represent a wide range of similar initiatives in place in many schools, and are already familiar to most teachers. Instead, the purpose, following a brief description, is to focus on the outcomes and impacts on pupils in terms of attitude and achievement, and in particular to examine the claim that they could impact positively on under-achieving boys.

Although school councils were initially more common in secondary schools, they are now becoming a feature of primary schools too, within the context of citizenship education (Taylor with Johnson 2002). They provided the initial focus of the socio-cultural strategies in the West

**Table 5.1** Citizenship initiatives evaluated in RBA schools

| Type of initiative | Triad schools involved |
| --- | --- |
| School Councils | West Midlands: introduced into all three schools academic year, 2001–2 |
| | Inner South London: established in Originator and Partner 1; introduced into Partner 2 academic year, 2001–2 |
| Circle Time | West Midlands: established in all three schools but expanded and developed alongside School Council initiative from 2001–2 |
| 'You Can Do It' | West Midlands: established in one Partner School; introduced into other two schools, academic year, 2002–3 |
| Pupil Responsibilities | West Midlands: established in Originator School, but re-focused 2001–2; introduced into Partner Schools academic year, 2002–3 |

Midlands schools, and were introduced with the principal aim of empowering children to make choices, to think, to reflect on the reasons for particular choices, to ask questions and to take risks within a supported, disciplined environment. The Project schools were keen to enable children to make a difference to what happened in their schools and to ensure that all were fully involved and had a voice. As a result, two of the schools moved fairly quickly to a situation where pupils chaired the school council and were responsible for keeping minutes.

Partner School 2 in the South London triad also introduced a school council as part of the RBA initiative. Here the process of setting up the council was established through the transfer of ideas from the other two triad schools, while in the West Midlands, the headteacher of the Originator School agreed to organize an after-school session for the staff of all three schools to develop understanding of school councils and to share experiences, with video materials used to demonstrate different models. Practical advice on setting up the councils was obtained from the School Council's UK website[1] and from the NSPCC publication, *School Councils: The View of Students and Teachers* (Baginsky and Hannam 1999). Visits to other local schools by children as well as staff also took place to observe good practice.

An integral aspect of the School Councils in the West Midlands was Circle Time. At its best, Mosley (1996) argues that Circle Time is a form of circular discussion, a forum for individual and organizational change, promoting self-esteem, self-discipline and responsibility towards others, building a sense of team and developing social skills. It is based on respect for the whole person, enabling people to deal with underlying factors that cause poor behaviour and result in low achievement (Mosley 1998). However, although increasingly popular in primary schools (Galton and Fogelman 1998), Taylor's (2003) research found a lack of an integrated, cohesive and inclusive whole-school approach to Circle Time, and a lack of training among staff. She also expressed some scepticism over teachers' claims that Circle Time can enhance academic performance through increased self-esteem, self-confidence and communication skills. Circle Time was in place in all three of the West Midlands schools, but in each school it was re-orientated as part of the RBA initiative to become a whole-school approach, and to evolve as an essential classroom-based forum to discuss School Council ideas as well as other issues. All staff received training and were encouraged to use Circle Time in this way, and initially to discuss the qualities needed to make a good councillor, and how manifestos might be created. However, while the teachers in Taylor's (2003) study expressed their aims mainly in social terms, in the West Midlands schools it was also decided specifically to monitor and encourage under-achieving boys' participation in Circle Times in a bid to raise achievement.

The West Midlands schools also took on the scheme, 'You Can Do It' (YCDI), which was in some cases incorporated into Circle Time. The scheme had been adopted by the local education authority as its programme for Personal Social and Health Education, and one of the Partner Schools had initially taken part as a trial school. Developed by Michael Bernard (Bernard et al. 1987), YCDI is a theory which identifies four 'Foundations' as necessary for achievement and socio-emotional-behavioural well-being: Confidence, Persistence, Organization and Getting Along. These foundations are said to be nurtured through 11 habits of mind and together they produce a positive mindset. Also identified is a negative mindset, consisting of four 'Blockers' that contribute to poor psychological health, under-achievement and disaffection: Low Self-Esteem–Anxiety, General Work Avoidance, General Disorganization and Rebelliousness–Anger, and these are supported and nourished by 11 negative habits of mind. The aim of the scheme, therefore, is to provide the foundations for achievement and social-emotional-behavioural well-being (Bernard 1996, 2000; see also the You Can Do It website[2]).

Alongside these was the pupil responsibilities initiative: responsibilities were discussed in the school councils and in Circle Times, and allocated through elections, through teacher appointments, through pulling names out of hats or through volunteering. They therefore involved all children, but provided the opportunity for teachers to target particular children who were under-achieving, disengaged or lacking in self-esteem. Responsibilities included playground buddies, library, tuck-shop and computer monitors, children serving on fundraising and welcoming committees and being part of a 'green team' responsible for keeping the school tidy. Training was given with Year 9 students from the nearby comprehensive school, for example, being involved in training buddies to support other children during playtime. The jobs were seen as having status and something to be aspired to, and could be withdrawn as a result of bad behaviour or lack of commitment.

### Impact of citizenship initiatives

It is clearly not possible to isolate a set of strategies and to hold them solely responsible for any change in pupils' engagement in school, increased self-esteem for learning, or improved achievement, particularly if, as was the case with most of the schools participating in the Project, they are engaged in more than one initiative. In addition, most of the strategies had been in place for a relatively short time – some for only a year – and would need time to embed themselves and for any problems to be addressed. This notwithstanding, we would argue that the intensive qualitative research which members of the Project team undertook, together with some quantitative evidence, allow us to make some valid judgements about the effects of the initiatives that were undertaken.

All four schools which introduced school councils as part of the RBA Project felt they were an important part of a range of strategies that create a more inclusive school environment. School councils enabled all children to learn that resolving issues is not simple, because of the need to reconcile many different views. They therefore learnt to listen, to discuss, to compromise, to resolve complicated issues, to work collaboratively. The introduction of a school council at the South London Partner School was seen in positive terms by the great majority of children. Questionnaires to Year 5 and Year 6 children expressed broad satisfaction with the council, the councillors and with the achievements to date. Interviews with the groups of girls and boys were also positive: they were enthusiastic about having a formal opportunity to talk with other children about issues they were concerned about, rather than taking them straight to a teacher. Having a council did seem to give them a say in how the school was run, and several pupils talked about how their own ideas had contributed to change. There are obvious advantages for the councillors themselves, in building self-confidence and self-esteem and developing responsibility. As one councillor explained, 'It makes you feel really good about yourself, and confident to speak out.' This has an impact on behaviour and engenders a sense of responsibility within the school community. Thus, we concur with Taylor and Johnson (2002: 119), who suggest that 'school councils appear to be successful in initiating positive, tangible change within primary schools'.

However, despite these positive impacts on the school as a whole, and on councillors in particular, in some ways school councils might be seen as less successful in improving the engagement of under-achieving children because such children may not be directly involved as councillors, while others believe their voices remain unheard. Nevertheless, when an under-achieving child *is* elected as a school councillor, it is possible that the skills learnt may impact positively on learning, and this did seem to be the case, at least to some extent, with the two boys in the focus group at the South London Partner School who were elected councillors. One boy in particular was evidently pleased, saying that being a councillor made him feel good, and that his mother was proud of him. He had felt too shy to stand the first year, but enjoyed taking part in the council and liaising with his class. His teacher subsequently reported that being a councillor had made a real difference to the boy's attitude towards school and work.

At a broader level, under-achievers who lack involvement in school and engagement in school work can benefit from a school council if the structures are in place, not only to *enable* them to participate, but to *actively encourage* them to take part properly. In some triads, teachers had clearly helped boys learn the language of negotiation, asking, for example, 'So how *do* you encourage cooperative behaviour?'. Active encouragement is not always easy, however, as one teacher commented:

> He gets very involved in Circle Time discussions, but often shouts out without considering others' points of view. He has been inattentive and disengaged, but he is now becoming a much more interested participant in discussions, though he still sometimes distracts others and does not engage in a cooperative way.

In the South London Originator School (which had a long-standing school council), there was a great deal of individual encouragement to become involved in council activities, while in the West Midlands Originator School teachers were asked particularly to monitor and encourage under-achievers to listen, question and engage in a positive way during Circle Times, and ensure that all were involved in writing manifestos, voting and participating in discussion. As a result, children in both schools felt fully involved and saw the school council as relevant and meaningful to them. Most of the focus group boys were keen to be councillors, with five out of eight of the boys at the West Midlands Originator School putting themselves forward. In the South London Originator, six of the focus group boys had been councillors and all had enjoyed the experience, said it increased levels of confidence and felt they did a good job. One boy who had not been a councillor said he was too shy to be one, although he did put ideas forward and people listened to him so he felt he could make a difference in this way. All the others who had not been councillors wanted the opportunity and thought they would have the right qualities, although there is a danger in some contexts that vocal and engaged boys might squeeze out the contributions of more reticent ones.

In contrast, in the South London Partner School, where there were less formal arrangements for children to discuss school council business, and no agreed commitment to target the participation of under-achievers, the focus group boys appeared less involved. Although all thought the school council was a good idea, and that some changes for the better had taken place, most lacked the self-confidence to participate: some were not sure that if they put forward ideas they would really be listened to, and some said they did not join in discussion because they had no good ideas. Of the original group of ten boys, six of them did not put themselves forward to be councillors in either Year 5 or Year 6, although three said they would like to be a councillor. All talked about being too shy to stand for election, or not having any good ideas, saying they were not good enough or did not feel confident speaking in front of other people. As one of them said, 'I'm not one of them people.' It is perhaps the case that in this school, where other strategies such as YCDI and Circle Time were not in place, that the boys' levels of confidence and self-assurance were less well developed when it came to taking on a high profile role.

In the West Midlands triad the majority of boys who were tracked across Years 5 and 6 were very positive about the range of strategies used to involve them in school life. Discussion with them suggested that there was development in the following areas:

- *Trust between pupils*: boys identified Circle Time as a time when they could tell the truth, speak out and look at problems: 'The class will look out for you.'
- *Trust between pupils and staff*: boys perceived a greater degree of openness between them and teachers, and better relationships ensued. Responsibilities were welcomed as an indication of teachers' trust: 'They trust us now we're in Year 6, to look after the younger kids and show them a good example.'
- *Confidence, pride and self-belief*: the language of YCDI, reinforced by teachers and through assemblies, alongside other strategies, led to increased levels of confidence: 'It helps you to be confident and get to know people better, and not to be nervous.' Several boys felt this would be particularly helpful in moving to secondary school.
- *Pride in individual areas of responsibility*: several boys were pleased that time had been invested in training them for particular responsibilities, and those who had not been given a responsibility were keen to prove themselves worthy of one.
- *Articulacy*: boys found it easier to express ideas orally, in Circle Time and through YCDI, than in writing and enjoyed doing so. By the final interviews they were noticeably more able to articulate their feelings.
- *Positive language*: the boys talked enthusiastically about the positive and negative statements of YCDI – even boys who had not enjoyed the programme were clearly influenced by its positive language.

- *Listening and feeling listened to*: the boys recognized school councils as a forum for their views. Circle Time was seen as facilitating the resolution of problems, and it was clear that the boys appreciated having to talk about themselves.
- *Ability to reflect*: YCDI and Circle Time helped develop the ability to reflect on ideas, so the boys talked about learning about themselves and others. They were able to identify which 'mind sets' they were best at, which required improvement, and how to improve.
- *Organization*: YCDI helped with organizational skills, which were recognized as important for academic improvement.
- *Self-control*: several boys said they learnt through YCDI how to control their behaviour and avoid fights.

Some teachers thought that giving children specific responsibilities around the school had made a significant difference to some under-achievers, though only when they felt their contribution had been valued, and when enthusiasm and commitment could be maintained. However, like the boys, teachers considered Circle Time and YCDI the most successful of the strategies implemented. These were seen as particularly valuable because they offered all boys the opportunities to voice their opinions within a secure classroom environment:

> Teachers are able to use planned activities and focused questioning to ensure all pupils are engaged and feel included and valued.

> There is an element of trust that allows boys to voice their opinions without fear of ridicule.

It was thought that Circle Time allowed the under-achieving boys to become engaged in issues relating to themselves and the school in general, and the focus group boys across all three schools responded well, although some boys did view Circle Time as an opportunity to entertain an 'audience'. Those who were inclined to act as class clowns had a tendency to dominate and not stick to agreed rules unless a firm hand was taken by the teacher.

Although introduced only recently in two of the schools, the YCDI scheme was felt to be effective in each of the schools because it gave the boys a chance to reflect on their behaviour and put the emphasis on positive achievement rather than failure:

It provides them with regular opportunities to become involved in lessons that focus on promoting positive self-images. The non-academic focus engages their interest and draws on their experiences.

It is all about recognizing who you are and beginning to value yourself, which for the 'classic under-achiever' has a positive impact.

YCDI was seen as effective in providing children with regular opportunities to become involved in non-academic lessons that focused on promoting positive self-images, engaged their interest and drew on their experiences. It was seen to have a significant impact in these schools because of the whole-hearted commitment of staff to reinforce aspects of the scheme across the whole curriculum. Furthermore, the schools had responded to pupil feedback and reduced the number of repetitive work-sheets which the children had found boring, emphasizing instead the brainstorming and group activities that the boys in particular enjoyed. Such an approach, therefore, was not just about trying to moderate boys' behaviour, but amending teaching approaches which themselves could lead to disaffection or disengagement.

Thus, the headteachers of the Originator and both Partner Schools saw clear benefits for the under-achieving boys from the YCDI and Circle Time initiatives. These benefits were seen as:

- *Improved behaviour*: all felt that the behaviour of the majority of the under-achieving boys had improved. In one of the Partner Schools, where most of the group of boys had previously been regular visitors at the Head's office to discuss behaviour issues, such visits had become rare.
- *More positive attitudes towards school and a greater commitment to school work*: with some boys, staff were able to see real changes in attitude towards school. The boys enjoyed the focus on oral participation and, as would be expected, responded well when action followed the suggestions they made.

It is possible, furthermore, to provide an indication of academic progress for the focus group boys, using DfES tables,[3] to calculate the 'value added' score of each child between Key Stages 1 and 2, and to compare the average progress of the focus group boys with the value-added score for the school as a whole. The resulting figures must be treated with great caution, both because of the very small size of the sample group of boys, and because of our earlier expressed reservation about the validity of value-added approaches (see Chapter 2, together with points raised by Tymms and Dean 2004). This notwithstanding, however, they show (Table 5.2) that in Partner School 1, and particularly in the Originator School, the focus group boys progressed at a greater rate than children in the school(s) as a whole. In Partner School 2 the progress made by the focus group boys was at a similar rate to other children, which was itself in line with the national average (between 99.3 and 100.7), despite the fact that the initial identification of these boys was based on their 'under-achievement', and they would therefore have been expected to achieve less well than the cohort as a whole.

In terms of overall results at Key Stage 2, the Originator School continued to perform strongly, achieving at levels not only better than average for similar schools, but exceeding the national average, and improving steadily year-on-year. While the gender gap widened, we would argue that continuing improvement for both sexes is a cause for celebration. Overall results in the Partner Schools continued to fluctuate, with results in Partner School 2 reflecting, in part, serious deficiencies in staffing. Partner School 1, however, achieved its best ever Key Stage 2 results in 2003, with results in English and science, exceeding the national average.

It must be stressed again that it is not possible, of course, to assert that the changes noted above are directly the result of the socio-cultural strategies put in place in these schools: other school effects such as booster classes, changes of teacher between Years 5 and 6 and increased pressure as National Curriculum tests drew near, as well as factors affecting individuals such as greater levels of maturity by the end of Year 6 and the influence of pupils' home environments, all affect a child's behaviour, commitment to school work and academic progress. Furthermore, the strategies themselves are still evolving, and need time to become embedded into the culture of the schools. This is particularly so in Partner School 2, where evidence pointed to much more positive attitudes among boys as a whole, but this was not yet being translated into significant academic improvement. Despite these caveats, we believe that it is possible to make some claims about the success of this

**Table 5.2** Key Stage 1 to Key Stage 2 Progress – West Midlands Focus Group Boys

| Value-added measure | Originator School | Partner 1 | Partner 2 |
| --- | --- | --- | --- |
| Whole school | 100.5 | 101.2 | 99.3 |
| Focus group boys | 105.0 | 101.5 | 99.2 |

Note: 'Expected value added measure', using DfES criteria, = 100.0

group of strategies. We would agree with Taylor (2003) in her reservations about claiming that any one initiative on its own (in Taylor's case, Circle Time) can have an impact on under-achievement. Nevertheless, our findings did concur with those of Crick et al. (2005), who list a number of positive outcomes of citizenship education, including, for example, enhancing students' learning and achievement and empowerment leading to increased self-confidence. Where these kinds of initiative form part of wider pedagogic practices and form an integrated, whole-school approach to citizenship and PSHE, where teachers receive adequate training, and – in particular – where there is full commitment on the part of every member of staff to making the approach work, then we believe that such strategies *can* play a key role in raising achievement.

## Breaking down barriers to learning through involvement in the arts

In 2000, following a review of the National Curriculum, primary schools were told that they could reduce provision in subjects such as art and music in order to concentrate on literacy and numeracy, although even by that date evidence was emerging that the Literacy and Numeracy Strategies were causing an imbalance in the curriculum of primary schools (Brehony 2005). Evidence was produced, for example, by Galton and MacBeath (2002), who argued that the introduction of the National Curriculum had led to the erosion of a broad and balanced curriculum and a decline in curriculum time available for creative subjects such as art, drama and music. Their study of 267 primary schools showed, for example, that music received the least amount of curriculum time during a typical week, with a median figure of just half an hour. Many teachers in the study said that the creative subjects were being squeezed out, with the consequence that there were fewer opportunities for children to be good at something, to succeed or to excel. The regret expressed by these teachers is justified, given findings from the literature which stress the importance of the arts in schools. Headteachers who took part in a study by Downing, Johnson and Kaur (2003), for example, believed that the arts could contribute to increased motivation, behaviour, attendance and self-esteem, and were essential to raising standards in school. Further evidence is available from Walker (1996), who argues that music contributes to socializing and pleasurable experiences in a group, to personal fulfilment and positive attitudes towards school.

While this is the case at the general level, it might be seen as particularly important for those who are less academically able or who are excluded in some way from mainstream society. Drama, for example, leads to learning that is not simply intellectual, but affective; it is therefore essential for pupils who, in the widest sense, have 'special needs' (Jones et al. 1996). It helps to develop a strong sense of group identity, Jones et al. argue, involving participants in negotiation and planning, in assertion and compromise and in the clarification of individual values. Music, too, can be a means to social inclusion (Allen and Cope 2004). The positive effects of a strong programme of arts education, such as improved self-esteem and personal and social development, have been described by Harland et al.'s (2000) research in secondary schools as highly pertinent to the task of tackling social exclusion among young people, a view reinforced by Ofsted's (2003a) report on the role of the arts in improving city schools. Describing his early years growing up as the son of a poor white single mother in one of Chicago's most notorious ghettoes, renowned sociologist Richard Sennett recalls how in his experience an inner sense of dignity comes from developing a skill:

> the development of any talent involves an element of craft, of doing something well for its own sake, and it is this craft element which provides the individual with an inner sense of self-respect. The craft of music made that gift to me.
>
> (2003: 14)

Sennett goes on to say that finally managing a good vibrato after several years of practice was 'an epochal event for me, as important a milestone as becoming good at games would be for another child' (p. 14). Unfortunately, however, as Sennett himself points out, class prejudice often stands in the way of developing that inner motivation among poor children. It is therefore perhaps unsurprising that Harland et al.'s (1995) study of 700 young people in five regions of England, found that the most likely candidates for non-enjoyment of the arts were males from partly skilled and unskilled backgrounds, where fewer than one in a hundred felt that primary school arts had been an occasion for realizing talent, and fewer than one in ten saw primary school arts as producing any significant skill acquisition. Over a quarter of respondents said they had not enjoyed or valued arts in their primary school.

As discussed above, the three schools in the South London triad served areas of significant social deprivation – areas similar to those where Harland et al. found young men turned off the arts by their primary schools. When the Project began, however, all three schools had a long-standing commitment to a broad curriculum, with a strong emphasis on the arts, particularly music and drama. While such a focus has more recently become government orthodoxy in England and Wales (DfES, 2003), the stance of these three schools at the time was unusual, as Galton and MacBeath's (2002) research suggests. The headteachers were experienced heads, describing themselves as 'maverick': all had confidence in their own leadership and all were willing to take risks and stand out from the crowd. (None of the schools, for example, had implemented the National Literacy Strategy, and yet Key Stage 2 results in English were above the national average.) Their schools promoted an ethos similar to the 'creative school' described by Jeffrey and Woods (2003) as 'a new kind of primary school, one which both takes note of the official policy discourse and reconstructs that discourse in line with their own cherished values'. Given their long-standing commitment to the arts, together with the strong belief in the promotion of the arts as a means of stimulating greater involvement in school and hence in learning, it was decided that this would be the main focus for the intervention strategy in these schools. The purpose was to help to articulate, and to evaluate the policy which already existed; it was also to provide evidence to support the 'gut instincts' based on the head-teachers' experience over the years, evidence which, despite such headteachers' convictions, is often hard to pin down (Ofsted 2003a). Evaluation focused both on specific aspects of arts activities engaged in by a range of children, and through focus groups of 8–12 boys.

These schools regularly engaged in a wide range of activities related to the creative and performance arts, as well as encouraging visits to the school by professional artists and visits by the children to galleries and exhibitions. In each school, the arts curriculum was designed to reflect the richness provided by the cultural diversity in which the schools were located. Both the Originator School and Partner School 1 took advantage of opportunities for their children to take part in the production of Shakespeare plays at the Globe Theatre in London. In addition, Partner School 1 had been successful in bidding for a grant from Creative Partnerships,[4] which enabled it to participate more fully in visual arts, drama and musical activities, including dance projects for each class. All three schools enabled children to have music lessons, with the Head-teacher in Partner School 2 himself teaching guitar lessons. This school also held an annual poetry week which involved all children, staff, some governors and parents, which focused on the performance of poetry through class presentations to the whole school. Another focus for arts-based activities in the Originator School was the annual celebration of Black History Month.

With the exception of poetry week and learning to play the recorder, participation in arts activities which extended beyond the normal curriculum was voluntary in Partner School 2. Children opted into music lessons and auditions for Christmas and summer plays, and were chosen according to aptitude. The other two schools had policies of trying to engage individual under-achievers through specific activities as a way of raising their self-esteem as learners, stimulating engagement and helping children to find something they could excel in.

### Impact of arts-focused initiatives

Analysis of the focus in these schools on the wider curriculum showed there to be impacts on the schools as a whole. The most recent Ofsted Report for the Originator School freely uses adjectives such as 'excellent' and 'outstanding', referring to an 'atmosphere of celebration of the achievements of all pupils', with pupils encouraged to think and to express their thoughts and feelings from the time they enter school, and so develop self-confidence as learners. The Report also commends the way in which

> the involvement in music and drama makes an excellent contribution to the self-esteem of pupils, which in turn has a very good impact on the standards that they achieve ... The range of activities is wide enough to enable every pupil to find a strength.

Common across achievers *and* low-achievers was a real feeling of involvement in school:

> Most of the time I like school because you get a proper education. This is a brilliant school. The best thing is the fun activities, and the way they teach you is fun. There's no worst thing about school. ... I've been told when I'm out of the school the teacher says she misses my ideas, so I always feel I'm part of the school.
>
> (Paul, end of Year 5)

Drama and various extra-curricular activities were clearly important to the children, with some boys citing 'all the fun activities' and school trips as the best thing about school. They talked about the enjoyment they felt when playing music, the feeling of being 'relaxed and happy' and the pleasure of performing in front of other people. All the boys who were interviewed in this school said they enjoyed drama, and several talked animatedly about their previous play, with even the least positive boy becoming excited: he had found Dahl's *Charlie and the Chocolate Factory* 'excellent', and said he learnt how to act and developed new skills without even realizing he was learning. They articulated the benefits of drama as enjoyment ('because we did it once in a real theatre'), learning to become more self-confident, 'to be brave and speak out loudly', 'not to laugh even when you're performing something really silly', 'to control yourself and perform in front of the whole school' and 'to do things as a team'. All but one said that taking part in productions made them feel more a part of school. As one boy said, 'Plays make the school a better place.' By the final interviews, the homework clubs which had focused on English and Maths before the National Curriculum tests had changed to offer art, drama and keep fit, and most of the focus group boys were attending these, and were enthusiastic about how much fun they were.

A sense of community within the school was further engendered through activities such as Black History month, when the children enjoyed various activities from making puppets, hand-painting, dressing up, and listening to and watching visiting groups who told stories, sang and danced. The boys talked about this being fun and enjoyable, and exciting to learn about different cultures, as well as learning about the good and bad things in black history, which 'helps you to understand how you should get on with everyone, not just people of the same colour and with the same accent – it's about getting on with people from different cultures'. One of the least able boys was able to talk about Martin Luther King standing up for freedom and the rights of people of colour. Others talked about the importance of not judging people by their colour: 'our school celebrates all different types of culture', and that it was important 'to go on learning not to be racist'.

In Partner School 2, two groups of three girls and four groups of three boys from Years 5 and 6 were interviewed at the end of Poetry Week. This activity was seen by the children in very positive terms:

- It was seen principally as fun and enjoyable, by boys as much as girls.
- It engendered a sense of community, partly because it involved the whole school, but more importantly because it brought the whole class together. One girls' group spoke of boys in their class cheering them on so they would not be shy, and telling them afterwards how good they were. A boys' group said that although they did not enjoy poetry in general, and would not read it at home, they enjoyed performing it as a class. The children talked about enjoying working as a team, listening to each other and co-operating together as they practised.
- Performing the poems built up self-confidence, and watching others perform helped them to appreciate a variety of poetry.

These examples show that the activities that form part of the wider curriculum do help children to feel involved in school. They are seen as enjoyable as well as teaching a range of skills which the children themselves could identify. For example, they talked about being part of a team and developing skills of organization:

> Dancing teaches you how to work in a group because you have to co-operate with other people, especially if some people in the group are not so keen.

> When you're playing the steel pans you have to care about the other people and not just yourself, so you learn to co-operate and develop a sense of commitment to the group.

In addition to acquiring new skills and knowledge in specific areas, such as 'the difference between funny and serious acting', the children also developed skills and qualities that would be useful in other contexts: they mentioned voice projection and learning how to express themselves well, for example, and one said that with dancing you have to think a lot about what to do, so it helped with thinking skills in the classroom.

While interviews with pupils indicated very positive attitudes towards the arts-based activities described above, benefiting the school in general (as with the drama strategy described in Chapter 7), we also contend that such a strategy can have a specific effect on underachievers because it has the important effect of breaking down a range of barriers to learning. The headteacher in each school talked about particular pupils whose attitudes and achievement had been turned round as barriers had been broken down. One boy who was part of the focus group in the Originator School had had considerable emotional and behavioural problems, and giving him a lead role in the class play had proved to be a really motivating experience for him. He no longer exhibited volatile and unpredictable behaviour and, although it was a real challenge for him to learn his lines, he had become 'a totally different child, completely focused on his work'. The boy himself was hugely enthusiastic:

> The first time I thought, oh no, not drama, but since I've been doing it, I want to do it all the time and go to drama school. I really love acting. I'm not shy, I'm brave going up there and I'll do whatever I want. I can do all sorts of different acting in school and I'm proud of being able to act. My Mum says she might get me into a club outside school, but she hasn't even bothered, but

she's got a lot of things on her mind. I likes singing as well, and I've sung in front of the school, lots of teachers, parents, and the teachers said I was one of the best singers and that made me really happy.

Another boy in the same school had become much more engaged in school at the beginning of Year 6, to the extent that his mother had come into school worried that he had become more interested in reading than in playing football! It is worth underlining again here the point about *active* involvement of under-achievers in these kinds of activities: both schools were explicitly choosing under-achieving pupils to enable them to take advantage of opportunities for arts-based engagement, through key roles in drama or dance productions, for specialist music tuition, or to be part of school bands. This is a crucial difference from what takes place in other schools, where it is the pupils who show more talent or greater promise who are singled out.

The example of Partner School 1 shows how this policy played out in practice among the nine under-achieving boys who formed the focus group there. These were boys who were variously described by their teachers at the beginning of Year 5 in the following terms: 'extremely lacking in self-confidence', 'uses his charm to avoid concentrating on tasks and getting involved in learning', 'has a self-image as very popular "jack-the-lad"', 'very volatile and takes a long time to calm down and engage in learning', 'lacks involvement in learning and has low self-esteem' and 'finds concentration extremely difficult'. In the initial interviews with the Project researcher, it was apparent that although all knew it was important to do well at school, various barriers to learning were clearly evident among these boys, and some were explicitly articulated:

I could probably improve a little bit because I do get told off quite a bit for not concentrating hard enough.

I could pay more attention because there's a person behind me and he always makes me turn round so I'm not facing the right way. He's always distracting me.

I could help myself and everyone around me if I didn't lose my temper.

Several of the boys talked particularly about arguments at playtime, especially over football, and how these spilled over into the classroom, making it difficult for them to focus on their work. They were well aware of what stood in the way of them achieving as well as they might, and tracking them across the two years showed the impact of some of the arts-focused activities in breaking down these barriers.

In their second term in Year 5, all pupils at the school were involved in the production of Shakespeare's *Twelfth Night* at the Globe Theatre in London. One of the focus group boys had a solo musician's part, and four were chosen to take main speaking parts, not because of their acting ability, but because they were perceived by their teachers to be in need of greater self-esteem and confidence. Being chosen therefore immediately boosted their confidence, and all expressed surprise at being selected to take part, particularly because they felt there were other children who would have been more obvious choices. They said they felt better about themselves because they had been able to learn their lines, or because people praised them for their achievements. Finding they could be good at something made them feel more confident in relation to their peers or in the eyes of their families. What was particularly impressive was that six months after the Globe production, the boys could still articulate the lasting effect of the skills and qualities they had learnt.

The other activity involving all the pupils when in Year 6 was a series of dance projects linked to the Creative Partnerships scheme. Castle et al. (2002) describe dance as having a distinctive role in education, as a holistic artform involving mind, body and spirit, as a cultural ambassador communicating different cultures and as a 'non-verbal' artform requiring physical and mental concentration and developing cooperation and collaboration. Several of the boys had not expected to enjoy dancing, and had been surprised to find that they did so. They were also positive about how it made them feel: 'The first time I danced I thought it's going to make me sad, but when I danced it made me happy, and it makes you laugh too.' Even the boy who had been most reluctant to participate in the dance project ('jack-the-lad') said he would take up the chance to dance if it were offered in his secondary school, and had a star part in the end-of-year dance evening put on for parents.

In addition, four of the boys had been selected to be in the Djembe drumming club, and three were in the school's steel band. Another boy had been chosen through the Royal Ballet's Chance to Dance scheme, with a three-year commitment to ballet lessons. Again, all felt honoured to have been selected from among the large numbers wanting to take part in these activities, and had clearly gained a huge amount of enjoyment from the opportunities they had been given. They talked about the fun of performance, the excitement of everyone's eyes being upon them, the frustration of sometimes not being able to get something quite right, and the importance of hard work and commitment to the group as a whole. Table 5.3 articulates the impact of these various activities in the boys' own words.

**Table 5.3** Breaking down the barriers in the boys' own words

| Barriers to learning | Impact of activities |
| --- | --- |
| Lack of concentration | In the steel band you learn to concentrate, and you learn to listen to what the pans are doing and think about other people. |
| Lack of self-control | Sometimes I get a bit angry at school, and that stops me doing well, but I don't get angry doing music – it helps me to feel calm. |
| Impatience | Acting is really hard because you have to do things again and again and again, and sometimes you do get fed up, but it really teaches you patience. |
| | When I started ballet I wanted to quit because I couldn't do it, but I kept going, and as it got better and I started performing I felt good about myself. |
| Low self-esteem | I didn't think I'd be chosen because I'm not very good. I thought my teacher had made a mistake, but when I got in the play I just wanted to jump up and burst out laughing. |
| | I've always wanted to be in the steel band and never thought I would be. When my teacher told me I'd been chosen I was so shocked, and I went back to my house that day and I screamed and ran up and down the hill and all around the place because I was so happy. |
| Lack of self-confidence | I learnt all the lines and it went well. I felt very nervous beforehand, but I felt proud afterwards. Acting gives you a sense of boldness. |
| | I feel like I've achieved something, because when I first started I wasn't really that good, but I've got better. I think I've achieved this year and done better in nearly everything. I feel good about myself. |
| Lack of engagement with school | When we do things like that, and I come back to the classroom, I think, that was done with the school, and I've started to think I really like school because if our teacher can organize really fun things like that, she knows what children are like, and I think, that's good. |
| Inability to express themselves | I remember the kind of emotion when I was at the Globe Theatre. It taught me that it does really really good to really express my emotion. Afterwards I felt like I'd revealed everything and had expressed myself in front of everyone. |

It was very noticeable how much most of the boys in the Partner School 1 focus group changed during the two years, so that by the final interviews they really did seem to have grown in self-esteem and to have become more self-confident. For those boys who do not usually excel in the classroom, finding something they could be good at made them feel better in relation to their peers as well as pleasing teachers and families. They found themselves becoming less angry in the playground and more able to reflect about how to deal with difficult situations. Involvement in dancing had also challenged some stereotypical views about what was suitable for boys and girls. It was clearly evident that the boys became more and more positive about school during the time we were interviewing them. Even one of the most difficult of the boys, who talked openly how 'bad' he was in Year 5, to the point of stealing some money from a teacher's purse, ended the last interview with the comment that at school 'everything's perfect' – and he also managed to raise his academic attainment from level 1 at KS1 to level 4s at KS2.

Similarly, in the Originator School, all 12 boys felt they had changed in positive ways between the beginning of Year 5 and the end of Year 6, and all but one said their confidence had increased. For some, changes had to do with working a lot harder, or growing up and becoming more mature. Some said their behaviour had improved, both in the classroom and outside; they said there was less fighting, and greater ability to sort out their own problems and reach agreement without teacher input. One talked extensively about his change in attitude:

> In Year 5 I wouldn't stop talking, I kept answering questions wrong and I never finished my work. I've changed my behaviour 2000% because I used to mess about and kept getting told off.

In Partner School 2, where involvement in extra-curricular drama or music was voluntary, pupils' reactions were less positive, and half of the focus group boys said during the early interviews that they did not like either drama or music and would not wish to take part in activities outside the classroom. By the final interviews only two of the boys had had a part in a major dramatic production, and the boys' views about arts activities had not changed. As a group, there appeared to be less change between Years 5 and 6 than in the other two schools. Although all said they had worked harder during Year 6, only half said that their work had improved and that they felt more confident as a result. One said he had become more focused and another talked about increased levels of concentration. In contrast, three of the boys in this group were not particularly communicative, and two remained quite negative about school.

The changing attitudes of the focus group boys are reflected in their attainment at Key Stage 2, as indicated in Table 5.4. In the Originator School, as already mentioned, the focus group was made up of 'low' and 'high' achievers, rather than under-achievers, since the school was confident in the effectiveness of the strategies it had put into place to tackle any sign of under-achievement before pupils reached the final two years of primary schooling. In this school, value-added measures were high, and, as expected, improvements among the focus group boys were in line with those of the cohort as a whole. In Partner School 1, where the targeting of under-achieving boys in arts projects was a major focus from midway through Year 5 and into Year 6, the focus group boys made significant progress. In Partner School 2, average value-added measures were achieved in the cohort as a whole, perhaps reflecting in part the whole-school policies of inclusion fostered through an explicit focus on the arts. Value-added measures for the focus group boys were very slightly lower: these boys experienced the whole-school approaches, but were not targeted to take part in activities as in Partner School 2.

Key Stage 2 results overall for these schools showed some variation from year to year, with the Originator School having a blip in its English and mathematics results in 2002, linked to that particular cohort of pupils. Its results in 2004 and 2005, however, clearly exceeded the national average for all schools in England and the gender gap remained neglible. Results for Partner School 1 continued to improve: they were particularly impressive in 2005 (Figure 5.3), with achievement clearly exceeding the national average, despite the challenging environment within which the school is situated. Not only did the pupils in this cohort perform particularly well in terms of the proportion gaining the benchmark level 4, but significant proportions attained the higher level 5 (Figure 5.4).

Giving a high profile to good quality drama, dance, music and visual art provision clearly provides enjoyment, as well as a range of skills specific to each activity, and, as other studies show (Ofsted 2004a), should be promoted. In the RBA Project, evidence from children's testimony showed that participation in the wider curriculum made them

**Table 5.4:** Key Stage 1 to Key Stage 2 progress – South London focus group boys

| Value-added measure | Originator School | Partner School 1 | Partner School 2 |
|---|---|---|---|
| Whole school | 100.8 | 99.2 | 99.9 |
| Focus group boys | 100.9 | 101.3 | 99.7 |

Note: 'Expected value added measure', using DfES criteria, = 100.0

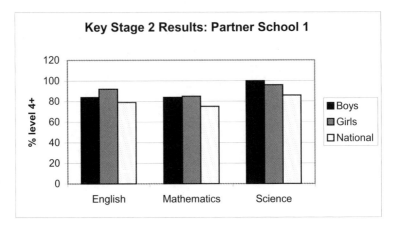

**Figure 5.3** South London Partner School Results 2005: pupils attaining level 4+

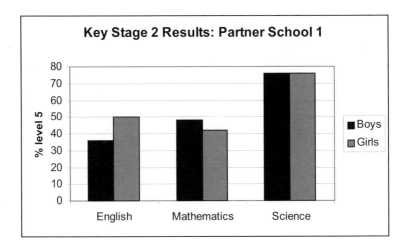

**Figure 5.4** South London Partner School Results 2005: pupils attaining level 5

feel more fully involved in school. Furthermore, the research in these three schools shows that the targeting of under-achievers for specific involvement in arts-based activities can bring not only personal and social benefits, but can also lead to a greater engagement in learning and contribute to higher levels of attainment. Choosing such boys for this kind of involvement is not enough in itself, however: it needs to be accompanied by an explicit recognition by teachers that these boys will need help and encouragement to perform the role *well*. There is no sense in which the pupils are 'set up to fail'; instead time and effort are invested to ensure success, and a very real sense of achievement. This, of course, needs a real commitment by all staff involved, together with a willingness to take risks. The real essence of the strategy, then, relates back to the ethos established by the headteacher, and the sense of dedication to tackling under-achievement through a variety of means. We would therefore argue that where boys are targeted to take part in particular activities, where they are supported to ensure they succeed, and where they are helped to overcome lack of confidence, shyness or self-esteem, there are positive outcomes in terms of engagement. Breaking down the barriers to learning appears to lead to higher levels of achievement among boys who may otherwise fall short of their potential.

## Conclusion

The various strategies pursued in these six schools have the potential to go some way to addressing conflicts between the values of school and wider society which can result in a lack of engagement and involvement in school. These conflicts need to be explicitly acknowledged and addressed, we contend, if attitudes are to change, because it is only when attitudes to school are positive that learning can be maximized. The positive impacts noted above suggest that there are benefits to be gained from such strategies. They must, however, be embedded in schools which prioritize the development of an ethos where individuals are valued, where children are given responsibility, and where there is a sense of community and teamwork, alongside a culture of equality. They work best where there is strong leadership, and a commitment among all staff to putting the strategies into practice. Where these preconditions are in place, then we believe that there is sufficient evidence to point to the effectiveness of this group of strategies in promoting greater involvement in school, more positive attitudes and increased levels of confidence and self-esteem gained through learning.

These are the foundations for academic success and benefit all children, but the schools which saw the greatest shift in attainment between Key Stages 1 and 2 among the under-achievers, were those which (while not disadvantaging other pupils) focused the strategy explicitly on these boys. This does not mean privileging a particular group of pupils, but ensuring that they have the same opportunities as other pupils in the class. The Originator School in the West Midlands used each of the citizenship initiatives as an opportunity overtly to engage the boys, and Partner School 1 in inner London targeted under-achievers for participation in arts projects even if they did not appear at first to have the aptitude for the various activities. In each school, this targeting appeared to have positive impacts on both involvement and achievement:

> I've grown intellectually and become more mature, and I've got smarter – more well behaved, more concentrated. I think I've achieved this year and done better in nearly everything. I feel good about myself.
> (Focus group boy, South London Partner School 2,
> at the end of Year 6)

## Notes

1   http://www.schoolcouncils.org (last accessed 20 July, 2005).
2   http://www.youcandoiteducation.com/index.html (last accessed 27 September, 2005).
3   http://www.dfes.gov.uk/performancetables/primary_04/p8.shtml (last accessed 29 September, 2005).
4   http://www.creative-partnerships.com/ (last accessed 20 July, 2005).

# 6 'Now I can read faster'

## Reading communities and partnerships

This chapter provides a link between the previous and the next chapter, in that it bridges triad activity on socio-cultural strategies and on literacy, which were the two key foci of research within the primary schools. The chapter considers the work of two triads, both of which were engaged in strategies focused on reading. Both of the triads were concerned to develop enjoyment and engagement in literature – what Wolfendale (1996) calls 'literacy for life', and as part of this process, both took on the notion of reading communities and partnerships, thus promoting experiences of shared learning: teachers, parents and other adult readers sharing reading with pupils, and pupils sharing reading with other pupils. Within this overall approach, the main aim of one triad was to improve boys' reading, measuring changes in reading levels and engagement. In the other triad, the key aim was essentially socio-cultural in nature, measuring changes in attitudes and self-esteem for learning, in the expectation that raising academic self-esteem would translate into improved attainment, both in reading and more widely. Bringing these two triads together gives a more holistic overview of the wider possible impact of these approaches.

### Context and background

The first triad to be considered in this chapter comprised three large schools, one primary (4–11), one junior (7–11) and one infant (4–7) school, located in an inner borough of East London. They were situated in an area characterized as having very high levels of multiple deprivation: the primary and infant school were in the bottom 3 per cent of wards in England in terms of multiple deprivation, while the junior school fell in the bottom 7 per cent, according to the 2000 Index of Deprivation. A very high proportion of pupils were bilingual or multilingual, particularly in the Originator School, where 86 per cent did not have English as their first language. One-third of pupils in the school were from Indian backgrounds, a quarter from Pakistani backgrounds and only 4 per cent were of white UK heritage. In the extension stage of the project, the Originator School continued to work with a further three schools serving similar socio-economic and cultural catchment areas.

Despite a catchment area comprising all the characteristics associated with lower than average attainment (see Chapter 2), overall performance in the East London Originator School at Key Stage 2 was consistently well above the national average, and performance data at the beginning of the project showed a steady improvement in both boys' and girls' results. In English, there had been a gender gap in favour of boys in three of the preceding four years (Figure 6.1). In the junior school (Partner School 1) the achievements of both sexes also increased from 1996, with a very slight gender gap in favour of girls in English in 2000, though a lower level of performance than that in the Originator School.

The second triad considered here consisted of three 7–11 junior schools and was located in West Yorkshire. The Originator School and Partner School 1 were situated in former mill towns and served mixed, mainly white, lower middle- and working-class catchments, with small proportions of pupils from Asian backgrounds. Partner School 2, although in the same local education authority, was situated in a relatively isolated village and served a white population of distinct communities, including children of affluent middle-class commuters, and families living on a local authority housing estate, often re-housed

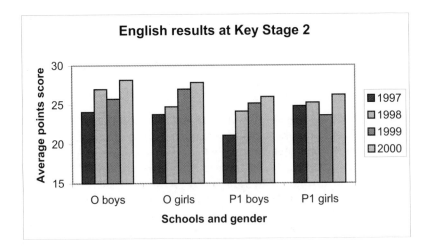

**Figure 6.1**   Key Stage 2 results, East London primary schools
*Note*: O = Originator, P1 = Partner School 1

from elsewhere. All three schools were around the national average in terms of the proportion of children eligible for free school meals, with slightly above average proportions of pupils having special educational needs.

In this triad, performance in National Curriculum tests at Key Stage 2 at the start of the project was well above the average in the Originator School, which had seen a narrowing of the gender gap and an upward trajectory of performance for both girls and boys; in English, as Figure 6.2 shows, performance in 2000 was similar for both sexes. English results for Partner School 1 showed boys out-performing girls in 1997 and 1998, possibly as a result of the heavy focus on boys linked to a local authority initiative in this period, but girls' results had then improved significantly, to overtake those of boys in 1999 and 2000. English results for Partner School 2 had also seen improvement, but with girls out-performing boys in all four years.

Both of these triads, then, had seen improvement in Key Stage 2 test results in the four years preceding the start of the project, and yet in each of them results in English were generally below those in mathematics and science. The two triads were quite different from each other, however, in terms of their location and the contrasting socio-economic and ethnic composition of their relative catchment areas. While the

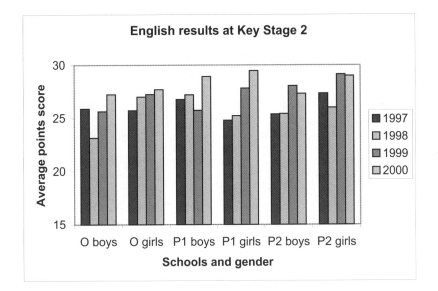

**Figure 6.2**  Keys Stage 2 results, West Yorkshire triad
*Note*: O = Originator, P1 = Partner School 1, P2 = Partner School 2

London schools drew their children from particularly deprived areas of the country, with high proportions of ethnic minority pupils, those in West Yorkshire were in areas closer to the national average in terms of deprivation levels, and served mainly white communities. It was these different cultural contexts that determined the direction that the intervention strategies were to take.

## Defining the intervention strategies

### Boys and reading

*Barriers for reading*

While English results in the East London schools had shown improvement, what was particularly intriguing in all three schools was that, in contrast with national figures where achievement in reading is commonly better than that in writing (see Figure 2.4), boys achieved less well in reading than in writing. Trying to understand the reasons for this therefore became an obvious initial focus, and so the first phase of the project and the early stage of the extension year were concerned with data gathering. The schools conducted surveys about reading among pupils, and interviews with focus groups of boys in the three triad schools and three extension schools sought to understand their perceptions of themselves as readers, their preferred reading material and the extent to which they read at home. In addition, a questionnaire was devised to provide information about attitudes to reading among carers, together with their own literacy experiences and preferences.

It is important to acknowledge that some boys do *not* present problems in their approaches to literacy (Moss 2000). Indeed, interviews with Year 5 boys showed examples of engagement and enjoyment of literature, seeing reading as far more than a technical exercise. Asked why he thought people needed to be able to read, one boy replied:

> So that when they get older they can get a good job, and for their knowledge, so that they can get more knowledge, and books are very inspiring, because I once read an autobiography, and you look up to the person you want to be like.

The findings from the intensive survey and interview research did, however, point to several factors that might hinder the development of reading for *some* boys:

- Boys associated difficulties in reading not with reading itself, but with 'getting the words right': in other words, they were

*Shouting*

concerned with the instrumental aspects of reading. The early surveys, both in the main stage of the project and later in the extension phase, indicated a high 'fear factor' where boys often said that they were embarrassed to read aloud in class: 'Sometimes I get confused if I read it out. Some people laugh if you read out loud. It's out of order. It makes me upset.' This is not in itself surprising, but the significant factor is that these responses were made by boys who had not been required to read aloud in class for several years. They seemed to be carrying deeply felt worries from early school experience.

- Reading may be seen by boys as a female activity, with female members of the family (and primary school teachers who are more likely to be female) providing the prime support for reading and the most common role models as readers (Millard 1997). In one school, over half the boys (though less than a quarter of girls) said their mothers had taught them to read. Mothers, too, were more likely to hear a child read: 'My mum reads to me and I read to my mum. She give me, like, how good I am out of ten and my mum reads to me and I have to give her how good she is out of ten.' Although this can often be a positive experience, some boys may fail to see reading as a valuable and high status activity, and sometimes simply, as Millard suggests, as 'a stage to go through': once they can read, some feel they no longer need to do so.

- Boys appear to have restricted views of reading, and read a narrower range of texts than girls (Davies and Brember 1993; Millard 1997; Hall and Coles 1999; Maynard 2002). Many of the boys who were interviewed mentioned comics and magazines as their preferred reading. Such reading preferences seemed to mirror those of adults at home, where boys invariably described male members of the household as mainly reading newspapers and female members as reading mainly books: 'My mum reads cooking books ... also when she's up at one o'clock she reads Jacqueline Wilson's books. My dad reads football stuff and newspapers.'

- In under-achieving boys, literacy appeared to offer little satisfaction even at the infant school: they had gone beyond initial decoding in learning to read, but had not gained any fluency or pleasure in reading. If this was the picture at the age of 5 or 6, then the future for these boys' reading was threatened.

Besides these more general factors the surveys and interviews revealed some more specific factors that might also have a bearing on understanding the unusual profile in these schools of boys attaining lower

PTO.

levels of success in reading than in writing. While there are no clear explanations, details from questionnaires to families suggested that some male family members were less committed to school literacy than the women and girls. In one school, relatively large numbers (a quarter of boys and a third of girls in one school) said that nobody read with them at home: at 6 years old this is significant.

One particular feature which emerged early on in discussion was that all members of the triad had in common a desire to get the wider community involved in their respective schools. Both the Originator School and Partner School 1 already had well-developed family links and had endeavoured to establish equal opportunities policies and practice based on a good knowledge of children's home and community language experiences. There had been specific plans to involve more parents, targeting English as an Additional Language funding and staff to set up English language classes and activities such as ICT in the Originator School. At Partner School 1, an outreach worker who spoke several Asian languages took on a liaison role with families. The infant school had further to go in assuming family involvement in school, but like the other two schools was keen to develop such links.

With an awareness of the contextual factors, therefore, it was decided that the intervention strategy would have as its aim the raising of boys' achievements in reading, both through looking at ways of widening the scope of reading in the classroom, but also with an emphasis on involving male family members (parents/carers, older brothers, grandparents) in classroom reading. The intention was to track the effectiveness of these approaches through compiling reading profiles and monitoring the impact on focus groups of boys – in the Originator School on Year 2/3 boys, in the junior school on Year 5/6 pupils and in the infant school on reception class children.

## Boys and self-esteem for learning

It was the sharing of a similar ethos that became the starting-point for discussion of an appropriate intervention strategy in the West Yorkshire schools. The headteacher of the Originator School saw a culture which celebrated success, praise and high expectations for every child as key to the school's success, and as fundamental to raising achievement. As in the South London Originator School discussed in the preceding chapter, he articulated a philosophy in which children were seen as individuals, with efforts made to find out what each child was good at and to use this positively to develop confidence and self-esteem for learning. There had, nevertheless, been an increasing awareness of the differing attitudes of boys and girls to school and learning, and a recent analysis of performance data had suggested that boys' attainments in English were generally lower than those of girls. Partner School 1 had a long-standing commitment to raising boys' achievement, and had embarked on a range of strategies such as an Executive Scheme of giving pupils special responsibilities (similar to that used in the West Midlands triad discussed in Chapter 5). Like the Originator School, this school also saw its ethos of valuing individual children, showing them respect and giving them a voice, as lying at the root of its success. Under a previous headteacher, standards at Partner School 2 had been very low and relations with the local community were poor, but while results had improved, there was evidence of boys' under-achievement, and the recently appointed headteacher felt that the school ethos and community relations needed to be tackled if the school was to achieve its targets, and she had begun to take steps to celebrate achievement and promote responsibility.

Besides a focus on school ethos, all three schools shared the view that much under-achievement was the consequence of poor academic self-esteem where pupils did not perceive themselves as learners – an issue which was frequently more pertinent to boys than to girls – and they quickly agreed that the approach they wanted to take in the Raising Boys' Achievement project was one that would endeavour to tackle that issue. Bearing in mind criticisms noted by Skelton (2004) over the use of the term 'self-esteem', we see it here in the context of a dissonance between the culture of the school and that of the local community with respect to learning. The hegemonic masculinity of 'laddishness' that is becoming apparent as boys pass through the later stages of primary schooling demands that boys who seek to adopt this identity reject academic achievement, and seek self-esteem in other areas, such as sporting prowess (particularly evident in this strong rugby league area). Such boys therefore, as discussed in the previous chapter, do not necessarily lack self-esteem; rather, their self-esteem is gained through consumer goods, or through actions which are oppositional to school, and can result in under-achievement as boys distance themselves from learning (see Chapter 1). Furthermore, because some of these boys are influential within the cohort, this can lead to others opting out and also under-achieving. Other children, by no means exclusively boys, may have a more global low self-esteem, including low academic self-esteem, and hence tackling self-esteem can be important in combating under-achievement more widely. In this triad, although there was less of a conflict between the values of school and community than in the triads discussed in the preceding chapter, the headteacher of the Originator School was concerned about a small number of key leaders, usually boys, who were very influential in the classroom, and sometimes had a negative impact on learning. In Partner School 2, with a very mixed catchment, there was also a concern over boys' behaviour in the playground, leading to a lack of concentration in the classroom and disruption at the start of the afternoon session.

In addition to a common ethos and a concern to establish self-esteem for learning, the schools in the West Yorkshire triad were keen to develop something they were already familiar with, rather than introduce an entirely new initiative, since they stressed that if the project were to be successful, the strategy would need to be coherent with initiatives they already had in place. The decision was therefore taken to put in a programme of peer support: this was firmly established at the Originator School in the form of a shared reading programme and had also been tried in the past at Partner School 1.

The proposed intervention strategies in both of these triads demonstrated, therefore, links between reading and culture. Schools in both triads recognized the existence of under-achievement in literacy – one of boys specifically in reading, attributed partly to cultural factors, and the other thought to be associated with a lack of self-esteem for learning. Both the triads therefore sought to establish reading communities or partnerships in order, directly or indirectly, to raise attainment.

## Reading communities: adult role models

As Driessen et al. (2005: 509) point out, 'expanding the involvement of parents in the education of their children has recently been viewed as an important strategy to advance the effectiveness and improve the quality of education'. Thus, not only in Britain, but in various other countries, have initiatives been taken to establish educational partnerships (Sanders and Epstein 1998). Within this broader context, various authors have, since the mid-1980s, highlighted the importance of parental involvement in developing literacy, with writers such as Wells (1985), Tizard et al. (1988) and Weinberger (1996) all arguing that literacy activities developed and introduced by parents have a direct bearing on later literacy achievement. Baker (1999), furthermore, stresses the importance of talking about reading with a range of different people, suggesting that the number of different people students react with in literacy activities has a real effect on reading development. Thus, Minns argues that: 'As long as experienced readers consciously and unconsciously act as reading models for children, young readers will learn from adults they wish to emulate' (1997: 136). Taking this a step further, Wolfendale (1996) argues for a need to move to a point where family literacy activities are so embedded within, and integral to, school, home and community, that the word 'initiative' becomes inappropriate. None of this literature, however, appears to focus explicitly on the role of fathers and other adult males in developing children's literacy.

While earlier discussion indicated that one factor that might contribute towards lower attainment in reading for some boys was their perception of reading as a feminized activity, findings from the initial survey of parents and carers in the East London schools also suggested that a number of men appeared to enjoy home-based reading, and in one school, a survey of the nearest male carer of 20 Year 5 boys revealed that more of the Pakistani-Urdu speakers had fathers who read with them. Many of the male carers saw reading as life-enhancing, and because of this evident involvement in reading, there seemed to be particular value in emphasizing the role model provided by male carers. The aim was that they would share their reading habits and literature in order to stimulate reading as a valued male activity and to establish networks of assured and enthusiastic readers among families. In the junior school, male carers were encouraged to come into school, while the Originator School prepared a leaflet for parents and carers in an appropriate range of languages, inviting them to attend reading workshops held in community languages. The purpose was to introduce parents to the kinds of reading experiences the children had at school and to encourage them to read with the children at home. Parents of pupils who said that no-one read to them at home were particularly targeted.

In the infant school, reading groups were established, led by members of the school community who were not teachers (for example, a facilities manager or welfare assistant). Both girls' groups (led by a woman) and boys' groups (led by a man) were set up. These were small groups where there was no overt 'teaching' but rather a general sharing of reading pleasure, based on all kinds of texts. Adults were invited into classrooms on a regular basis (at least once a fortnight), not to 'hear children read', but to read to the children and to talk about books and other forms of written text which children were encouraged to bring in. Thus pupils were exposed to adults reading *with* them, rather than testing them by getting them to read aloud from an unfamiliar text.

Evaluation of this last initiative, based on discussions with some of the adult readers, together with observation of the pupils' responses, showed that, where the groups met consistently (unfortunately some adult readers were unable to keep up the commitment), the children soon became engaged and enthusiastic. Reflecting on her experiences, one adult reader said that 'half the battle is listening' – both the children listening to the stories and to each other, and the adult being prepared to listen to the children's opinions: 'you've got to listen to what they're saying'. She had encouraged the group to give their views and, while she sometimes stopped to explain something or talk about ideas, she explained that, 'generally I'm waiting for them to ask about things'. She noticed a change in her group's reading behaviours, in that they settled more quickly through time, and were alert and eager to hear the stories. One of the male readers commented on his surprise over the attitudes of some boys in his group, with contributions from some he would not have expected to participate. He had shared his own interests in reading, particularly in magazines about hobbies and the boys had brought in their own comics and had shown generally more involved interest in reading. One became excited about writing stories and another (who had been almost incomprehensible in his speedy delivery) began to show more ability to communicate at an understandable pace.

While it is not easy to attribute improvements simply to the reading group experience, such changes in attitude towards reading suggest that there are important indicators here about the treatment of reading as a shared enjoyable experience, rather than as something to be laboured over, tested and measured. The adult readers treated the children as equal partners in the reading experience, honouring their opinions and preferences and showing that they valued what they had to say, and, as a result of being with adults who talked about what they read, the pupils increased their ability to talk about reading. Improvements in reading were linked with improvements in being able to talk about reading, as pupils move from 'learning to read' to 'becoming a reader'.

## Boys becoming readers

It was this attempt to move from 'learning to read' (technical skills) to 'becoming a reader' (reading with understanding) and developing a wider view of reading that became the over-arching strategy adopted by the East London triad. The aim was to develop critical and committed readership in boys, and while it recognized that all the relevant reading skills had to be in place, even for the youngest pupils, the focus was less on decoding the text on the page than on real engagement with the text. Thus, talk and reflection about reading, and sharing ideas between adults and pupils about what was enjoyable to read were given a high profile, and were the means by which the technical skills were absorbed. In sum, the approach aimed to meet the concerns expressed by the Qualifications and Curriculum Authority in its 2002/3 annual report on English in primary schools, and the Office for Standards in Education is its study comparing schools achieving very high standards in reading with those in similar circumstances where standards were low, that:

There are too few opportunities for pupils to become engrossed in reading or for being read a variety of rich texts; nor is there sufficient time allocated to allow pupils to discuss texts that interest and inspire them.

(QCA 2004: 7)

Although some schools were successfully raising reading attainment ... few were successfully engaging the interest of those who, though competent readers, did not read for pleasure. Schools seldom build on pupils' own reading interests and the range of reading material they read outside school.

(Ofsted 2004b: 4)

Besides the development of reading partnerships discussed above, this broad overall strategy came to embrace a number of other components:

- The reading repertoires of all boys, but specifically the most fluent readers, were enhanced and extended by the provision of books which include boys' preferences.
- The use of reading journals was introduced on a regular but not routine basis as a reflective space to record, by choice, responses to texts. Discussion in staff development sessions had led to an agreement that these journals would be working documents which may include brief comments, illustrations, more carefully structured reviews and recommendations.
- Explicit attention was paid to teachers modelling ways of responding to the meaning and content of books, not just decoding the text.
- Homework was set which specifically encouraged pupils to read all kinds of texts.
- Guided reading groups were revived as a focus for helping pupils read for inference and not only for accuracy, with an emphasis on identifying individual targets and the use of fun stickers as a means of motivation and of affirming when pupils reached their particular targets.
- Year 6 literacy teaching became genre-based and planned in extended units of work. These combined reading, writing, speaking and listening in an integrated programme to allow for familiarization with the genre, capturing ideas through discussion and role play and leading to writing which is more enlivened by familiarity with the genre features and the opportunities to experiment with the genre. Particular emphasis was given to talking about texts.

Not all schools in the triad put each of these initiatives in place, but all worked within a framework that aimed to create a climate of high expectations and to enable boys to become successful and satisfied readers.

## Boys supporting boys: improving reading through shared reading partnerships

Besides putting in place some of the initiatives itemized in the previous section, the Originator School in the East London triad followed a similar rationale to the involvement of adult males discussed above, but in this case the decision was taken to employ a 'boys supporting boys' programme, where older boys (brothers where possible, and with pairings matched according to home language) mentored, and acted as reading role models, for younger readers. Shared reading, as mentioned earlier, was also the strategy chosen by all three schools in the West Yorkshire triad, and is discussed below.

As with the literature on the role of parental involvement in literacy, an interest in shared reading dates from the early 1980s, in the form of paired reading, peer tutoring and peer-assisted learning. While these approaches vary in detail, they all imply the notion of children becoming each others teachers, in the belief that learning encounters without an adult present can be especially important (Forman and Cazden 1985). Based on Vygotsky's (1978) social interactionist view of cognitive development, with social interaction as the key through which learning takes place, the complementary relationships which develop between knowledgeable and less knowledgeable partners, between expert and less expert, are at the heart of peer tutoring (Foot and Howe 1998). Peer tutoring may take place at any age and in any subject (see, for example, Goodlad and Hirst 1990; Morrison et al. 2000; Evans et al. 2001; Topping et al. 2003, 2004), but has perhaps most frequently been employed in the development of reading skills. Topping (1990), reviewing ten projects, describes peer-tutored paired reading as having 'substantial promise', with both tutors and tutees gaining in reading skill at approximately four times 'normal' rates. Paired reading, Topping and Bryce argue, is 'a well-researched structured method for supported or assisted reading in cross-ability pairs, ... with many controlled studies demonstrating its effectiveness principally, but not exclusively, on traditional norm-referenced tests of reading comprehension' (2004: 599). Tutors have been found to gain more on average than tutees, and tutees in cross-age projects appear to gain more than tutees in age-peer projects (Topping 1990).

As noted above, paired reading is not simply 'anything that two people do together with a book' (Topping 1998: 87), but must be a *structured* and well-organized approach if it is to have the desired outcomes. In the East London school, shared reading was centred on Year 3/6 partnerships, with under-achieving Year 6 boys identified as reading 'buddies' to partner Year 3 boys. In the first instance, ten pairs were selected and the older boys received training and were provided with special files, pens, record sheets on which to record the progress of the Year 3 boys, and stickers to use as rewards. The aim was principally to raise the achievement of the Year 6 boys, but also to develop a wider view of reading for both groups. The 'reading club' was held twice a week for 20 minutes at lunchtime, and its impact was monitored through observation and interviews.

Observation of some of the shared reading sessions noted the older boys' ability to support the younger boys' reading. In interview Mark (Year 6) commented that 'I was impressed with what he [Mohammad, Year 3] could remember'. During the reading session he prompted for initial sounds, picture clues, letter clusters, meaning and analogies with other words. Mark felt that it was a good idea to have reading buddies 'because it helps people to like reading'. Mohammad was also positive about his experiences because 'If somebody doesn't like reading then they read more and more ... and then they like to read'. Graham, another Year 6 mentor, said that Sumeet, his younger partner, was 'more fluent now' and 'used picture clues more'. He noticed that Sumeet 'doesn't seem to know his letters', and so he suggested that he might 'make it fun by putting it in pictures ... and making it more physical to help him learn'. Another Year 6 boy, Jonathan, summed up his view of reading buddies:

> I think reading buddies are good because more children in the community will learn to read and write and when you grow up you might see or hear from them saying 'Thank you for helping me in reading, and now I've got a great job because of your help.

While greater engagement in reading, more enjoyment and increasingly positive attitudes towards reading were the overall aim of the initiatives put into place in the East London triad, the strategy was driven in the first place by the fact of boys' lower achievement levels in reading at Key Stages 1 and 2. Here the findings of the research as a whole were also positive. While over two years an average pupil's attainment would be expected to improve by one National Curriculum level (DfES 2004b), teacher assessments of two focus groups of boys, whose progress was tracked in the primary and junior schools in this triad from the summer term of Year 5 to the summer term of Year 6, showed much greater levels of improvement (Table 6.1), with over half the group far exceeding the expected yearly progress.

**Table 6.1** Teacher assessments of reading progress among Year 6 focus group boys in National Curriculum Levels (no. of pupils)

| 1/3rd level | 2/3rd level | 1 level | Between 1 and 2 levels | 2 levels | More than 2 levels |
|---|---|---|---|---|---|
| 2 | 11 | 9 | 3 | 2 | 2 |

*Note*: Table shows thirds of levels in line with usual class teachers' record keeping practices.

### Sustainability and transferability

After the main two-year intervention stage of the triad, the Originator School was keen to continue its involvement, both in terms of refining its 'Boys Supporting Boys' programme, and transferring it, with the support of the local education authority, to three neighbouring schools. The dissemination process began with a meeting of representatives from the three schools with the Originator School. An information pack was provided, and Originator School representatives gave a positive and motivating talk which also stressed some of the problems that might occur and suggested ways to overcome them.

Being proactive in setting up links with the other schools undoubtedly helped the Originator School in maintaining the momentum of the initiative, which was extended to encompass a larger group of boys. Almost all the Year 6 boys made significant improvement with reading in just one year (Table 6.2), friendship groups between the Year 3 and Year 6 boys developed, and even attendance improved. Teachers also noted that the boys involved became more thoughtful, and being a good role model helped some immature boys to develop more independence. Boys themselves commented favourably on the experience: 'I think reading buddies is interesting and it helps children to improve their reading skills. I have improved on the meaning of the hard work.'

**Table 6.2** Teacher assessments of reading progress among Year 6 focus group boys in National Curriculum Levels (no. of pupils)

| 1/3rd level | 2/3rd level | 1 level | Between 1 and 2 levels | No change |
|---|---|---|---|---|
| 4 | 5 | 3 | 1 | 1 |

*Note*: Table shows thirds of levels in line with usual class teachers' record keeping practices.

This final year of research into the 'Boys Supporting Boys' initiative enabled some observations to be made about the process and success of transfer. First, it is pertinent to note that the transfer schools were working on the strategy for only one year, so there was less time to embed the strategy, and some of the pre-conditions necessary for successful transfer might not have been in place. Second, however, is the question of what counts as success. In one of the transfer schools, the teacher attending the final meeting of the group of schools, while aware of some problems, viewed the outcomes as 'really positive', citing measurable improvements in reading levels for all 12 Year 6 boys, as well as gains in self-esteem. The boys themselves, however, when interviewed, clearly felt that the scheme had been imposed upon them against their will and resented giving up their lunchtimes to attend, as this conversation shows:

*Alex*:    If you don't feel like going you are reported to the headteacher, and if we bunk off.

*Jesse*:    And the headteacher said if we don't go we have got to read a book, and we'd miss our play and our lunch.

*Alex*:    The worst thing is that they say you have to read for 20 minutes and when it's one o'clock we're meant to go back down and have 15 minutes more for lunchtime, but the Year 3s come late – sometimes they even come at one o'clock, and we have to wait for them, then after that our time gets wasted.

*Derek*:    People mess around sometimes when the person that takes care of the reading club asks people to come, they [Year 3 pupils] don't come.

Only one of these boys said he liked the reading club and all said they disliked school; there was very little change in their attitudes towards reading between the interviews before and after the strategy and only three admitted to an improvement in their reading.

The different perspectives here between the teacher representative and the focus group boys highlights a core concern of the Raising Boys' Achievement Project. While it is possible to achieve 'success' in quantitative terms, the central aim must be to embrace a wider view of success, engaging pupils as learners, and as committed readers. If we take seriously the views of pupils, the outcome cannot be seen as wholly successful if their attitudes towards school and reading remain negative – even if seven boys who had not been predicted to do so at the beginning of the year attained the benchmark level 4 in their National Curriculum reading test. On the contrary, we would suggest that this extension of the initiative had at best been of limited success, partly because of staffing and organization: when the member of staff who took charge of the reading scheme left, there was no handover information for her successor. Furthermore, the actual running of the reading club had been handed over to a teaching assistant, who had been unable to maintain discipline or ensure the younger boys arrived on time. More important was the notion of compulsion and punishment, which seemed to be at the root of the boys' disaffection. Rather than portraying the reading club in positive terms, for the boys' own benefit, they said they had been chosen because they were poor readers and felt they were being punished for this by having to miss their lunchtime play. Even worse in terms of perhaps destroying any notion of reading as enjoyable was, as Alex and Jesse recounted, having to 'read a book' as a punishment for failing to turn up!

It seems clear that, if boys who show some reluctance to engage in school-based literacy are to be asked to give up their lunchtime play period to participate in a reading club, then they need to be persuaded of the positive reasons for doing so. Seeing it as a punishment, or, as was the case in two other schools, being 'bribed' to attend through the promise of a trip at the end, does not provide the ideal motivation. The Originator School, on the other hand, had sold the idea to the Year 6 boys not only in terms of helping them, but of helping someone else to read. The boys were not put on the football rota on reading club days, and a small party was held at the last session, with dictionaries given to the Year 6 boys and certificates to the Year 3 boys. There had been no insistence over the participation of the one boy who was adamant about not taking part; his non-involvement was accepted as his choice. These boys did not express resentment over giving up some of their lunchtimes, but saw the reading club as something which teachers had put in place to help them.

The experiences of these four schools enable us to say with confidence that shared reading can have a positive impact on the older boys' attainment in reading. If the strategy is well organized, if there is a wide range of reading material for the boys to choose from, and if the member of staff involved ensures that the Year 3 pupils cooperate, then the Year 6 boys can themselves recognize the positive impacts. In addition to positive feedback from boys in the Originator School, nine out of ten boys in one of the extension schools said they had enjoyed reading club and seven felt their own reading had improved. More importantly, our research has shown that these kinds of initiative can engender greater enjoyment of reading:

> At the beginning, when we started talking about what kind of books we liked, my partner used to just bring books what I didn't

like, but then I started liking it because I used to read it, and he used to read it as well, so I quite like the stories and how they used the words. So now I really like different kinds of books as well.

Going to reading club makes me want to read more.

Reading is fun. I like reading long books and comics and books from films.

There are, furthermore, wider benefits. As already mentioned in relation to the Originator School, boys' behaviour improved, confidence was built up, and new friendships were formed across year groups. One of the most positive aspects for all the groups of boys who were interviewed was the pleasure they got from helping a younger child, so that even in the school where only one boy had enjoyed the reading club, all felt pleased and proud to have helped the Year 3 pupils to improve:

The best thing is that I get to help people that don't know how to read. I can explain some words that they don't know and they can understand.

When I give my partner a sticker I feel good about him, I feel good that he's learning more stuff from reading books.

## Building self-esteem for learning through shared reading partnerships

These wider benefits of peer tutoring have been well documented. While standards have been shown to rise, peer tutoring also seeks to empower students, and so it can be used not just to increase knowledge and skills, but to promote engagement and self-assurance: even if support is of a lesser quality than that offered by adult teachers, this might be compensated, Topping and Ehly (1998) suggest, in terms of increased motivation and confidence. In addition, tutors learn to be nurturing towards tutees, and in so doing, develop a sense of pride and responsibility; relationships between pupils become more positive (Topping and Bryce 2004), and self-esteem is said to be enhanced (Charlton 1998). Nugent (2001), in her study of cross-age paired reading in a school for pupils with moderate learning difficulties, also refers to the multiple benefits that accrue: besides progress in reading, she reports enhanced feelings of self-worth, as well as more positive attitudes towards school.

It is the wider benefits that were the main reason why the West Yorkshire triad chose to implement shared reading, and it is to their experiences that we now turn. Although in one sense the West Yorkshire triad followed the originator-partner in that the strategy came from the Originator School and was taken on by the two partner schools, in fact, Partner School 1 quickly assumed a more proactive leadership role. This was partly because of an Ofsted inspection in the Originator School during the first year. Thus Partner School 1 trialled the strategy that term with a group of Year 5 boys who were chosen because they were perceived to have low self-esteem with respect to learning, and paired with Year 3 children who were felt to be poor readers. Pairings were done carefully, taking personality as well as reading ability into consideration. The older boys participated in an intensive training programme for several weeks to learn how to be a listener and were given a shared reading folder including a manual for reference. The local education authority's Shared Reading Scheme materials were used as a resource. Shared reading sessions then took place twice a week for a period of six weeks (in class time) and involved older children sharing books of their choosing with their partners, younger children bringing books to read aloud and the reading together of wall displays throughout each school. At the end of each session the Year 5 children completed a record sheet, marking out of five their partner's reading, attitude, interest, degree of involvement and effort. The older children were encouraged to reward their partner with stickers, and wrote reports for parents at the end of each six-week programme. This format was subsequently repeated with the whole of the Year 5/Year 3 cohorts in all three schools. A unique feature of the scheme in the Originator School was a reading pack which each Year 5 child had put together themselves over the previous term for use with their partner. These packs included a number of activities with a literacy focus, such as puzzles, word searches and games, and the children were allowed to use the activities towards the end of each shared reading session once the teachers felt sufficient reading had been accomplished.

Triad meetings discussed problems and how to resolve them in response to pupil feedback, and awareness of some of the difficulties that were encountered helped to inform the schools' planning for the subsequent year. For example, the role of teachers during the shared reading sessions, the children's preferences for same-sex partners and the need to develop questioning skills among the older children were all discussed. In both the Partner Schools the same cohorts of children took part in shared reading in the following year, (Year 6/4 pairs), but the Originator School chose not to run the programme in the Project's second year because of time constraints and pressures that the shared reading scheme created on other aspects of the curriculum. This in itself is an interesting outcome, to which we return later.

### 'It makes you feel proud of yourself': evaluating a socio-cultural approach to shared reading

While in each school the programme involved whole classes, in order to evaluate the effectiveness of the strategy, a group of between eight and ten boys in Year 5 (and later when they were in Year 6) were selected as key informants in each school. The main criterion for selection was that the boys were thought to have low self-esteem as learners, and several were potential peer leaders. Interviews were conducted at the start and end of each shared reading cycle and each boy completed a tick-box questionnaire. The class teachers involved were also interviewed at the end of the scheme. In addition, an attitude survey seeking views on the shared reading initiative was undertaken across the cohorts by the schools themselves. A self-esteem survey (using the B/G STEEM questionnaire developed by Maines and Robinson 1988) was also conducted by Partner School 2 at the beginning and end of Year 6.

Interviews with the focus group boys indicated that shared reading had a positive impact on nearly all the boys, who were able to identify a number of benefits (Table 6.3), showing that the aims of the strategy – to contribute to increased levels of confidence and self-esteem for learning – were being realized.

Overall, therefore, while some of the focus group boys had been ambivalent about the shared reading scheme at the outset, and were doubtful about their ability to help the younger children, and while some encountered difficulties with their partners, all were able to articulate a number of benefits. Furthermore, questionnaires showed that almost all the focus group boys across the three schools had enjoyed doing the shared reading and thought their partner had enjoyed reading to them.

Interviews by the research team, together with evaluations undertaken by each school, showed that the staff involved concurred with the positive aspects of the scheme listed in Table 6.3. They were in no doubt that it enhanced the self-esteem of both older and younger children and were delighted with the way in which older children rose to the occasion – 'even those children that you might have concerns about':

> It gave a really good self-esteem boost to the boys in my class: the ones that were picked initially [pilot focus group] aren't strong readers themselves. For them to train the rest of the class how to do it – it worked really really well.
>
> (Class teacher 1, Partner School 1)

**Table 6.3**  Summary of positive impacts of shared reading expressed by focus group boys

| Positive impact | Comment |
| --- | --- |
| Sense of 'can do it' | Fears about not being able to help partners quickly disappeared. Self-belief developed as boys able to share knowledge with, and motivate, younger children: 'I've learnt that I can work with small kids, and I can say that if there's a little kid in trouble with his work, I have to help him; I know what to say and I can help him.' Boys talked of strategies they had used, such as how to cope when neither boy could initially read a particular word. |
| Sense of responsibility for another's learning | Took role as listeners seriously: 'You had to really concentrate. You couldn't look around or anything in case they got stuck on a word.' Most thought partners had made progress and felt they could take some credit for this. |
| Developing social skills | Most dealt successfully with situations where partner refused to cooperate, and had been able to negotiate appropriate reading materials with partner. |
| Developing relationships | Despite earlier fears about not getting on with partners, most had got on well, and playground relationships improved. |
| Feelings of pride | All experienced pride through sense of accomplishment and from being looked up to by younger child, enjoying their status as expert: 'It makes you feel proud of yourself because you've helped someone younger than you to read.' |
| Enhanced self-esteem and sense of self as learner | Several said directly that shared reading helped them to feel good about themselves, and contributed to increased confidence: 'I think I can learn better now, and I feel more confident because I've been able to help my partner, so that feels good.' |

Some were very impressed at the way in which the Year 5 children had taken on the responsibility of ensuring their partners were reading at a suitable level, suggesting another book if they could see their partners struggling, or negotiating with staff to try a more challenging book if they were doing well. An enhancement of social skills were felt by all staff to be a real strength of the scheme, with children getting to know each other well, and older children proving good role models:

The respect given to their peers is noticeable, with the younger pupil working hard to gain the highest mark and the older taking everything into consideration to award what they deem to be appropriate.

(Class teacher 3, Partner School 1)

One teacher talked about the quality of interaction as being 'amazing':

Mark [Year 6] and Michael [Year 3] have been brilliant. Mark has, in the past, had real behaviour problems, but he's been absolutely fantastic with this – really, really, amazing, so patient, and just loving it. Michael was a really poor reader, and it's really worked for him.

(Class teacher 2, Partner School 2)

In one instance, when a Year 3 child with social and emotional difficulties was misbehaving in the classroom, his Year 6 partner, with whom he had formed an extremely good relationship, was called in to calm the situation. Some teachers felt the Year 5 children had developed an awareness of how people learn, and were able to apply the range of skills learnt in shared reading to their own learning in class. Several also noticed a more positive attitude towards school in some children.

While the emphasis in this triad was on the socio-cultural impacts of shared reading, some positives impact on reading were also apparent, with the results of the schools' whole-class attitude survey showing that 88 per cent of boys felt their partner had got better at reading. In interview, most of the focus group boys in the Originator School expressed the view that their reading had improved as a consequence of shared reading: they had learnt new vocabulary and a number felt they could apply the strategies they had learnt to help their partner's reading. By the end of Year 6, boys in Partner School 2 also felt their reading had improved considerably through learning new words and listening to someone else read. In Partner School 1, however, although the majority of focus group boys suggested that they felt more positive about reading as a consequence of doing shared reading, most denied their reading had improved, and said they would still prefer on the whole to do other things than read, given the choice. Despite this, teachers felt, on the whole, that the shared reading scheme had raised the profile of reading, promoting both interest and enjoyment of reading as well as greater levels of competence and technical skills such as using much more expression in their reading. One teacher thought the programme had inspired some less able readers, mainly boys, to read more at home.

In addition to this qualitative evidence of change in both social and academic spheres, some quantitative data are available from the self-esteem questionnaire conducted by Partner School 2. At the beginning of Year 6, only two-thirds of focus group boys were actually classified as having low global self-esteem, indicating that the emphasis on raising self-esteem in Year 5 may already have had some effect. A comparison with scores at the end of Year 6 suggested that further progress had been made: while the self-esteem scores for the year group as a whole had not changed, those of the boys in the focus group had increased. Although these increases might relate to maturation, the fact that the year group overall did not change suggests this explanation is unlikely: the most likely explanation for improved levels of self-esteem among the focus group boys is the work the school did with the boys over the year, of which shared reading played a key part.

Furthermore, as with the other triads pursuing socio-cultural strategies, some comments can be made on value-added data for the focus group boys. As Table 6.4 shows, boys in the Partner Schools made significant progress compared with the school as a whole. This was particularly the case in Partner School 1, where the focus group had originally been those boys with whom the strategy had been trialled. Here the pilot group felt special because they had been chosen to take part in the first phase of shared reading. All were delighted to be chosen, saying that their family and friends were pleased and that others had been envious. Indeed, one commented that his friend was surprised he had been chosen because he was a 'bad boy'. Partner School 1 was proactive in sharing resources and ideas and was, like the other Partner School, keen to effect change. It attained its best ever Key Stage 2 results in 2003, with all girls and 85 per cent of boys attaining at least level 4 in English. Its 2004 results were even better, with 96 per cent of all pupils attaining at least level 4 in English (compared with a national figure of 78 per cent), and a third attaining level 5 (compared to a fifth nationally). Although Partner 2's overall results dipped slightly in 2003, it too attained its best ever results in English in 2004.

However, while the Originator School maintained a negligible gender gap in its overall results, its English results at Key Stage 2 actually declined during the two years of the project, and were not only below those of the two partner schools, but also below the national average in 2004. The school, although very willing to share ideas and playing an active part in triad meetings, appeared reluctant to commit the school to too much change. Thus, while in one sense the shared reading strategy was 'embedded' (see Chapter 4), in that it had been in place in the Originator School for a number of years, there appeared to be insufficient confidence in its impacts to 'risk' putting it in place with Year 6 pupils, and so the programme ran only once, when the focus group boys were in

**Table 6.4** Key Stage 1 to Key Stage 2 attainment for West Yorkshire focus group boys

| Expected Value-Added Measure | Originator School | Partner School 1 | Partner School 2 |
| --- | --- | --- | --- |
| Whole school | 99.2 | 101.6 | 100.3 |
| Focus group boys | 98.7 | 103.2 | 102.3 |

Note: 'Expected value-added measure', using DfES criteria, = 100.0

Year 5. It is obviously inappropriate to attribute the lower levels of attainment in English to that decision, but the fact that no shared reading took place in Year 6, might in part explain the lower value-added score for the focus group boys in the Originator School.

## Shared reading: pre-conditions

Shared reading can be a short-term strategy, relatively straightforward to put in place, and without massive resource implications, and the evidence from the two triads discussed here indicates that it can, as other studies have shown, boost self-esteem and improve reading among boys, as well as having a number of other positive benefits. It does not, however, automatically bring success. This depends on being able to define clearly the rationale underpinning the strategy, which underpins how the strategy is implemented and worked out, and how effective it turns out to be. It is not simply a case of implementing peer support for reading, for example, but how and why it is implemented. Certain pre-conditions must therefore be met:

- Both older and younger children must be told the purpose of shared reading and what is expected of them. This needs to be presented positively, in terms of how the experience will help them.
- Pairs need to be chosen carefully: where whole classes are involved, same-sex pairings appear to be preferred by pupils, a finding also noted by Morrison et al. (2000), and matching pupils by home language was found to be beneficial.
- It is important that the older child believes he or she is better at reading than their partner; it would appear to be helpful to set the older child up as an expert and role model.
- Training is crucially important (Foot and Howe 1998; Dearden

1998): older pupils need to be clear what their role is and how to run the session; they need to be trained in how to apply relevant strategies to help their partner, how to deal with off-task behaviour, how to give positive feedback and how to create trust and confidence in their partners.

- The programme needs to be teacher-led and well organized, rather than being delegated to someone with less authority and expertise. Difficulties were encountered in both triads where older pupils were unable to deal with bad behaviour by their younger partners, and if serious, this could put them off the idea of shared reading.
- Timetabling can be an issue (Topping and Bryce 2004), and ideally sessions should take place in school time, rather than depriving pupils of lunchtime breaks. If this is not possible, pupils need to be convinced that the programme is there for their benefit.

## Conclusion

This chapter has sought to demonstrate again the importance of schools' own cultural contexts in determining both what they need to focus on and what is right for them. Both of the triads discussed here chose to focus on reading communities and partnerships – one in order to raise boys' attainment in reading; the other to raise self-esteem for learning. To implement these initiatives in the contexts defined here, and to monitor their impacts, demands time, detailed planning and careful implementation. As we have noted, these demands were ultimately seen as too time-consuming and distracting in the West Yorkshire Originator School. Overall, however, in the shorter term, research in these two triads has supported other studies in showing that shared reading programmes can raise achievement in reading *and* have impact on self-esteem. In the longer term, giving pupils the opportunities to develop the meta-language to talk about reading (particularly through the wider range of initiatives described in the East London triad), lays the foundation for pupils to go beyond learning to read, to become readers, and, for the older boys, to become male role models of the future. Thus, we would argue that the research presented here represents, first of all, a more holistic approach to reading. Second, we would suggest that it takes the existing gender-neutral literature forward through its evaluation of shared reading partnerships specifically between boys.

# 7 'I like the good words I use..

## Becoming writers

Concerns about boys' achievements in literacy are not new. As we indicate in earlier chapters, the nature of the gender gap at Key Stage 2 has focused attention directly on the relative under-performance of boys in English in general and in writing in particular. Indeed, to some commentators, this relative failure of boys to match girls' achievements in reading and writing lies at the heart of the gender debate in primary schools. Yet studies about boys' reading and writing suggests that such broad generalizations about boys' under-achievement in literacy are unhelpful. Research on boys' reading (Moss 2000; Moss and McDonald 2004; Smith 2004) suggests the need to acknowledge that some boys do not present problems in their approaches to literacy. Similarly, the Ofsted report (2003b) focuses on schools where boys perform well in writing. One of the underlying premises of the RBA project, then, was to provide a more sophisticated and carefully researched analysis of factors which might support boys' and girls' successful literacy development.

In supporting and extending school-based research into how best to promote boys' achievements in literacy, therefore, it was important to avoid over-simplification and to focus instead on diversity. The Project as a whole found differences in masculine cultures and attitudes across geographical regions and even between schools within local authorities. There were also individual differences to be taken into account: not all boys were unmotivated readers and writers, and even within the groups of boys who were described by their teachers as under-achieving in literacy, there were noticeable differences in attitudes, aspirations and commitment.

Such diversity of attitudes and perceptions is matched by the range of types of evidence which have informed debate about boys' performance in literacy (Daly 2003). Some is based on national testing data; some on teacher research or action research; some on observational data. Literacy itself is a shifting concept and evidence of achievement in literacy can be variously conceived (Safford et al. 2004). The products of literacy – scores in National Curriculum reading and writing tests, for example – offer different kinds of evidence from teachers' observations of the processes of literacy and the behaviours which learners have to adopt if they are to become confidently literate. This range of evidence identifies two main areas of concern: one is the everyday classroom observation that boys seem unmotivated and 'switched off' from literacy, with writing the particular area where boys show lack of motivation. The other focus has been on boys' under-performance in national tests which is most noticeable – and persistent – in writing.

## Context and background

Two primary school triads and one special school focused on writing although each took different routes to raising boys' achievement. Both primary triads included Key Stage 1 pupils at some stage of their work while the special school had pupils of all ages. All three worked on an initial phase of intervention followed by a shorter second extension phase.

The first triad was located in an outer London borough, and consisted of a large junior school and an infant school (Partner School 1) which shared the same site, together with a one-form entry faith school (Partner School 2). According to the 2000 Index of Multiple Deprivation, these schools were situated within the 12 per cent most affluent wards in England. The proportion of pupils eligible for free school meals was less than half the national average. Most pupils were of white UK heritage (93–94 per cent), and the percentage of pupils identified as having special educational needs was below the national average in each school. In the Originator School, overall performance in National Curriculum tests at Key Stage 2 was consistently well above average for similar schools. Boys' results in English had increased steadily in the period 1996–2000, with a narrowing gender gap (Figure 7.1). Overall performance at Key Stage 2 in Partner School 2 was above the national average for similar schools, with a gender gap in favour of girls in English, but an overall gap in favour of boys because of boys' performance in science and particularly in mathematics consistently exceeding that of girls.

The second triad to focus on writing was made up of three primary schools situated in the south coast area of Sussex. The Originator School served a mixed urban catchment area, with pupils from a wide range of family and ethnic backgrounds, including a substantial refugee population. Both this school and Partner School 1 had higher than average numbers of pupils with special educational needs. Partner School 1, in a neighbouring town, also had pupils from a range of social backgrounds and above average numbers of pupils with special educational needs but

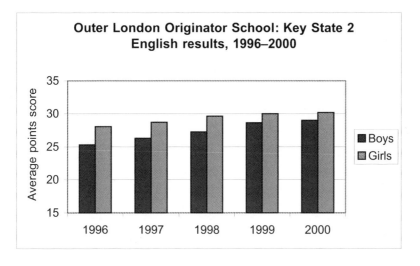

**Figure 7.1** Key Stage 2 results, Outer London Originator School

very few ethnic minority pupils. Partner School 2 was located in a small, prosperous seaside town serving a mainly white community, and with average levels of special educational needs. Key Stage 2 results for the Originator School were well above average for similar schools in 2000 (Figure 7.2), when the RBA project began, while those in both partner schools were around the average for similar schools.

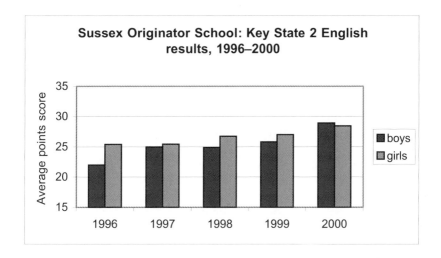

**Figure 7.2** Key Stage 2 results, Sussex Originator School

# Defining the intervention strategies

## A focus on talk

Perhaps unsurprisingly, over the time schools worked on the project, it became clear that local, even school-specific, situations varied greatly and had their effect on achievement and that issues about raising standards of literacy cannot be separated from wider socio-cultural issues. The diversity of the settings and circumstances of the schools involved in the project was matched by the diversity of the findings. Nevertheless, some common threads emerged, particularly in the role which talk, including drama, plays in promoting successful writing.

The importance of talk in developing literacy may not seem like news. In a general way, speaking and listening have for some time been identified as important for writing (Corden 2000; Alexander 2003; Carter 2004) and specifically for boys' writing (Barrs and Pidgeon 2002; Essex Writing Project 2002, 2003). Drama has equally been acknowledged for its significant role in supporting boys' literacy (Barrs and Cork 2001; PNS/UKLA 2004; Safford et al. 2004). However, much of the research on talk and gender has focused on the behaviours associated with class discussion, particularly on talk for learning (Ofsted 1993; Noble and Bradford 2000); other work emphasizes the construction and negotiation of gender roles through language (Connell 1995; Francis 2000; Renold 2004a). There has been little long-term empirical work associating spoken forms of language with written forms.

The Raising Boys' Achievement project provided a chance to take a more detailed look at the relationship between talk and literacy. Schools where boys and girls have been most successful in writing are those where they have had consistent opportunities for different kinds of talk, including drama, throughout their schooling. They are also places where the teachers' use of talk acts as a model for pupils' development of different types of spoken language. The case studies in this chapter describe school and classroom approaches which have contributed to the growing evidence of talk as an essential factor in raising achievements in writing. Further, the findings offer a more subtle view of the different types of talk which can best support the development of successful and satisfying literacy.

Any research into promoting standards of writing has to confront some complex inter-relationships: between teaching writing and how pupils learn to become writers, and between writing as a finished product and writing as a process. Underpinning the first is yet another complex relationship – between teaching the technical aspects of writing and encouraging a sense that writing should have conviction, voice and purpose. Over-emphasis on technical aspects can result in lifeless writing; over-emphasis on self-expression can result in technically imperfect writing. Teaching writing means more than instruction in technicalities, it means providing a balance between helping young writers develop a personal voice and ensuring that they also know how to present well-structured and accurately written texts. In terms of the second, for many years writing in schools has been seen as representing the end point of an activity. It is the basis for assessment of learning. However, writing is also a process through which writers develop, extend and realize their ideas. In order to provide evidence of how standards of achievement and attainment in writing might be secured, the research and intervention plans of the project schools had to consider what is involved in 'becoming a writer' and to look at how they saw writing both as a process towards learning and a product which demonstrates learning.

A starting-point for all the schools was to identify just what they understood as 'under-achievement' in writing. Under-achieving pupils were identified by a combination of judgements based on:

- assessments in English which allow for progress to be forecast, using computer software provided by the Qualifications and Curriculum Authority;
- comparisons with national or local LEA data, although these may not necessarily signal under-achievement since fluency in English, for example, is not taken into account in such figures;
- the teachers' view of the individual's potential: a 'vision' of what this child might achieve often related to formative assessments. These were usually expressed through National Curriculum levels (and sub-levels) of attainment.
- broader perspectives about social or emotional relationships or judgements about pupils who appeared to lack confidence or who did not enjoy their work.

Although specific teaching approaches aimed to improve writing were used with whole classes, in order to measure improvement each of the teachers involved identified focus groups of under-achieving boys who were interviewed at several points in each year of the project. Early discussions between the schools in each triad led to plans for specific investigations and interventions aimed at raising standards of writing, particularly for boys. Attainment scores based on National Curriculum levels were kept throughout the project and teacher assessments, and interviews and classroom observations conducted by a researcher, provided qualitative data. The initial project work was planned for two years. Extension projects then followed up aspects of the work which had emerged as offering potential for more detailed or sustained investigation.

## Boys talking about writing

Before starting on classroom interventions, all the pupils in the focus groups were interviewed about their views on writing and their perceptions of themselves as writers. This provided qualitative baseline data for comparison after each phase of the project and ensured a combination of teacher, researcher and pupils' voices in evaluation and analysis.[1] In early interviews, the focus groups presented views which were very much in line with earlier research into pupils' perceptions (National Writing Project 1990). Many disliked writing, with the exception of stories, and their view of writing was mostly focused on technical or secretarial features or on the tensions associated with actually holding a writing implement. Handwriting, spelling and punctuation were the most disliked aspects but the boys also mentioned problems about writing at length, not knowing what to write and not having any choice:

> I'm rubbish at spelling.
> > (Year 4 boy)

> When you're writing in class, your arm starts aching.
> > (Year 4 boy)

> We never get to write what we want to write.
> > (Year 5 boy)

At this stage of the work, these young writers indicated a restricted view of what writing in school meant. One question in the interviews asked pupils to give advice to younger writers about how to improve their writing. Responses to this question in initial interviews revealed similar limited views of writing:

> Tell them to get a pen/pencil grip to help them hold it properly.
> > (Year 4 boy)

> Teach them how to write words. Teach them spellings.
> > (Year 6 boy)

The older, secondary-aged boys in the special school saw writing as hard, commenting:

> Hard – writing lines and spelling and full stops and everything.
>
> (Year 10 boy)

> I find it difficult sometimes. I like writing something that I'm interested in rather than what we have to do in class.
>
> (Year 10 boy)

Their advice to younger writers was similar in its scope, although they showed greater reflection on motivation:

> Don't worry about the spellings or anything.
>
> (Year 10 boy)

> Find something you're interested in and write about that because if they don't know about it they're not going to try very hard and it won't be any good.
>
> (Year 10 boy)

The youngest writers in the project were more positive about their writing. Most of the boys interviewed in Years 1 and 2 thought they were good at writing and enjoyed it. Where the Key Stage 1 pupils gave negative responses to writing in school, they saw writing in much the same way as the older boys, as largely to do with the technical aspects of handwriting and spelling:

> I always get my ds and bs wrong.
>
> (Year 1 boy)

> No, it's boring – all you have to do is sit down and write some words.
>
> (Year 2 boy)

There were also some mixed messages, as indicated by these two Year 2 boys:

> I love writing but I hate school. Sometimes I don't go out to play [he is occasionally kept in to finish writing].

> I just hate it. I'm quite good ... when my teacher makes me do it I am.

These comments align with differences in the boys' attitudes in general to writing at home and at school. Most of them said that they did some writing (or drawing plus writing, particularly with the younger boys) at home and were far more positive in their views:

I like writing letters and cards.

(Year 2 boy)

Yea, I do write at home. I've got this cousin in Australia ... I usually get replies but sometimes I don't ... I like drawing cartoons and making comics as well.

(Year 4 boy)

Sometimes I like write little stories ... I get ideas from outside in the woods ... Sometimes my mum and my dad read them.

(Year 5 boy)

The boys' responses indicated a commonly found disjunction between attitudes to writing at home and at school, reflecting very similar views to those recorded in the large scale research into writing carried out by the National Writing Project (1990) between 1986–89. It is not surprising that pupils prefer writing at home where they can choose when and what they want to write and are not constrained by curriculum requirements to write in particular forms or to pay attention to technical aspects. In school, however, many of the boys who were identified as under-achieving seemed unmotivated, or unwilling to take risks with their writing. The teachers saw the differences between boys being prepared to be adventurous at home yet reluctant to write at school as a matter of concern.

By the end of the first two years of the project there had been significant shifts in the boys' views of their writing. Overall, the boys in Key Stage 2 had become more assured in talking about writing. They referred not just to the technical/secretarial aspects of writing but to the satisfactions of crafting a piece of writing, getting their ideas across and engaging the interest of the reader:

I like the good words I used ... 'the wind whistling through his fingers'.

(Year 4 boy)

I've got better at setting a scene and explaining what I think.

(Year 6 boy)

You've got to make something happen to keep people interested.

(Year 6 boy)

At Key Stage 1 most of the boys also felt that their writing had improved:

Yes. I'm good at remembering my full stops and capital letters.

(Year 2 boy)

I love stories ... I've made a book.

(Year 2 boy)

I'm way better at ideas.

(Year 2 boy)

While there were still indications of concerns about secretarial aspects, by the end of phase one of the project, the boys talked about matters of authorship as well as technicalities. Across the sample as a whole, many unequivocally said they liked writing, and very few still disliked writing. There was no clear pattern of narrative or non-fiction preferences although there was a sense that choice – of subject, type of writing and content – was an important factor in satisfaction.

Equally revealing about attitudes were the end-of-project responses given to the question about advice they might offer to younger pupils to help them improve their writing. Even the youngest in the sample had moved from a major focus on secretarial aspects to thinking more about the process of learning to be a writer. By Year 6 the advice to younger writers showed much greater understanding about the pleasures and challenges of composing whole texts than in the initial interviews. The boys' comments indicate a shift from their earlier concerns about surface features of writing – learning to write – towards a clear sense of what being a writer involves:

The ideas. Everyone's ideas. Listen to other people's ideas.

(Year 2 boy)

Use your imaginations and see what actually happens in your head. Write something you want to write.

(Year 6 boy)

Use bullet points in non-fiction writing because they make sure you say the facts.

(Year 6 boy)

Plan out before writing a story. Try and pick out the key events. Describe the setting and feeling well. See and picture it.

(Year 6 boy)

These comments indicate that over the course of the project the boys developed a vocabulary through which they could express their views about writing. This in itself is an important marker of progress. The case studies which follow give more of the detail provided by the research in identifying factors which can lead to progress in boys' attitudes to themselves as writers and their attainment in writing.

# An integrated approach to literacy

### Phase 1: Practices in the triad schools

Since all three schools in the outer London triad had higher than average national test results in English, particularly for boys, a first stage before developing strategies to improve writing in this particular triad was a rigorous examination of school and classroom factors which may have contributed to this success. The self-scrutiny undertaken by the schools allowed them to focus more precisely on areas of writing which might be improved. The schools carried out perceptions surveys with pupils identified as under-achieving but also held discussions with staff about their concerns about teaching writing and looked critically at the boys' writing. Analysis of writing samples showed some common features in the writing of those boys identified as under-achieving: a lack of personal voice; a lack of awareness that the piece was meant to communicate with a reader; and insecure structure in terms of paragraphs and punctuation. There was also a tendency to write from inner visual images and a failure to translate these into coherent written form.

Speaking and listening were an established regular feature of literacy sessions in the junior school and the inclusion of talk increasingly became a focus of attention in the triad. The aim was to develop a coherent and integrated approach to literacy in its broadest sense, seeing reading, writing, speaking and listening not as separate components, but as inter-related. Teaching approaches which would be developed during the project put emphasis on:

- greater attention to paired and group talk and drama; more oral preparation for narrative;
- work on the elements of narrative; more explicit discussion of character, plot, setting, structure and vocabulary;
- teacher demonstration: reading, discussing and analysing ideas, 'thinking aloud';
- aligning each curriculum area with a specific text type as designated by the Literacy Framework to consolidate literacy work in specific terms for each year group;
- the visual as a source of inspiration for writing and use of visual approaches to planning and note-making.

At the end of phase 1 of the project, classroom observations indicated the successful implementation of many of these teaching approaches, identifying common features which contributed to high standards of writing. These connect with research into effective teaching of literacy

(Wray et al. 2002) including planning for longer-term literacy learning; making explicit connections between reading, writing, speaking and listening; developing a classroom culture of high expectations; and having a clear knowledge of every pupil's capabilities so that teaching could challenge high achievers and support less assured learners.

End of phase 1 analysis of the pupils' writing showed marked improvements in narrative organization and structure as well as identifiable individual preferences and strengths, for example, character depiction; evoking atmosphere; using dialogue as a narrative device. In non-fiction writing there was a marked awareness of the needs of a reader and the extent and clarity of information required to communicate effectively. Most particularly, the writing showed far greater assurance in pace, voice and viewpoint – all indicators of a writer's sense of how best to engage a reader's attention, and all suggesting connections between text structure and experience in speaking and listening. Such evidence from the writing gave the prompt for more focused attention on talk and writing in the extension phase of the project.

### Phase 2: Planning for speaking and listening

Building on their preliminary work about boys' writing, in phase 2, the junior and primary school gave explicit attention to talk as a means of supporting writing. They also aimed to extend the work beyond Years 5 and 6 to include Year 3 pupils. In the junior school, this meant a thorough review of planning specifically to incorporate forms of speaking and listening which would directly support the teaching of particular text types. This was an extension of the existing link between the planned management of teaching text types both in literacy sessions and in other specified areas of the curriculum. In the primary school, the emphasis was on developing collaborative talk partnerships, beginning with Years 3 and 6.

Teachers in both schools with Key Stage 2 pupils were positive about the effects on their professional development:

It's added a new dimension because it fits with the Strategy's speaking and listening focus.
This integrated approach of speaking and listening as an automatic part of literacy work is now part of my normal planning and teaching.

Pupil interviews also showed that the younger boys (Year 3) who had been working with talk partners felt that it had helped with their writing:

> When you're talking it makes you have more ideas and if you have a partner it makes you feel more confident.

> When you're working ... when you're writing it's like you're learning as well at the same time. You always have to talk to yourself and your friend about something.

> If you don't really know what you're doing, you should talk.

In Year 6, there was even more conviction about how talk contributes to learning and writing:

> It does help a lot ... if you explain to others you understand it.

> Yes it can, when you're talking to yourself ... telling yourself how to do it.

> I like writing with my friend – I love it.

Apart from giving the teachers confidence to expand their planning to take account of speaking and listening, the work very clearly boosted the confidence of individual boys. The security of sharing ideas before writing had helped them to be more adventurous, taking greater risks both in the language they were using and the structure of their work as a whole. They had established a language to say what they wanted to say and had used talk as a way of drafting their writing. There was also evidence of greater enjoyment and a sense of *I can do it*. In addition, during the course of the year, teacher assessments showed that the writing of many of the boys had improved more than expected, specifically in the development of pace and individual voice in their writing; the establishment of atmosphere; a clearer structure and improved punctuation and paragraphing.

By the end of the three-year project, this triad identified key factors in improving attitudes and performance in writing as:

- organizing literacy sessions to incorporate a range of speaking and listening activities – formative, informative, performative and evaluative;
- an emphasis on talk and time to reflect – finding ways to talk about learning and literacy;
- the importance of 'companionable' writing through using response partners and groupwork;
- teachers being prepared to take risks in bringing more creativity to literacy sessions;

- teachers writing themselves, modelling writing and showing how it is constructed;
- using a variety of activities: at times these might be short, specific focused writing tasks; at other times they would allow time for boys to return to writing over a period of time;
- balancing attention to accuracy and neatness with a sense of fitness for purpose and knowing when it is important to 'get writing right';
- not engaging in purposeless writing – less writing, but writing which matters and which is relevant to the learners;
- more transparent assessment and marking with targets shared and negotiated with the pupils;
- having some sense of how literacy is perceived and supported at home.

## Drama as a focus for writing

In October 2001, drama was becoming a focus for the Sussex triad. The Originator School had already been working on integrating drama into literacy and the local education authority drama advisor was proactive in getting the other two schools interested in a more creative approach to teaching literacy. In the first phase of the project, the teachers wanted to combine the successful factors of the National Literacy Strategy (for example, termly objectives and a planned progression of skills) and the knowledge that a creative approach to teaching literacy may further enhance learning. For writing, drama was used to provide pupils with first-hand experiences to stimulate imagination and help them formulate and plan their writing; to allow them to rehearse and draft writing through talk and work collaboratively on written tasks. It also gave them opportunities to write for a range of purposes in role so that their writing would spring from experiences which felt 'real'.

At the end of the first phase, observations of the boys during drama sessions in the Originator School showed them to be enthusiastic and engaged. When interviewed following drama work involving texts and writing, the boys said that drama helped them have an idea of how a character would feel. They also thought that acting out parts of the story or freeze-framing helped them to remember key events:

> The drama has helped me to understand the story and to get my ideas organized. It's all in your head when you're writing.
>
> (Year 4 boy)

I prefer doing drama in the class than writing straight away.

(Year 5 boy)

Drama helped me to write in the first person because it gives you an idea of what it would be like and their feelings.

(Year 6 boy)

The boys in Partner Schools had not completed as many drama activities during literacy sessions as the boys in the Originator School but they thought that drama had helped them with their writing. The focus group boys in all three schools achieved a higher standard of work than their teachers had expected following literacy activities involving drama.

By the end of the first phase, the Originator School had established drama as an integral feature of literacy teaching units for each year group and was working with advisors from the LEA to raise awareness of the use of drama across the county. In the other schools, there had not been quite such an in-depth impact although several teachers had begun to integrate drama regularly into their literacy sessions. The opportunity for a further year's work allowed the triad to evaluate how far any gains by teachers and pupils were being sustained and how the approaches might be developed. A particular focus was to look at how the established work on using drama to support writing could be embedded into the curriculum and extended to give other teachers confidence in using drama approaches, since integrating drama into regular classroom literacy activities is seen by many teachers as high risk.

After a term's work one school was unable to continue involvement; however, by the end of phase two the aims had largely been met in the two schools which remained involved. There had been some very successful joint planning sessions that had allowed the teachers to identify success factors for future development of across-school planning and there had been definite gains in the boys' achievements in writing. Teachers commented that there had been noticeable improvements in attitudes and motivation and the boys' confidence had increased. Over one year, the boys' writing showed clearer voice, structure and pace; vocabulary was being used more precisely and punctuation more varied and consistently included.

### Finding a voice: one writer's progress

One example indicates the kinds of gains made. In October, Robert (aged 9) had written his Seaside Adventure (Figure 7.3). Although Robert shows some sense of trying to gain the reader's attention (by the use of capitals and punctuation, for example) the writing is generally disorganized and

October

Robert

## <u>Seaside Adventure</u>

Last summer mum and Dad took us to Drymacker for the summer
and Fred and (Rosmery) took a boat with them.
                        *rosemery*

Thay (bedal) far for a way then the waves woo coming.
        *paddle*

The boat was rocking and Fred nerley fell out thay shouted

"HeLP" thay said help! but no one houd

them so thay worry Left alon but then thay houd

a sound like a boat it was the life boat

"HRay" (the) thay said thay got on the boat and

went Back home.

### The End

thay next summer we saty home and had a

barbea.

And it was fred birthday.

*Last summer mum and dad took us to Grymacker for the summer and Fred and Rosemary took a boat with them.*
*Thay paddle far far away then the waves was coming.*
*The boat was rocking and Fred nearly fell out thay shouted*
*"HELP!" thay said help! But no one houd*
*them so thay wos left alon but then thay houd*
*a sound like a boat it was the lifeboat*
*"HRay!" thay said thay got on the boat and*
*went back home*
*The End*
*That next summer we saty home and had a barbeq*
*And it was fred birthday.*

**Figure 7.3**  Robert's Seaside Adventure

lacks coherence. The section about the boat capsizing bears the unmistakable mark of a young writer who has the pictures in his head but does not realize the amount of detail he has to give the reader so that they, too, can get a sense of the action. By early March, Robert had made considerable progress. The class had been reading *The Iron Man* by Ted Hughes and had used a range of drama activities to support their understanding of the narrative. Towards the end of the story, the Iron Man is called upon to save the world from an invading monster. Figure 7.4 gives an extract from Robert's letter appealing to the Iron Man for help.

The rhetorical pace of this piece very clearly reflects the experience of the drama. Repetition, sentence length and vocabulary are all used for effect in a highly persuasive piece of writing, very different from the insecure writing of six months ago. Robert is by no means a special case; many of the boys in the second phase of the project made significant gains in the conviction and organization of their writing.

The development of this triad's approach indicates some key factors for effective curriculum development in raising standards of writing through integrating drama with literacy. Clearly, it is important to establish a school culture which can support teachers as they take more curriculum 'risks', as they often see it, in bringing drama into a more central place in their teaching. This seems to be linked with the role of the headteacher. Where there is an established expectation and under-standing, the headteacher is likely to be in a better position to challenge teachers to develop their teaching approaches. The most effective teachers were those who were already enthusiastic about developing their professional expertise by using drama. Once they felt more secure,

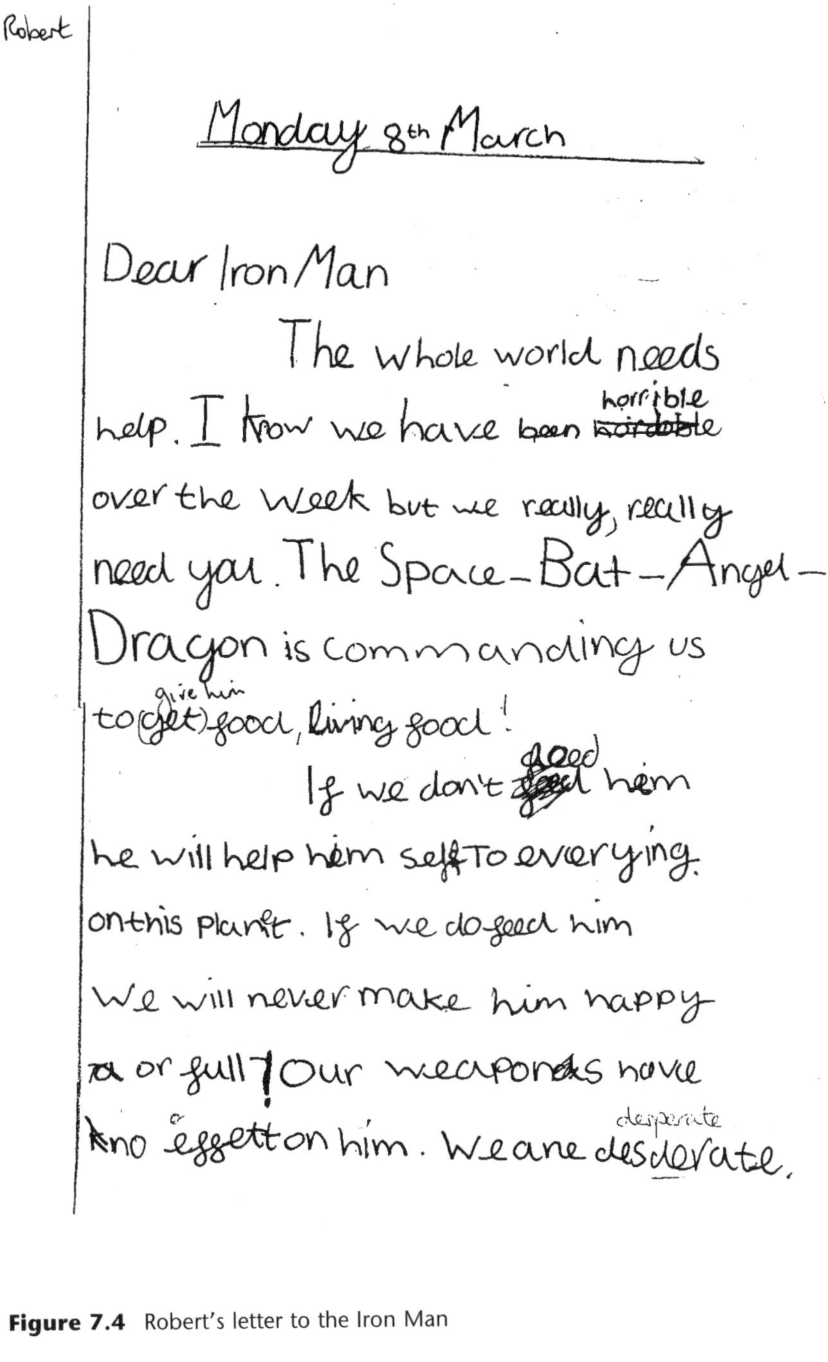

Robert

## Monday 8th March

Dear Iron Man

The whole world needs help. I know we have been ~~horible~~ horrible over the week but we really, really need you. The Space-Bat-Angel-Dragon is commanding us to ~~(get)~~ give him food, living food!

If we don't ~~feed~~ feed him he will help him self To everying. on this planet. If we do feed him We will never make him happy ~~a~~ or full! Our weaponds have ~~kno~~ no ~~eggett~~ effect on him. We are ~~desderate~~ desperate.

**Figure 7.4** Robert's letter to the Iron Man

they could then support others who were more tentative but prepared to try things out.

The steady embedding of drama into the curriculum is a matter of 'evolution not imposition' (Ofsted 2003c). Any initiative which means a fundamental shift of teaching approach will take time to develop with individuals before taking the approaches further and wider in the school (and, more significantly, across schools) and has to be made possible by senior management. In this triad, another important factor in developing work across schools was the support from local authority advisers and in-service providers. These conclusions are supported by other research work on drama and writing (PNS/UKLA 2004).

## Reflecting on writing in a special school

In addition to the work undertaken in the triads discussed above, one of the special schools involved in the project took writing as a key focus. In this all-age school in an East Anglian seaside town, the research project aimed not only to investigate teaching approaches which would support improvement in boys' writing, but to investigate how far the boys themselves could reflect on their learning. In the initial stages the work was carried out with one Year 10 class where the pupils were described as having a range of emotional, health and learning difficulties and whose literacy achievement was at National Curriculum Levels 2 to 3 in English. Most of them took a cautious approach to writing, unadventurous with vocabulary or spelling in case they made mistakes.

In a similar way to teachers in the mainstream schools involved, the class teacher adopted an integrated approach to English, including careful scaffolding of tasks over a period of several weeks leading to a specific genre outcome. She used visual and aural approaches, making learning approaches explicit and aiming to help pupils develop self-evaluation strategies. Attention was given primarily to close monitoring of the pupils' responses to teaching, particularly their increasing capacity to write confidently, talk about their writing and to understand that writing is meant to reflect their own thoughts, ideas and feelings. At three points in the two-year project, samples of writing were analysed and the pupils were interviewed about their attitudes to writing and the processes of their learning. In the first year, it was found that all of the pupils had made significant moves in their approach to writing, their attainment levels, their independence, pride and assurance as writers. Specifically, there were indications of greater fluency in the language that they used to talk about their writing, and in awareness that writing should reflect their own thoughts, ideas and feelings.

Many of the boys mentioned that their spelling and handwriting had improved over the year. Talking about surface feature technicalities can indicate lack of a wider vocabulary to talk about meaning, readership or purpose and concern about spelling, handwriting and punctuation can mean a restricted view of learning. However, for this group of students, the concern about technicalities was very much bound up with their experience as writers so far in their school careers. Almost all of them were fearful of making mistakes. For them, the inability to get their writing right was a recurrent reminder of frustrations and failures. This suggests that while they needed continued practice and experience in talking about the meaning and purpose of their writing, they also needed to be constantly reassured that they would be able to achieve accuracy. Without this, they would continue to be locked in a cycle of fearing to try out ideas which in turn meant that they would not have experience in taking risks to express their ideas and thoughts in writing.

Two short vignettes illustrate the kinds of shifts that boys of significantly different levels of fluency and assurance in writing made over a year and a half. They indicate progress in attitudes to their writing, the ability to evaluate their own work and the development of ways of talking about writing. These thumbnail sketches are drawn from field notes and video recordings of interviews throughout the project:

Dan was probably the most assured writer among the boys and in the first interview was very good in talking about the process of picture planning which his teacher had used as a way to support narrative writing. He was able to comment on characters, plot and setting, knowing what these meant in a piece of narrative writing. By the summer he was even more fluent and assured. Again he was able to describe his process of writing (information writing this time). He had become far more aware that writing is intended for different readers and needs to be shaped accordingly: 'I've learned how to write letters and communicate my ideas to people' and he commented several times on his increased independence as a writer and learner. His teacher assessment moved from 3a (lowest NC sub-level of Level 3) to 3c (highest) in the course of the year – a greater improvement than might be expected at this stage. In the second year of the project he became even more aware of his control over his writing, commenting on 'making it better by putting in paragraphs' and 'I've explained it more – more detail'. He gave a very clear explanation of his proof-reading and re-drafting:

> Read through aloud quietly ... that helps quite a bit to see
> when something's wrong ... And I do another neat copy.

By midway through Year 11 he was regularly writing at NC level
4b.

Luke had distinct emotional and learning difficulties. In the first
interview he showed very 'closed-in' body posture yet told, at
some length, a story about an old man who was isolated and
lonely then found help from a social worker. It was evident as he
was telling the story that he was drawing on his visual
imagination and probably his own experience. He was clearly
frustrated by his inability to spell and form letters accurately,
although he came alive when talking about his pictures (he is a
good artist). By the summer his body language was much more
relaxed and expansive. He liked the content of his information
texts and the fact that he had punctuated his sentences. He still
found spelling a hurdle and liked someone to scribe for him. He
was very clear about the purpose and process of the pamphlet he
had recently been writing and was quick to respond that his
writing had improved:

> It's tidier and neater and I can read it better. Teachers can read
> it and they don't have to ask you.

During the year his writing assessment moved from 1a (National
Curriculum sub-level ) to 1c. By Year 11 he was even more ready
to talk about his writing, showing great pride in work he had
done on the computer (partly because it looked neat and error
free) although his National Curriculum assessment was still 1c.

## Developing communication in special school settings

Assessments of the whole group at the end of Year 10 showed that four of
the six boys involved had moved at least two National Curriculum sub-
levels during the year. This contrasts sharply with the expected timescale
of two years for this rate of progress. Analysis of the writing showed
developments in overall fluency and assurance, the technicalities of
spelling and punctuation, and the range of different types of text
tackled. The teaching strategy had also helped the pupils to work
collaboratively. This progress continued as the pupils went into Year 11.
Teacher assessment at the end of the year showed that two of the boys
had maintained the gains made during the previous year and that four of
them had made a third or two-thirds of a level more progress.

In the second year of the project, however, the new Year 10 group did not replicate the previous year's experience of greater control over writing or their progress in developing a metalanguage to talk about writing. The boys remained preoccupied with the surface features of handwriting and spelling, and the discernible progress was only in terms of handwriting and control of sentences and paragraphs. The particular special needs of these pupils and the relationships within the group seemed to hinder the boys' progress. Despite the teacher's efforts, the boys in the second cohort did not move very far towards greater independence as learners or writers, in contrast to the first cohort.

The contrasts between each year group of boys indicates that developing intervention strategies to help raise the standards of boys' literacy in special school settings is particularly complex. The two year groups differed not only in levels of achievement but also in their capacity to talk about the content and intentions of their writing. Where the boys in the first cohort noticeably grew in confidence and a sense of self-efficacy, most of the boys in the second cohort failed to thrive in these respects. The improvements made by the girls in the second group indicate that it is likely that there were no great differences in the teaching approaches used, but that the nature of the learners and their needs was a key factor in success. This is a strong indicator of the 'specialness' of special education. While some of the successful approaches used in mainstream classes can be equally effective in both types of school, the special nature of the learners themselves means that initiatives to improve boys' writing need to take account of individual learning needs. In addition, although it can be recognized that talk, both as a medium of teaching and learning and a way of reflecting on learning, is a key factor in improving literacy, communication difficulties are likely to be more in evidence in special schools. The findings from the special school project suggest the need for further work about the relationship between oracy and improvements in literacy in special education settings.

## A more detailed view of talk and literacy

Recent attention to talk (Carter 2004) has emphasized its creative role: talk as contributing to the formation of ideas. These *formative* uses of talk are important in learning, just as the *informative* aspects of explaining ideas can reveal what has been learned. However, there is one other use of talk which has not been given as much attention over recent years – the *performative* aspect of oral storytelling, debate and reporting. Finally, there are the *evaluative* aspects of talk, allowing reflection on learning. The

Raising Boys' Achievement project has identified all of these functions of talk as critical in developing assured literacy, particularly the last two categories: performative and reflective/evaluative talk. In addition, the work has emphasized teachers' (and other adults') use of language in providing opportunities for pupils to extend their spoken repertoires.

## Formative talk

Exploratory, formative talk helps to capture shape and develop ideas in the opening stages of any teaching and learning experience. However, teachers have to plan deliberately to include opportunities for tentative thinking through talk; in groupwork formulating ideas is much more likely to happen if individuals have access to a language of negotiation and cooperation. In terms of boys' development of strategies to support effective literacy learning, emphasis on social interaction and practice in more tentative forms of language, for example, attentive listening and supportive speaking styles have been identified as offering beneficial ways of negotiating gender roles (Malone 1997; Renold 2004a). Teachers and other adults in the project modelled these ways of talking: *I wonder if we could ...? Perhaps this might work ...? What do you think ...?* and demonstrated supportive response: *Could you explain that a bit more ...? What might be a way forward now ...? What else might work ...?* Drama approaches as part of planned teaching and learning sequences were specifically selected to help pupils formulate ideas, offering useful opportunities for speculation and hypothesis.

## Informative talk

One of the most familiar aspects of any classroom is the constant exchange of question and answer – mostly questions from the teacher and answers from pupils. Such informative talk is part of everyday teaching and learning and might enter the planning and teaching sequence at any point. Recent work (Alexander 2004b) strongly suggests the value of longer stretches of informative dialogue where teachers offer opportunities for pupils to explain ideas in some detail and challenge their thinking further. As already indicated, questions from teachers and pupils emerged as significant for the development of assured literacy. In particular, there was evidence that the chance for pupils to ask questions is an important contributor to boys' engagement with learning. In triad 2, drama strategies were used to encourage extended stretches of talk. Greater readiness to share ideas and express opinions in front of others indicated growing confidence and assurance which had its effects on achievements in reading and writing.

## Performative talk

The emphasis on practice in whole stretches of talk which parallel written text types is an under-researched aspect of the talk curriculum in general although it is gradually gaining attention as important in supporting boys' literacy (PNS/UKLA 2004). In contrast to the more tentative and conditional aspects of formative talk and the explanatory elements of informative talk, performative or presentational talk involves longer stretches of oral narrative, instructional or persuasive types of text. Sometimes this can be achieved through drama, as in simulations which involve the adoption of specific roles, but very often performative talk means pupils rehearsing whole stretches of a text type through talk. In those schools where literacy was specifically planned to link with other curriculum areas, opportunities were offered through re-enactments of historical incidents, descriptions of scientific experiments or the rehearsal of arguments about moral issues in personal and social education. Although at first some boys felt exposed by the presentational element of lessons, in a supportive and challenging environment a culture is established that 'it's cool' to be seen publicly as good at something and that even if you might be feeling insecure inside, there can be satisfaction in taking on a challenge.

In schools in the project where boys' standards of literacy matched those of the girls, and both were high, performative talk was a feature from early in school experience. When it comes to writing, the opportunity to rehearse whole stretches of text takes the heat off the more usual practice of expecting pupils to hold in their minds both the structure of the text type and the specific content which the writer wants to include. Knowledge of the shape of the whole text means that greater attention can be given both to content and stylistic features during writing. It was clear that in those schools where performative talk had been a feature, the pupils' written work was much more likely to be well structured and punctuated, with greater control of point of view, pace and voice.

## Reflective/evaluative talk

Evidence from all schools involved in the aspect of the project which focused on writing, particularly the special school, strongly suggests that reflection and evaluation allowed the boys to take on a broader view of what writing might offer. Many of the boys involved had started the project with anxieties about secretarial and physical aspects of writing, confining themselves to accuracy of words and sentences. Invitations to think and talk about writing as a means of communication released them from some of these initial fears so that their writing became much more a matter of personal expression and satisfaction. Where drama was used, it offered ideal opportunities for reflection and evaluation, both within the drama and when commenting on the effectiveness of the work. The establishment of response partners added to opportunities for learning generally, but particularly for attentive review and editing of writing. Developing strategies for useful response helped the boys become more focused about the specific aspects of their work which they wanted to improve.

The teachers' own use of language was essential to the process of developing a more attentively evaluative approach, for example, by vocalizing their own thought processes and giving their own opinions: *I think this is a better way of saying it because ...* and *I hadn't got this quite right so I tried it another way ...* They not only demonstrated reflective and evaluative types of language but used a technical vocabulary to describe the repertoire and processes of writing. All the evidence from focus group pupils indicated improvements in their use of a metalanguage to talk about writing. Teachers' automatic and regular use of specific terminology about texts and about language itself, afforded the pupils a vocabulary through which they could express ideas about their own writing. The pupils' use of metalanguage became one of the key measurement tools for gauging the success of the approaches used in each school.

## Conclusion

Throughout the project's literacy strand, in a generally rich and layered set of evidence, two key themes emerge: the importance of integrated, planned, systematic management and organization – at whole-school level as well as in classroom literacy teaching and learning – and the valuable role of spoken language and expressive elements of the literacy curriculum. In terms of intervention strategies, the work has shown the importance of balancing teaching the skills of writing with attention to the processes of learning to be successful and satisfied writers.

Speaking and listening have emerged as central to this process. In terms of reading this means finding the space to foster opinion and reflection on what has been read, not as a routine 'read it then write about it' practice but as part of a genuine exchange of views. Reflection on writing is important, but other aspects of talk have emerged as crucial: the opportunity to draft and redraft orally, to get a sense of the shape of a text before having to grapple with the language used to express it. In all aspects of literacy, the development of a metalanguage

has become a major factor in success. The ability to descri
aspects of writing which need attention shifts thinking up
enables both deeper and more focused understanding o
improve.

Equally, the opportunities to enact ideas though drama has proved a
key feature in boys' development of more secure literacy. This is not only
a matter of getting in touch with personal feelings, but of opportunities
to take on the role of others, thus helping boys tackle issues of 'self-worth
protection' (Jackson 2003). Behavioural factors are often associated with
motivation, and schools which used drama, role play and enactment as
part of their literacy teaching found gains not only in achievement but
in attitude and feelings of self-efficacy and value.

None of these strategic interventions will genuinely take hold,
however, unless they are part of a systematic, planned and holistic
pedagogy. Those schools where boys and girls make the most gains are
those where the teachers have adopted a wider view of teaching literacy
which includes visual, creative and talk-based approaches. In terms of
school organization, these teaching approaches have even more effect
when they are part of a planned and progressive curriculum which seeks
to integrate pupils' learning experiences. The role of management is
central here. The most successful initiatives have emerged from those
schools which have a developed culture of mutual respect not only
between head and teaching colleagues but between adults, children and
the community served by the school. A culture like this allows for
understanding that sustained and effective achievement is based on a
view of long-term learning goals supported by a thorough and detailed
knowledge of the progress of each individual pupil. In terms of the
markers of under-achievement which the teachers identified at the
outset of the project, there was evidence of the approaches leading not
only to higher levels of attainment in writing but to the boys having
greater assurance and sense of personal satisfaction as writers.

# Note

1   There were 76 boys interviewed in the first two-year phase of the project (12
    in Years 1–2; 56 in Years 5–6; 8 in Year 10) and a further 60 (24 in Years 1 and
    2; 8 in Year 3; 12 in Year 4; 10 in Year 6; 6 in Year 10) in the one-year
    extension phase. The summary of perceptions draws on both cohorts
    interviewed.

# 8 'The teachers do try and make it enjoyable for us and make learning fun'

## A focus on pedagogy

### A focus on learning styles

> It has been estimated that up to 37% of the population are kinaesthetic learners ... Boys are more likely than girls to be kinaesthetic learners.
>
> (Suffolk County Council, 2002)

> Boys are more kinaesthetic learners than girls, and value the opportunity to do something rather than listen to it.
>
> (North Somerset Education Department, 2002)

Much interest has been generated in the last decade, in both primary and secondary schools in England, by work on children's preferred learning styles, particularly in the context of accelerated learning (Smith 1997, 1998), and Gardner's (1983, 1999) work on multiple intelligences. There has been widespread adoption and adaptation of these ideas, and enthusiastic promotion by local education authorities, by government agencies and by educational consultancies. Work on developing teaching strategies which access visual, auditory and kinaesthetic opportunities for learning has become widespread, evolving in part from Smith's accelerated learning framework. The notion of accelerated learning schools (Wise and Lovatt 2001) has been espoused by Ofsted and by DfES, and the associated teacher effectiveness enhancement programmes have been welcomed as presenting exciting and innovative ways of enabling pupils' 'critical skills' and 'thinking skills' (TEEP 2005). Similarly, the DfES website on learning styles and brain-based learning references 38 programmes for teachers to resource, and talks of how brain-based learning is 'a powerful means of engaging teachers and pupils in improving the quality of learning in classrooms' (DfES 2004c).

Likewise, support information produced by London Challenge includes materials on students' preferred learning styles and on visual, auditory and kinaesthetic learning which 'can be particularly powerful when shared with learners' (DfES/London Challenge 2004: 17). Indeed, the essence of many of these ideas accords well with teachers' professional knowledge, understanding and intuition, and relates well to current concepts of intelligence which we refer to in Chapter 2.

At the same time, there has been increasing unease that classroom-based strategies derived from these notions of multiple intelligences have sometimes strayed significantly from the original conceptions of those who derived the ideas, and the subsequent classroom approaches have frequently been presented uncritically and without reference to the context from which they have been derived (Younger et al. 2005a). Thus, Gardner himself has written of programmes derived from his original work which have left him uncomfortable: 'much of the program [in an Australian state] was a mishmash of practices, with neither scientific foundation nor clinical warrant ... approaches commingled with dazzling promiscuity' (quoted in report of the Demos Learning Working Group 2004: 15). Similarly, Coffield et al., in a wide-ranging review of research into learning styles, speak of the extravagant claims made by some leading learning theorists, of the lack of reliability and validity of some models, of 'advice offered to practitioners which is too vague and unspecific to be helpful' (2004: 37). They argue that, after more than three decades of research, 'no consensus has been reached about the most effective instrument for measuring learning styles and no agreement about the most appropriate pedagogical interventions' (2004: 55). In a strong critique of the use of learning styles work in classrooms in England, the Demos Report suggests that the research evidence about the effectiveness of learning styles approaches is 'highly variable' and 'very slender', *especially* when such schemes are applied in classrooms: 'there is usually even less evidence that these schemes really do help to enhance the character of teaching so that learning is improved' (2004: 11). Furthermore, the authors of the report argue that 'some teachers, despite the best of intentions, are using learning styles in ways that constitute poor professional practice' (2004: 11).

It remains true, however, that in the past decade many primary schools have implemented teaching approaches derived from work on learning styles, and there has been a belief, based on teachers' experiences and pupils' responses, that such approaches have been instrumental in enhancing boys' and girls' motivation and engagement, and in raising achievement in end-of-Key-Stage tests. Such was the case in one of the Originators and so, given our commitment within the RBA project to identify pedagogic initiatives which appeared, *from the perspective of schools,* to have such potential, learning styles became the focus in one triad. Our aims here were three-fold:

- to assess how far it was possible accurately to identify the learning styles of primary school children;
- to develop and refine teaching and learning strategies derived from approaches that focused on accelerated learning and multiple intelligences;
- to identify evidence of the impact (or not) of such pedagogic approaches on children's motivation and achievement.

## The case studies

The triad in question consisted of three large primary schools in mixed urban/rural catchments in one local education authority in Suffolk, where the LEA had been proactive in initiating evaluation and dissemination of ideas associated with multiple intelligences among its schools. The Originator School was situated on the outskirts of a large town while Partner School 1 was located in a coastal town. Pupils at both these schools were mostly of white British heritage, the proportion of pupils eligible for free school meals was low, and there was an average number of pupils with special educational needs. Partner School 2 was situated in an urban area with above average free school meals and just over a quarter of its pupils from ethnic minority backgrounds. In the Originator School, as with other Originator Schools at the beginning of the project, achievement for both sexes in the core subjects at Key Stage 2 had shown a steady improvement, with a narrow gender gap (Figure 8.1).

There was a strong commitment in the Originator school to the promotion of multi-sensory approaches to learning, particularly within the context of kinaesthetic styles of learning. Teachers felt that this aspect of pedagogy had become increasingly neglected in the primary curriculum, and believed that the introduction of kinaesthetic modes of learning had impacted positively on boys' and girls' motivation and attainment at Key Stage 2. Particularly, there was a belief that:

> Kinaesthetic activities can be used effectively to change the mood in the classroom, to motivate, stimulate interest and re-engage, to give children opportunity to remember things by association.
>
> (Teacher from Originator School, speaking at RBA's cross-phase Learning Styles Conference, February 2003)

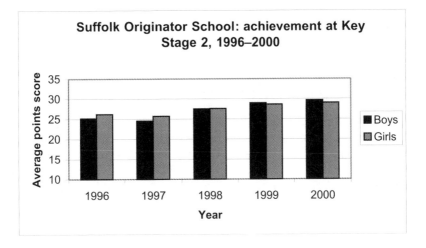

**Figure 8.1**  Key Stage 2 results, Suffolk Originator School (all core subjects)

Research took place during the main intervention stage of the project, and continued during the extension stage, when it was developed further in the context of two West Midlands 11–18 secondary schools which had been involved in learning styles work during the secondary project, and two of their feeder schools, one of which was a primary school and the other a junior school. These schools served inner city urban catchments, with high levels of social deprivation; the student intake was predominantly white working class, although in each school there was a significant proportion of students from minority ethnic backgrounds, mainly of Indian or black Caribbean heritage. The proportion of pupils eligible for free school meals ranged from 20 per cent to 40 per cent.

### Identification of pupils' learning styles

Central to learning styles work is the belief that it is possible to identify pupils' preferred learning styles, in terms of the balance between visual, auditory and kinaesthetic (VAK), and thus identify any marked dominance within the learning profiles of individuals. Once pupils are made aware of their learning styles, they can begin to reflect on their learning and extend their learning styles repertoire, and become more effective learners. In each school, the use of a commonly available questionnaire, a VAK test from Smith's Accelerated Learning Programme (ALP) (Smith 1998), enabled pupil profiles to be built up, in terms of learning styles dominances. These profiles were cross-referenced against interviews, which gave the children the opportunity to *talk* about their preferred modes of learning and whether they found certain skills easier to perform than others.

Analysis of the questionnaires and the interviews revealed interesting, and somewhat surprising, outcomes (Bricheno and Younger 2004). The analysis of data from the common VAK questionnaire suggested that – contrary to expectations derived from assertions within some of the literature – individual boys did not necessarily prefer a kinaesthetic learning style compared to visual or auditory (Table 8.1); indeed, data from across the schools revealed that few boys apparently held such preferences and that the proportions of boys and girls identified as having a kinaesthetic learning style were very similar. Where dominance could be identified, there was more of a tendency for girls to favour visual styles of learning, and boys auditory learning. Interviews with a sample of pupils confirmed these conclusions in one respect. When pupils were asked to respond to visual prompts and to say which skill (listening, looking carefully or doing/building/making) was easiest and hardest for them, their responses did not suggest that more boys than girls were kinaesthetic learners. Nonetheless, the 'doing' skill *was* most often regarded as the easiest skill by *both* boys and girls, although more girls than boys found the 'doing' skill hardest (see Table 8.2).

**Table 8.1**  Preferred learning styles assessed by ALP's VAK test

| Identified learning style | Boys (%) | Girls (%) |
|---|---|---|
| Visual (V) | 29 | 44 |
| Auditory (A) | 42 | 30 |
| Kinaesthetic (K) | 17 | 17 |
| Combinations (VA, AK, VK, VAK) | 12 | 9 |

**Table 8.2**  Skill preferences by gender: interview outcomes

| | Hardest skill | | Easiest skill | |
|---|---|---|---|---|
| | Boys (n) | Girls (n) | Boys (n) | Girls (n) |
| Listening | 12 | 12 | 7 | 9 |
| Looking | 7 | 8 | 7 | 12 |
| Doing | 6 | 11 | 12 | 13 |
| Equal | 5 | 3 | 4 | 1 |

In another respect, however, there was no obvious relationship between questionnaire results and the preferred skills that these pupils identified during interviews (Tables 8.3 and 8.4). It might be expected, for example, that most visual learners would choose 'looking carefully' as the easiest skill, but their preferences were almost equally divided between the three skills. However, it is interesting that none of those described as kinaesthetic learners chose 'doing' as the most difficult skill and most of them chose it as the easiest. On the whole, 'listening' was regarded as the most difficult skill and 'doing' the easiest:

> Yeah, carrying out tests and building and making things is the easiest, because once I start I get, like, stuck into it and plan to finish it.
>
> (Tracy)

> For me it [the most difficult] would have to be the listening skills because the boys, they don't let you learn . . . they're just so noisy and that's why I don't hear that much.
>
> (June)

**Table 8.3**  Easiest skill preferences by assessed learning style: interview outcomes

| Easiest skill | Visual learner | Auditory learner | Kinaesthetic learner | Combination (VAK) | Total |
|---|---|---|---|---|---|
| Listen | 5 | 2 | 0 | 1 | 8 |
| Look | 5 | 8 | 2 | 0 | 15 |
| Doing | 4 | 9 | 6 | 0 | 19 |
| Listening & looking | 0 | 0 | 0 | 3 | 3 |

**Table 8.4**  Hardest skill preferences by assessed learning style: interview outcomes

| Hardest skill | Visual learner | Auditory learner | Kinaesthetic learner | Combination (VAK) | Total |
|---|---|---|---|---|---|
| Listen | 6 | 9 | 7 | 0 | 22 |
| Look | 6 | 5 | 1 | 1 | 13 |
| Doing | 2 | 5 | 0 | 0 | 7 |
| Listening & looking | 0 | 0 | 1 | 3 | 4 |

We must be cautious, of course, because of the small numbers of pupils involved, but it is clear that there are dangers of over-simplification in much of the discussion about pupils' preferred learning styles. There is a presumption that it is relatively easy to establish preferred learning styles, but both in the mismatch between the questionnaire outcomes and the subsequent pupils interviews and in our experiences on the secondary project (where different questionnaires administered to the same groups of students actually yielded different results), we feel that 'VAK' tests and labels may be inadequate in representing pupils' learning preferences (Younger et al. 2005a). Equally, as in our secondary case studies, there was little substantive evidence from learning style questionnaires to suggest that individual boys necessarily preferred a kinaesthetic learning style compared to a visual or auditory one. In fact, the evidence pointed to a lack of gendered preferences; as with so many other stereotypes, the commonalities between genders were more significant than the differences (Wood 2003; Jones and Myhill 2004b).

A further element of complexity is introduced into the discussion if we consider pupils' responses to a question posed in interview about whether their learning was affected if a range of activities was used by the teacher, demanding a combination of skills rather than one explicit skill (Table 8.5). In both groups of schools, a significant number of the pupils spoke about the value of combining different sensory strategies to support their learning, but again there is little evidence to support a differential approach by gender. While it is true that more boys than girls preferred combining kinaesthetic approaches with other sensory strategies, this was a small percentage of the total interviewed (12 per cent of boys and 6 per cent of girls); indeed, almost equal percentages of boys and girls suggested that they found it more helpful to combine auditory and visual approaches to support their learning. Once again, this has resonance with one conclusion from our secondary case studies, and our warning against identifying 'the preferred learning style of a pupil (singular), without contextualising it within a more balanced approach which looks at the significance of each learning style within the student's overall dominance profile (plural)' (Younger et al. 2005a: 88–9). This point is likewise reinforced within the Demos Report: 'while it is true that some learners have a dominant learning style, a good education does not limit them to that style or type, but ensures that students have opportunities to strengthen the other learning styles' (2004: 11).

**Table 8.5** Pupils' perceptions of the value to learning of combining skills

| Comments about the value to learning of combining skills | Original Primary triad | | Extension cross-phase triad | | Total | |
|---|---|---|---|---|---|---|
| | Boys | Girls | Boys | Girls | All boys | All girls |
| | (%) | (%) | (%) | (%) | (%) | (%) |
| Better/made learning easier | 44 | 26 | 63 | 56 | 46 | 40 |
| Worse/made learning more difficult | 0 | 2 | 16 | 12 | 5 | 5 |
| Better because – combining auditory and visual | 31 | 21 | 37 | 33 | 29 | 26 |
| Better because – combining kinaesthetic with others | 3 | 0 | 26 | 12 | 12 | 6 |
| Total number of pupils interviewed | 62 | 43 | 38 | 43 | | |

*Notes*: Interviews in the extension cross-phase work (but not in the original primary triad) included an explicit question on the extent to which children used a combination of skills in their learning, so the responses of the children in the different interviews are not directly comparable.

## Teaching and learning strategies

Given the reservations expressed above about the difficulties of identifying pupils' learning *styles*, and the lack of evidence for gendered preferences, it became more fruitful to focus more on teaching and learning *strategies*. Teaching and learning strategies developed within this aspect of the RBA project have been rooted both in the realities of existing pedagogic practice within each school and with regard to initiatives developed in each of the local education authorities in which the triads were located. Thus, for example, the Suffolk triad drew inspiration and guidance from research and case studies in schools across the county, as the LEA sought to prompt debate about how best to support effective learning for all pupils. One aspect of this work was to offer a classification based upon the Gardner's work on multiple intelligences (1993), and to suggest how this might be exemplified through appropriate teaching approaches (see Figure 8.2). Similarly, the West Midlands schools engaged in the cross-phase extension work of the project used LEA inputs, together with the experiences gained from the secondary phase of the RBA project, developing pedagogic strategies such as jigsaw activities, drama and role play, brain gym, mindmapping,

| Intelligence | Characteristics | Appropriate Approaches |
|---|---|---|
| Linguistic | • Good with language/words<br>• Awareness of patterns<br>• Ability to reason<br>• Good memory for detail | • Brainstorming<br>• Discussing<br>• Writing<br>• Telling/reading stories<br>• Using a word-processor<br>• Doing puzzles, word games and memory games |
| Logical Mathematical | • Good with numbers<br>• Selecting patterns<br>• Identifying relationships<br>• Dealing in abstract notation<br>• Enjoys problem solving and logic<br>• Values precision | • Following instructions<br>• Problem solving<br>• Playing computer games<br>• Sequencing<br>• Classifying<br>• Predicting & hypothesizing<br>• Analysing/interpreting data<br>• Using reasoning & deductive thinking |
| Visual Spatial | • Good at visualizing in 3D<br>• Can manipulate mental images<br>• Good at interpreting diagrams, charts and maps<br>• Good at designing | • Using pictures<br>• Drawing diagrams<br>• Watching videos<br>• Using wall displays<br>• Highlighting with colour<br>• Using computer graphics<br>• Using concept mapping |
| Bodily Kinaesthetic | • Very good body control<br>• Enjoys physical movement<br>• Well-developed sense of touch<br>• Likes to manipulate objects | • Using movement/role play<br>• Using models<br>• Using games<br>• Construction and manipulative activities |
| Musical | • Sensitive to pitch, tone and rhythm<br>• Good sound discrimination<br>• Enjoys listening to music<br>• Ability to play musical instrument | • Using background music<br>• Singing and chanting<br>• Using raps to aid memory<br>• Using rhythm activities<br>• Composing & performing tunes and songs |
| Interpersonal | • Good understanding of people<br>• Can anticipate likely reactions<br>• Works well in a team<br>• Communicates well with others<br>• Enjoys company, sociable | • Working collaboratively<br>• Peer group tutoring<br>• Team games<br>• Group discussions and projects<br>• Role playing |

| Intrapersonal | • Well developed capacity for reflection<br>• Aware of own strengths and weaknesses<br>• Strong sense of identity<br>• Self-motivated | • Taking time for reflection<br>• Undertaking independent study<br>• Taking control of own learning<br>• Personal target-setting<br>• Autobiographical writing<br>• Self-evaluation |
|---|---|---|

**Figure 8.2**  Teaching strategies related to multiple intelligences
*Source*: Suffolk County Council (2002)

musical stimulation and practical design activities, to stimulate visual, auditory and kinaesthetic (VAK) learning (Smith 1997, 1998; Wise and Lovatt 2001). A subsequent cross-phase conference, held under the aegis of the RBA project in February 2003, developed these ideas further and explored how these strategies might be made more accessible to teachers *and* to children.

Any classification such as that set out in Figure 8.2 must recognize, as already discussed, the difficulty of identifying and defining the distinctiveness of each learning style or 'intelligence'. Many classroom-based activities involve a variety of different teaching strategies, and it can be argued that it is simplistic in the extreme to categorize specific activities as oriented only towards one learning style. We recognize, too, that most of these pedagogic strategies are neither original nor at the cutting edge of innovation. Given the approach we have taken, inevitably these strategies accord well with teachers' own experiences of classrooms, so much so that some teachers did not feel that they had adapted their teaching much, if at all, but had now acquired labels for what they were doing 'naturally':

> I think it was just that now there was a name for things that I was doing … it wasn't until working [on this project] did I realize that some of the things which I would do naturally anyway, I was then starting to be able to say, this is the learning style that I have always taught in, and you can label the parts now, and this one would come into here and so forth.
>
> (Teacher, West Midlands school)

On the other hand, classroom observations through time in a range of classrooms strongly suggested that there was a marked mismatch between the teaching styles which many teachers believed were appropriate, and what actually happened in classrooms (Younger and

Warrington 1999). Interviews with pupils frequently confirmed this perception, as in these interchanges between Hannah and Robert, and between Asha, Linda and Denise:

*Hannah*:   It's the listening ...
*Robert*:   Yeah, I don't mind doing the writing, its just listening, where you listen for ages.
*Hannah*:   ... and you sit there and listen for ages.

*Asha*:   We copy from the book, all the time, because there's no point in doing all that, when you're just, you're just wasting your time.
*Linda*:   What makes it dead is we just do writing and learning boring stuff, whereas if it was lively we would be able to make things, so we understand.
*Denise*:   Yes, I think the same, it is dead, we just sit there writing, and we've got a seating plan. I hate seating plans at school.

This mismatch between many teachers' beliefs and the reality in some classrooms has been emphasized in the context of primary school literacy by Wood:

> The pupils showed considerable consensus on the characteristics of a good lesson ... which was consistent with the kind of learning styles teachers believed are preferred by boys. However, the teachers' beliefs did not always translate into practice: whole class teaching episodes were dominated by question and answer sessions, by teacher talk or by discussion ... there were relatively few examples of practical activities involving the whole class.
>
> (2003: 377)

The challenge, then, has been to develop teaching strategies which have bridged this rhetoric–reality gap, to generate the active engagement in learning of boys and girls, and to recognize the wide range of strategies which might properly be used to stimulate different types of learning and understanding.

## Impact

It is difficult, within the context of primary schools with small pupil cohorts, to make meaningful comparisons in achievement data from year to year. In each school, both in the original primary triad and in the cross-phase extension work, average points scores varied from year to year, although in the Suffolk Originator School performance in National Curriculum tests remained above the national average, and gender parity between the performance of girls and boys in English was maintained through the lifetime of the project. As we have argued in other chapters, however, changing attitudes and motivation among pupils can provide useful evidence in evaluating the success of a particular approach. Thus, we focused one aspect of our research (in the Suffolk triad) around a number of Year 5 boys who seemed, in terms of the standard of the work they produced and their level of classroom engagement, to be under-achieving when compared with their performance at Key Stage 1. In each school, initial classroom observations suggested that these boys rarely participated in class discussions or acted in a proactive way during groupwork, were frequently off-task during lessons and often misinterpreted the requirements of activities set by the teacher. This passive disengagement contrasted markedly with the assertive and dominant role within the peer group which they assumed in other contexts, particularly in the playground and on the school field.

Within the framework of the research, the preferred learning styles of each of these boys were identified through questionnaire and response to pictorial stimuli and confirmed with each boy in subsequent individual interviews, in an attempt to provide each with more self-awareness of themselves as learners. At the same time, staff development work on preferred learning styles was initiated, in association with the LEA, to allow teachers to develop strategies which would cater for pupils' strengths and preferred learning styles, while at the same time enabling them to support pupils to work more effectively in their 'less preferred' styles. Throughout the two-year span of the research, the boys' attitudes, behaviour and attainment were tracked, so that an initial assessment of the impact of the intervention strategy could be made. The end of the two-year cycle was marked by interviews with pupils and teachers, and lesson observations were carried out by members of the research team.

Partner School 2 did not continue with the strategy into the second year, but end-of-project interviews in the other two schools suggested that the boys had markedly more positive attitudes about the curriculum and learning. Virtually all the focus group boys felt that their teachers were using a wider variety of teaching approaches within lessons, and there were explicit references to modes of learning:

We are learning but it's fun. There are more fun things in lessons now.

We use whiteboards to work out sums the quickest: it's bigger than a page.

> They've tried to help us by making the environment around us better.

> They set up activities and they know what we like.

> I like acting things out.

> You had to play with your mind to find stuff.

Equally, most of the boys felt that the teachers were more proactive in helping them access learning that they were finding difficult, and in supporting them in their weaker learning styles. The boys commented, for example, that:

> She makes me look carefully at what she is talking about.

> He helps me to work in a group.

> He shows me how to do the stuff. I learn best by looking.

> He points carefully to the things I need to look at.

It was clear that these boys were aware that teachers were planning lessons carefully to engage them in a variety of activities, and appreciated the efforts which teachers were making to support their specific learning needs, mentioning strategies such as role play, model-making, group work and carousel activities which involved searching the classroom for prompts and clues:

> In geography, we had to make our own city in Egypt that would be better than Cairo.

> We done more talking about *Twelfth Night*.

> In PSHE I got to be the teacher. I learnt how to lead a group.

It was also clear that these boys were more aware of themselves as learners, and understood more about the processes of learning, as a result of their involvement (and that of their teachers) in this pedagogic aspect of the RBA project. Interviews with them pointed to some positive attitudinal change towards schooling, and less disengagement and disillusionment with school. In each of the schools the focus group boys appeared more confident, had improved self-esteem as learners and were more willing to work collaboratively and supportively in groups. We cannot, of course, disentangle the specific impact of the intervention strategy from other whole-school effects, nor ignore the impact on these boys of their involvement in a project such as this. Positively, though, our interviews with teachers, and lesson observations at the end of the project suggested a number of significant changes within each school, as we report elsewhere (Younger et al. 2005b: 63), namely:

- Teachers planning and teaching in more cross-curricular ways, combining art and literacy, for example, or ICT and history, or science and literacy, to diversify the range of learning styles in lessons;
- Teachers' increased awareness of preferred learning styles of individual pupils, differentiating to build on strengths and establish confidence, and offering support to develop other, less favoured aspects of pupils' learning;
- More pupil engagement within lessons, with increased motivation, and a better understanding of the intentions of the teacher.

The impact of a learning styles approach on pupil engagement is worth some emphasis at this point, since the findings from the Suffolk triad are strongly corroborated by cross-phase work in the West Midlands. One aspect of this extension research involved the link researcher carrying out lesson observations of teaching in the different schools, focusing on the number of different learning styles being used by teachers and the degree of pupil engagement, as evidenced through a sample number of pupils in each classroom. Across the schools, there was a high and statistically significant correlation between the number of different learning styles apparent and the degree of pupil engagement (all other things being equal), with distracted and off-task behaviour falling with an increase in number of learning styles employed by the teacher (Figure 8.3). As with the initial identification of pupils' preferred learning styles, however, there was little differentiation by gender (Figure 8.4). This reinforces and complements our earlier point, where we reported pupils' views about the value of combining different sensory strategies to support their own learning (Table 8.5), and suggests that the more multi-sensory strategies are used, the less likely it is that pupils' disengagement and negative attitudes to learning will become embedded.

These positive impacts of learning style approaches are not confirmed, however, when we review achievement data. Here, value-added data for the focus group boys presented a rather different perspective on the 'success' of the intervention strategy in the Suffolk triad, since in the Originator School half of the boys under-performed in

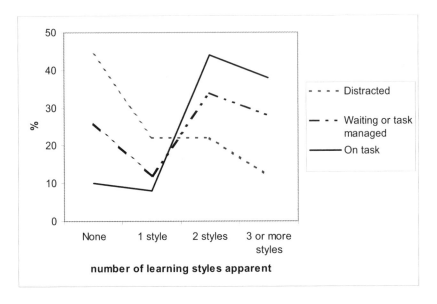

**Figure 8.3** The relationship between pupil engagement and number of learning styles apparent in lesson

terms of their 'expected' progress between Key Stages 1 and 2, and the progress of the boys was also disappointing in the Partner School which continued its involvement over two years. This again raises issues about what might be said to constitute success, which we discussed in Chapter 6 and explore further in Chapter 9. Yet despite the outcomes in achievement terms, we noted marked attitudinal change not only in these 'under-achieving' boys but across the year group as a whole. Equally, as part of the extension work of the project, these boys were tracked through their first year of secondary education, in two contrasting secondary schools. Although we need to be cautious when dealing with such small numbers, it appeared that 'the boys who had experienced the learning styles approach in their primary school were more able to express ideas about what helped them to learn and what made learning difficult' (Younger et al. 2005b: 64), so it may be that the learning styles approach had a positive effect in helping the boys to think about their own learning.

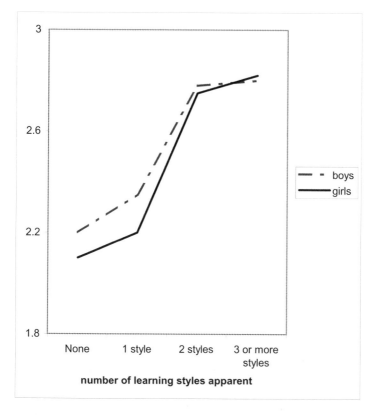

**Figure 8.4**  The relationship between pupil engagement (by gender) and number of learning styles apparent in lesson

*Note*: Systematic and regular observation of pupil activity during lessons was quantified, and defined as: 1 = distracted, 2 = waiting, 3 = engaged, so higher mean value equates to higher levels of engagement.

## Concluding reflections on learning styles approaches

> In misguided hands, learning styles could become not a means of personalising learning, but a new version of general intelligence that slots learners into preconceived categories and puts unwarranted ceilings on their intellectual development and achievement
>
> (Demos Report, 2004: 12)

Pedagogic initiatives based on learning styles approaches have become widespread in primary schools in England over the past decade, and the language, particularly of VAK, has become commonplace among both teachers *and* pupils. The evidence from these primary schools, albeit limited in scope and scale, suggests that there are some gains to be had from such an approach, particularly in terms of pupil engagement in learning, and their ability to articulate the ways in which they learn most effectively. Pupils who are aware of their own preferred learning styles (plural) are likely to feel more involved in their own learning, to have more control over that learning and to be empowered by knowledge of themselves as learners. Equally, there is evidence to suggest that those teachers who have a knowledge of learning styles research, either through continuing professional development activity or in their initial training, appear to have the skills and the understanding to develop a multi-sensory approach more effectively in their classrooms, and to have a wider repertoire of multi-sensory activities to call upon, which helps them plan more interesting lessons. Awareness of pupils' preferred learning styles enables teachers to offer more targeted support to pupils who have learning weaknesses in specific areas.

There are, though, some important words of caution which need to be acknowledged. First, we have emphasized throughout the plurality of learning styles, rather than focusing on a pupil's one preferred learning style. We have taken this position partly because we are not convinced of the validity or accuracy of commonly used tests and questionnaires which purport to identify a pupil's dominant learning style. Equally, our evidence suggests, not surprisingly, that children learn better when teachers use strategies that access a variety of learning styles in their lessons, whereas emphasis on a preferred learning style may be restrictive on learning rather than facilitatory. There is also the argument that preferred learning styles evolve through time, in response not only to maturation but to the teaching experiences which pupils encounter (Younger et al. 2005a), and are not fixed or innate. It is crucial, then, that we recognize that the essence of work on preferred learning styles is not to define and indulge a particular learning style, to which a pupil might apparently be predisposed at one time, because such categorization of students is inflexible and potentially misleading, but to emphasize a balance of different learning activities and teaching styles.

Second, our evidence from the primary schools, reinforced and supported by our work on the secondary RBA project, suggests very strongly that preferred learning styles are not gendered. Despite the implications in some texts and consultancy programmes, there is little evidence to suggest that boys are more kinaesthetically inclined than girls, or that boys favour kinaesthetic experiences rather than any other; in our experience, the appeal is in the context and the presentation, rather than in the teaching style. It follows, then, that the notion that there are boy-friendly and girl-friendly teaching pedagogies is difficult to justify.

Third, it is highly unlikely that work on preferred learning styles will be transformative in isolation. It is not a panacea for raising boys' and girls' achievement, but rather needs to be firmly located within a whole-school context, cross-referencing to integrated curriculum planning and to broader pedagogic issues. The central role of the class teacher in many primary schools means that the ethos and environment of the classroom are crucially important, too, because pedagogy and teaching style cannot be divorced from the overall tone and implicit messages that the children receive. More interactive learning styles, increased opportunities for groupwork and for talk to support learning, more physical breaks and opportunities for activities such as brain gym, will not be effective in isolation. All these activities can access learning for more children, whatever their preferred learning styles, but teachers need to support this by developing a classroom culture that encourages children to take increased responsibility for their own learning and to become more independent in their approach to learning.

David Hargreaves (2004) has asked: 'How much of all these new ideas and practices about learning is just fad or fashion? How much is snake-oil rather than evidence based improvement?'. This is a fundamental question, especially when teachers have encountered so much of the debate about learning styles, but in different guises. Are we simply repackaging the old to make it appear more eye-catching and more alluring? Indeed, teachers have frequently responded by telling us that 'That's what we do anyway!' There is more than a grain of truth in these reactions, but it appears to us that implementing a learning styles approach, within the context we have described above and noting the significant dangers we have outlined, can have some benefits. These will only be maximized, however, when the emphasis is placed on developing pupils' self-awareness as learners and their own sense of agency, when it encourages teachers to plan more varied lessons, assessing a greater range of teaching strategies and techniques, and when we free the discussion from ill-conceived gender-specific overtones.

# 9 Conclusion

## Overcoming the barriers

### No easy answers

This book reports the findings of intensive research with four pilot schools, an additional 21 triad schools, five extension phase schools and one special school, and builds on the extensive work we have done over the past decade or so on boys' achievement in primary and secondary state schools. The clearest outcome of the Raising Boys' Achievement Project was one that confirmed our earlier research, namely, that there are no 'quick fixes' to the issue of raising boys' achievement. There are no easy ways of breaking down the barriers to learning which some pupils experience, and so none of the strategies discussed in this book, whether we talk, for example, of citizenship or arts-based activities (Chapter 5), shared reading (Chapter 6), a focus on talk and drama (Chapter 7) or learning styles (Chapter 8) can, of itself, raise achievement levels. It is not possible, we argue, for a school to put in place any initiative and expect automatic success: the issue is much more complex than that. The key finding of our research, therefore, is the need for a *holistic* approach in raising the achievement of both boys and girls. This chapter brings together the components of such an approach, but first it is necessary to clarify what we mean by 'raising achievement'.

### What is success and how do we know it when we see it?

Since the introduction of National Curriculum tests and the publication of tables listing individual schools' results, there has been a tendency to judge schools on this criterion. Success for primary schools is therefore seen in terms of attainment at Key Stages 1 and 2, particularly the latter, as measured by the proportion of pupils attaining the standard level 4 in the core subjects of English, mathematics and science. Indeed, the government's own educational policy is frequently judged on the basis of test results, so that 'the pressure is mounting on schools to reach [the government's] higher targets ... with fears that many will fall far short'

(Freeman 2005). While, as we suggest in Chapter 1, we are disturbed by such an emphasis on testing, targets and league tables, measures of performativity *are* important in order to identify pupils' individual learning needs and give appropriate support, to provide feedback on progress which encourages dialogue, and to allow the performance of different groups to be compared. The most successful schools in the RBA project did indeed have an emphasis on the academic performance of *individual* pupils; only then is it possible to identify under-achievement, and begin to address it.

The project's original research design (Chapter 4) itself revealed, however, the difficulties that could arise through a rigid focus on attainment data over a short period, particularly in primary school contexts where small sample size places limits on the statistical reliability of data. One of our pilot schools was discounted as an Originator School in the second stage of the project because it did not meet the statistical criteria we had set ourselves, of both boys' and girls' achievement rising and a narrowing of the gender gap over the four preceding years. Chapter 2 outlines some of the problems surrounding the concept of a gender gap. In this instance, the school's year-to-year results over this short period fluctuated quite markedly, and so it became a Partner School in a triad where the Originator School conformed to the pattern we sought. Had the research begun four years later, however, we would have identified the Partner School and not the Originator, since the latter's results worsened in the subsequent two years, while those of the former continued to improve, and its gender gap narrowed. It was only by looking at the results over a much longer time span that we could see an overall trend of rising achievement for both sexes in the Partner School. Every school we have worked with over the course of the project has experienced these kind of fluctuations, linked to particular cohorts of pupils, or to factors that are difficult to control, such as long-term staff illness or problems of staff recruitment. In assessing performance, therefore, it is essential to look at long-term progress and, as Chapter 2 points out, to focus more on levels of performance rather than on a gender gap.

It is crucially important, furthermore, to move away from a narrow focus on academic performance and to engage with a broader concept of achievement, explicitly valuing not just academic attainment, but success in other areas, whether these be sporting or artistic, and in acknowledging social contributions to school life. We should judge 'success', not simply in terms of a certain level of attainment in National Curriculum tests, but of pupils' involvement in learning in its widest sense. While it is possible for there to be improvements in attainment among pupils with negative attitudes towards school, as one example in

Chapter 6 showed, such attainment is unlikely to translate into a zest for learning for its own sake and to provide the foundation for subsequent engagement with school. Equally, as we showed in Chapter 8, changing attitudes may not always immediately be translated into improved academic measures, since a longer time period may be necessary before real engagement in learning occurs, and academic results consequently improve. Unlike academic attainment, however, measuring changing attitudes is much more subjective, and it is only through listening intensively to pupils that it is possible really to assess their level of engagement with school and learning. Thus, as Chapter 4 underlines, the importance of *pupil voice* and the attempt to measure changing attitudes underpinned the whole project, and it is to this that we now turn.

## 'Girls are stronger on the inside, boys on the outside'

This comment was made by Ben, a boy from a rural Norfolk school where 99 per cent of pupils were of white UK heritage, and where the proportion of pupils eligible for free school meals was less than a third of the national average. Interviewed in a group at the beginning of Year 5, Ben, Lloyd and Martin thought school was 'OK most of the time' and particularly enjoyed games and physical education (where they were 'twice as fast as girls') because 'there you can get out and have a laugh by running around'. None of them liked literacy, especially not hand-writing. They thought that boys were better at mathematics, at geography ('because it's about coordinates') and at thinking, and that girls were better at literacy, particularly handwriting. They agreed that whether one sex worked harder than the other depended on the subject, with boys working harder than girls in lessons they thought would be useful in the future (such as mathematics) or lessons they found interesting or fun:

> When I'm doing something I enjoy – even in literacy – I do it *really* well: like what we're doing now – conversations and funny stories. But when we're doing lots and lots of writing, that does my head in and I don't like it.
>
> (Lloyd)

> If it's something I know we've got to take seriously I'll try as hard as I can, but other times, when I know I don't have to do as well, I'll take it a bit easier.
>
> (Martin)

Ben, who wanted to be a helicopter pilot, thought it was important to do well at school:

> Because if you want to earn money you've got to learn, 'cos school now is just a practice for your A-levels and O-levels [*sic*], for when you grow up and go to High School, because it's going to get really hard then.

Despite this, he did not always do as well as he could because,

> Sometimes it's just that I get distracted. If someone talks to me I can't just block them out. I have to turn round and talk to them.

Lloyd, on the other hand, admitted:

> It's usually me that distracts someone else, but when someone talks to me I just can't help it, I have to talk.

While Ben and Martin thought their teachers definitely cared about how well they did:

> She's always checking on us to see how well you do and she encourages you.

Lloyd was less certain:

> I'm not sure. My Dad says they don't care about what you do; they only care about their money.

Asked whether teachers treated boys and girls the same, there was some ambivalence:

*Martin*: Girls get on harder than boys and teachers come to like girls more than boys.

*Ben*: Girls are treated better in girly lessons like literacy.

*Lloyd*: Girls are treated exceptionally better. Say if you go into the classroom at lunchtime to fetch something, you never hear teachers talking about how well boys are doing. They're mostly talking about how well girls are doing. Teachers should take a bit more pride in the boys.

*Martin*: Boys get told off for things girls are allowed to do.

The discussion with these boys, identified by their teachers as 'under-achieving', typified the interviews which took place with over two hundred boys at the beginning of the intervention stage of the project. Despite coming from contrasting socio-economic backgrounds and attending 24 different schools across the country, certain commonalities were evident, encapsulated in the quote which provides the subheading for this section. This quote can be seen as reflecting in part the stereotypical view of boys as physically strong as evidenced by their prowess in sport (and in some schools by being 'better at fighting'). Thus, differences between the sexes were frequently exemplified in terms of sport, particularly football, which sometimes dominated the conversation regardless of the question asked. Most boys were keen to distance themselves from activities they saw as more fitting for girls – skipping, netball, dance and gymnastics – and sometimes even work:

> Boys' bodies are built for running round more; girls prefer doing work or playing skipping games with other girls.
>
> (Solomon, South London)

Subject preferences among other groups were generally similar to those of the Norfolk boys: a group from a town in West Yorkshire said that boys preferred mathematics to literacy 'because you use your brain more in maths', and in a London school the interviewer was told by boys that 'girls like doing simple things like English and biography. We do maths and sports things.'

Besides positioning boys as physically strong, Ben also referred to girls as 'strong on the inside', a reflection perhaps that he thought girls found it easier to resist peer pressure and not to succumb to the distractions which prevented boys from getting on with their work. Thus, boys from most schools talked about lack of concentration, of being distracted:

> by people who want to hide the fact that they don't understand the lesson by being silly.
>
> (David, Suffolk town)

Others admitted that their behaviour prevented them from learning:

> I could do a bit better and improve my knowledge and stop messing about and listen to the teacher.
>
> (Jamal, South London)

In some interviews the influence of needing to live up to a certain image was apparent, so that a West Midlands boy said he was expected to behave badly by his peers, and was teased when he tried to be good and work hard. Often there was the fear of ridicule if they deviated from the expected norm, as with the boys from a rural Suffolk school who said they did not like gymnastics 'because the girls laugh at us for moving around like that'. Other boys were well aware of the consequences of standing out against their peers:

> Girls work harder than boys – I work like a girl. I don't act like one but I like the choir, and they make fun of me.
>
> (John, West Sussex)

> When you're good at reading and proper brainy like me, people call you snobs. Sometimes you get the micky taken if you're brainy and called snobs if you're proper brainy ... proper brainy is when you know your big sums and stuff off by heart.
>
> (Kieran, West Yorkshire)

Thus we see among this sample of 9- and 10-year-old boys, most of whom had been identified as under-achieving by their teachers, evidence pointing to the social constructivist explanations of under-achievement discussed in Chapter 1. Many of the boys saw literacy as a feminized activity (Millard 1997), football was a central part of belonging and being accepted by other boys (Swain 2000) and disruptive behaviour in class led to them being constantly disciplined (Reay 2003). We found evidence of boys protecting a macho image to ensure acceptance of their social group (Skelton 2001) and being teased for choosing not to project acceptable forms of masculinity (Renold 2004a). In Lloyd's comment about his father's view of teachers, tension between the values of home and school was evident. One of the contentions of this book is that it is the social construction of gender by students, teachers and by wider society, contributes markedly to the attitudes which the different sexes have to learning. Already, by the age of 9 or 10, a number of boys in our sample had gendered attitudes towards some subjects. The perceived need to conform to the expectations of their peers was also evident in some interviews, as was the perception by some boys that their teachers valued girls more and liked them better because of their behaviour or their 'hard work'.

These perspectives may well have had an effect on their motivation and attainment in some subject areas.

However, it is also important to state, and to reiterate our discussion in Chapter 3, that not all boys conformed to these stereotypes, and it was noticeable that there were some schools where the emphasis on looking at the individual and on valuing and celebrating diversity had communicated itself to the pupils:

They play good games and we play good games. ... Girls work hard and boys work hard. It depends on the person ... Girls are sometimes silly and boys are too.

(East London Originator School)

These were the schools which epitomized the whole-school ethos we identified among the pilot schools (see Chapter 4) and which we sought among the Originator Schools, and while not every boy had fully imbibed their school's philosophy by the beginning of Year 5, they were, on the whole, less likely to express stereotyped views. In the South London Originator School, for example, while there were boys who were keen on football, there were others who were not interested, and all were definite that 'it doesn't matter if boys don't like football – you can do your own thing – no-one pushes you to play'. In the West Midlands pilot and later Originator School, the school ethos had been communicated to the pupils to the extent that they could articulate the core values clearly:

You definitely don't get racism or sexism here. Mr C doesn't allow it. Everyone respects each other in this school no matter what their race or their gender is.

In this school everyone wants to learn. ... We work together; we don't compete with each other, we work as a team. So if anyone gets stuck, or if anyone falls over in the playground, we help them, or if we've got crisps we share them.

Discussions with both boys and girls strongly suggested that this was not merely rhetoric, but the reality of school life. There were also a number of boys from across the schools who clearly did enjoy literacy. In one London school, for example, both groups of boys expressed enthusiasm for reading and were proud of being 'able to read even big books quickly'. All talked excitedly about poetry, with one reciting in interview a poem he had learnt by heart and another fetching his book to read a poem he had written at home.

It would be expected that attitudes towards school and learning would change during the final two years of primary schooling, partly due to increasing maturity, and partly as pupils became more focused on their Year 6 National Curriculum tests and on transferring to secondary school. Thus, for Ben, Lloyd and Martin, it was clear that the National Curriculum tests they had just taken, and the prospect of imminent transfer to a new school, had focused their minds. Although the strategy the school embarked upon (one of target-setting and mentoring) did not become sufficiently embedded to warrant its discussion in this book, the boys did, in the final interviews, feel they had improved during the year, they were more confident, better behaved (because of a 'strict' male teacher), and were more able to 'block things out' and get on with their work. None of them, however, really liked school (though Lloyd had begun to enjoy literacy), and still made stereotypical comments, such as boys doing better 'because of their competitive ways', and needing to talk less and take more time over their work instead of rushing to get it done.

In contrast, in the three triads where the principal aim was to promote greater engagement in school, and to foster self-esteem gained from learning rather than from peer culture (the West Midlands, South London and West Yorkshire), there were at least some boys whose attitudes to school did change for the better over the two years. This was markedly the case in one of the Partner Schools in the South London triad (see Chapter 5). Here, for example, Solomon, a black African boy (quoted above), held very gendered views in his first interview, but by the end of Year 6, when asked if one sex would do better in their tests than others, he replied:

> I really can't say, because some boys are good at things, and some girls are weak at things, and some girls are good at things and some boys are weak at things. Overall they're equal.

In the first interview, Solomon talked at length about getting 'over-tempered' in the playground, often over football, and how this not only got him into trouble, but distracted him when he returned to the classroom. Asked in his final interview whether he had changed over the two years, he replied:

> I've changed in my approach to my work and instead of getting angry quickly, I've learnt to slow down. I thought about the influence I was having on the younger children and thought it's not right that I should be behaving like this, so that's how I've cooled my anger down. Sometimes you don't even need to do anything, because it's not a big problem, it's just a little problem, and you can sort it out by yourself, and not need to go to the teacher. I've got things more in perspective.

There were other schools where changes in attitude were very noticeable. In an outer London Partner School, which had focused on literacy (Chapter 7), both groups were remarkably clear about the ways in which they had changed from the previous year:

I've dealt with some problems [of behaviour] and made a decision to move away from friends in class.

I always didn't care about my work. I think I'm actually starting to care.

I've matured and got more confident. I'll ask questions now.

I do some judo and when I was doing competitions I was scared – now I'm not scared. I take more risks and I feel like I've got more options.

While in both interviews boys from this school were welcoming and friendly, their attitudes were much more balanced and reflective in the final interview.

## A whole-school ethos of inclusion

Success, then, for the RBA project, was defined both in terms of academic achievement and in changes in pupil attitudes towards school and learning. In the preceding chapters we have discussed a range of possible approaches, each of which has the potential to contribute to that success. However, in line with our emphasis on a holistic approach to raising achievement, we argue that certain generic pre-conditions must be in place before any initiative can succeed (Figure 9.1). First, there is no one-size-fits-all strategy: it is essential that the *cultural context* in which a school is situated is taken into account. While the preceding discussion shows that there are certain common factors contributing to boys' under-achievement, some strategies will be more appropriate in some contexts than others, and so the RBA project, rather than imposing particular approaches or suggesting strategies from the outside, worked *with* schools to define and develop initiatives.

Central to the whole notion of success is a *whole-school ethos of inclusion*, entailing the establishment of a supportive but energetic and robust school culture with attention to pupils' and teachers' self-esteem, and which involves – and creates – trust between pupils and adults and creates a 'cycle of affirmation'. Such a culture embraces the following components:

- *Behaviour*: expectations of high levels of self-discipline established and supported by prompt attention to misdemeanours, follow-through in care and staff courtesy to pupils.

**Figure 9.1** Success factors and outcomes

- *Equal opportunities*: commitment to valuing diversity through curriculum content, classroom grouping arrangements, school activities and worship.
- *Fostering pride and achievement*: a school emphasis on pride in work and behaviour, high expectations of responsibility and independence. Pupils aware that staff care for their progress and happiness.
- *Imaginative thinking* about ways pupils can become engaged in life of the school together with a willingness to use ordinary activities to target and monitor individual pupils.
- *Values and aims*: which are transparent, consistent, shared by colleagues, and permeate all the work of the school.

We see three key contributors to this whole-school ethos of inclusion. First, we identify the headteacher as the lynchpin, and thus *leadership* as a crucial component. The most successful schools we encountered, as we discuss in Chapter 4, were those with participatory leaders, who had a strong emphasis on teamwork, putting into effect a transformational model focused on people and relationships, 'setting the tone' (Fielding et al. 2005) and willing to take risks. As far as the RBA project was concerned, such leaders were *proactive*: they did not simply 'give permission' for a strategy to be put in place, but actively supported it and ensured that time, appropriate training and resources were allocated. Important, too, is the need to be realistic about the school's weaknesses: as noted by Ofsted (2004b), effective schools in a study on reading were honest with themselves about where they were failing, and tackled weaknesses and problems knowledgeably. Crucially, such head-teachers were willing and able to use performance data rigorously, to appreciate the gains which had been brought by a renewed focus on assessment, but equally were sensitive to context and to other aspects of achievement. These headteachers had the confidence to challenge conventional wisdoms and strategy-based initiatives, as well as the assurance to accept new directives when they were seen to be appropriate to the context and needs of their own particular circumstances.

The second component contributing to success is undoubtedly a *pedagogy* which does not privilege one sex over the other, which is not expressed in boy-friendly or girl-friendly approaches, but which encompasses:

- *Continuity of experience*: not only for the pupils but for teachers so that there are links made between different aspects of pupils' learning experiences and the teaching, an awareness of integration rather than subject dislocation, and a feeling of coherence which makes sense to the pupils and gives meaning to the work.
- *A supportive classroom environment*: which encourages all pupils to be positive about their own and others' achievements while also considering how improvements might be made, and which celebrates pupils' successes regularly and explicitly through praise and display.
- *A commitment to developing pupils' self-awareness* as learners and their own sense of agency, to establish 'respectful pedagogies' (Martino and Pallotta-Chiarolli 2003: 209) where there is effective dialogue about the processes of learning in classrooms, so that pupils are enabled to become more independent in their approaches to learning.
- *The wider curriculum*: coherent and integrated planning and inclusion of ICT and creative aspects combined with opportunities for pupils' personal development beyond the scope of lessons.

- *Continuing reflective analysis of progress*: gives the opportunity to affirm effective practice, as well as to develop a process of focused development.
- *Active use of individual performance data*: to inform and monitor practice, with a commitment to address under-achievement at an individual level. High but realistic expectations accompanied by careful planning and monitoring of work and outcomes.

Third, we see *partnerships* on a number of levels as important. Positive relationships with parents and carers, effective teamwork between governors, staff and parents in determining school priorities, together with staff who plan as a team, all contribute towards success. Another layer in the RBA project was the partnerships which developed between schools and with researchers and the higher education institution, which, as we discuss in Chapter 4, were an integral contributor to the success of the various initiatives. Where strong partnerships were not established, we saw strategies being less firmly embedded, and much less change in pupil attitudes.

With these in place, the key outcomes are *achievement* – in its widest sense – and *empowerment* of both pupils and staff. Pupils become independent learners, empowered to take responsibility for their own learning, and hence well-equipped for the next stage in their education. Furthermore, staff feel valued and believe their contribution to be important, and hence morale is high. Parents, too, can feel empowered to contribute effective to their child's education.

All these factors are important: as Dyson et al. argue, in discussing the factors contributing to an inclusive culture:

> The attitudes and values shared by the staff, the level of collaboration and mutual trust, the sense of community and the capacity of leaders within the school to establish these cultural norms are crucial in determing how far a school will facilitate the participation of all its students.
>
> (2002: 39)

## Final reflections

Our involvement in this four-year project on Raising Boys' Achievement was sustained by the belief that educational research should both contribute to theory and offer help and guidance to policy-makers and to practitioners in schools and in local education authorities. We aimed to add to the development of a body of knowledge and understanding, based upon evidence of the effectiveness of intervention strategies in different school contexts, and on the identification of pre-conditions for their successful sustainability and transferability. We sought to work with schools on a variety of initiatives which were realistic in a practical sense, but also principled and theoretically coherent. During the course of this research, we were challenged as to the extent to which it was possible to direct a government-sponsored project such as the RBA project, and at the same time to preserve our own values and intellectual integrity. How far could we work in a policy context orientated strongly towards increased performativity (Arnot and Miles 2005) without becoming insiders and contributing to what Mahony has described as 'the morally bankrupt gender agenda currently being defined by policy-makers' in England (2003: 75)?

The preceding chapters chart the development of the RBA project developed over the four years 2000–4, both in terms of the theoretical underpinnings (Chapters 1–3) and in terms of the working relationships with schools and the intervention strategies which were developed and evaluated (Chapters 4–8), and define our response to these challenges. Our positioning of the project, within a concern for inclusivity, diversity and a lack of essentialism, is reiterated within these chapters. Through-out, our commitment has been to underline the complexities of raising achievement, for both boys and girls, and to recognize that 'under-achievement', however defined, is not an issue which rests solely with boys. Equally, though, our commitment to make the journey from research to policy and practice (Hammersley 2002) led us to re-examine some of the basic orthodoxies about boys' 'under-achievement' and to support teachers in evaluating practices and approaches based upon their own experiences and judgements. This concurred with our convictions that educational research should also strengthen teachers' commitment to remain resolute to their own values and ideas of good practice, to have confidence in their own judgements and experiences, and sometimes to question official discourses of good practice. Central to this is the acknowledgement that teachers' craft knowledge is often sophisticated and well developed to respond to different situations and contexts, that the worth of these teaching repertoires must be recognized and applauded, and that 'good practice is not just about what teachers *do*, but also what they do *not* do' (Hart et al. 2004: 263).

This project allowed us opportunity, then, in Mahony's words, 'to sup at the table of the patriarchal state' (2003: 76). We resolved the dilemmas implicit within this invitation, however, by focusing on girls as well as boys, and by espousing an overriding concern for social justice and equity for all pupils, joining with schools in their commitments to make a real difference to real pupils' lives. Within a context sensitive to ethnicity, gender, disability, social class or spatial location, we tried to develop approaches which would allow all pupils equal opportunity, recognizing that equal opportunity does not imply similar treatment or offer 'fixed solutions under the name of equality' (Daniels et al. 2001: 112), but a flexibility and diversity of approach.

During the four years of the RBA project, the response of the sponsoring United Kingdom government department (the DfES) changed, at least in some respects. In 2000, discussions with those who advised policy-makers were, in global terms, related to boys' under-achievement, to the need to develop practices which would *quickly* impact on *boys*, to different learning styles of boys, to single-sex classes for *boys*. By late 2005, inconsistencies still appeared in government publications, particularly in terms of pedagogy, quick-fix approaches and 'boy-friendly' reading lists (DfES 2005e) but the general tone of the Gender and Achievement website was more inclusive, with a more sophisticated tone to the analysis of the issues and a recognition that 'the crucial point is to ensure that policies designed to improve the performance of boys do not do so at the expense of girls' (DfES 2005e). While those of us who have worked on the RBA project would not wish to claim all the credit for a reorientation of the prevailing discourse on gender and achievement, it is likely that the engagement between education researchers and policy-makers did change the tone and direction of the debate.

Our final reflections suggest, though, that there is still some way to be travelled before the marriage of rhetoric and reality can be celebrated. Our fundamental conclusions from the RBA project, reiterated at the beginning of this chapter, point to the need for a holistic approach if strategies which have the potential to raise achievement for boys and girls are to be disseminated through the primary sector and sustained through time. Such strategies point to the need for a more integrated approach to the primary curriculum, the need to give higher status to arts-based subjects and projects, the need to give more opportunity to talk to support writing and learning. While *Excellence and Enjoyment* (DfES 2003) offers a rhetoric, it does not convince because it is so shrouded in the language of delivery, performance and compliance (Alexander 2004a). We need to recreate (and we choose the word carefully, given the course of primary education in England over the past 50 years) a curriculum which motivates and has meaning for young children, which builds upon the achievements of the past rather than ignores or derides them, and which offers every child an enhanced capacity for learning and achievement. We need to make certain that primary schools in England can offer, those 'moments in childhood when the door opens and lets the future in' (Graham Greene, *The Power and the Glory*).

# Bibliography

Ailwood, J. (2003) A national approach to gender equity policies in Australia: another ending, another opening? *Journal of Inclusive Education*, 7: 19–32.

Alexander, R. (2000) *Culture and Pedagogy: International Comparisons in Primary Education*. Oxford: Blackwell.

Alexander, R. (2003) Oracy, literacy and pedagogy: international perspectives, in E. Bearne, H. Dombey and T. Grainger (eds) *Classroom Interactions in Literacy*. Maidenhead: Open University Press.

Alexander, R. (2004a) Still no pedagogy? Principle, pragmatism and compliance in primary education, *Cambridge Journal of Education*, 34: 7–34.

Alexander, R. (2004b) *Towards Dialogic Teaching: Rethinking Classroom Talk*. Cambridge: Dialogos.

Alexander, R., Rose, J. and Woodhead, C. (1992) *Curriculum Organisation and Curriculum Practice in Primary Schools*. London: DES.

Ali, S. (2003) 'To be a girl': culture and class in schools, *Gender and Education*, 15: 269–83.

Allan, J. and Cope, P. (2004) If you can: inclusion in music making, *International Journal of Inclusive Education*, 8: 23–36.

Archer, J. (2004) The trouble with 'doing boy', *The Psychologist*, 17: 132–6.

Archer, J. and Francis, B. (2005) 'They never go off the rails like other ethnic groups': teachers' constructions of British Chinese pupils' gender identities and approaches to learning, *British Journal of the Sociology of Education*, 26: 165–82.

Archer, J. and Lloyd, B.B. (2002) *Sex and Gender*. Cambridge: Cambridge University Press.

Archer, L. (2004) *Race, Masculinity and Schooling*. Buckingham: Open University Press.

Archer, L. and Yamashita, H. (2003) Theorising inner-city masculinities: 'race', class, gender and education, *Gender and Education*, 15: 115–32.

Arnot, M. (2002) *Reproducing Gender? Essays on Educational Theory And Feminist Politics*. London: RoutledgeFalmer.

Arnot, M., David, M. and Weiner, G. (1996) *Educational Reform And Gender Equality in School*. Manchester: Equal Opportunities Commission.

Arnot, M., David, M. and Weiner, G. (1999) *Closing the Gender Gap: Postwar Education and Social Change.* Cambridge: Polity Press.

Arnot, M. and Gubb, J. (2001) *Adding Value to Boys' and Girls' Education: A Gender and Achievement Project in West Sussex.* Crawley: West Sussex County Council.

Arnot, M. and Miles, P. (2005) A reconstruction of the gender agenda: the contradictory gender dimensions in New Labour's educational and economic policy, *Oxford Review of Education,* 31: 173–89.

Arnot, M. and Weiner, G. (1987) *Gender and the Politics of Schooling.* London: Hutchinson.

Askew, S. and Ross, C. (1988) *Boys Don't Cry: Boys and Sexism in Education.* Milton Keynes: Open University Press.

Atkinson, E. (2000) In defence of ideas, or why 'what works' is not enough, *British Journal of the Sociology of Education,* 21: 317–30.

Baginsky, M. and Hannam, D. (1999) *School Councils: The View of Students and Teachers.* London: NSPCC.

Baker, L. (1999) Opportunities at home and in the community that foster reading engagement, in J. Guthrie and D. Alvermann (eds) *Engaged Reading: Processes, Practices, and Policy Implications.* New York: Teachers College Press.

Baron-Cohen, S. (2003) *Men, Women and the Extreme Male Brain.* London: Penguin.

Barrs, M. (1998) Texts and subtexts: literacy, gender and achievement, in M. Barrs and S. Pidgeon (eds) *Boys and Reading.* London: Centre for Language in Primary Education.

Barrs, M. and Cork, V. (2001) *The Reader in the Writer.* London: Centre for Language in Primary Education.

Barrs, M. and Pidgeon, S. (eds) (1998) *Boys and Reading.* London: Centre for Language in Primary Education.

Barrs, M. and Pidgeon, S. (eds) (2002) *Boys and Writing.* London: Centre for Literacy in Primary Education.

Beard, R. (1999) *National Literacy Strategy: Review of Research and Other Related Evidence.* London: DfEE/SEU.

Beck, C. (1999) Values, leadership and school renewal, in P. Bagley and P. Leonard (eds) *The Values of Educational Administration.* London: Falmer Press.

Beckett, L. (2001) Challenging boys: addressing issue of masculinity within a gender equity framework, in W. Martino and B. Meyenn (eds) *What About the Boys? Issues of Masculinity in Schools.* Buckingham: Open University Press.

Bell, D. (2004) The achievement of girls, Speech to the Fawcett Society, 8 March.

Bernard, M.E. (1996) *Improving Student Motivation and School Achievement:*

*A Professional Development Program for Teachers, Special Educators, School Administrators and Pupil Service Personnel.* Athens, ON: Hindle and Associates.

Bernard, M.E. (2000) *Providing All Children with the Foundations for Achievement.* Oakleigh, Victoria: Australian Scholarships Group.

Bernard, M.E., Hajzler, D.J. and Roberts, R. (1987) *You Can Do It! What Every Student (and Parent) Should Know about Success in School and Life.* Blackburn, Victoria: Collins Dove.

Best, R. (1983) *We've All Got Scars: What Boys and Girls Learn in Elementary School.* Bloomington, IN: Indiana University Press.

Biddulph, S. (1998a) *Manhood.* Stroud: Hawthorn.

Biddulph, S. (1998b) *Raising Boys: Why Boys Are Different – and How to Help Them Become Happy and Well-Balanced Men.* Sydney: Finch.

Black, P. and Wiliam, D. (1998) *Inside the Black Box: Raising Standards through Classroom Assessment.* London: King's College School of Education.

Bleach, K. (1998) *Raising Boys' Achievement in Schools.* Stoke-on-Trent: Trentham Books.

Blunkett, D. (2000) quoted in 'Single sex classes to help failing boys', *The Observer,* 20 August.

Boaler, J. (1997) Reclaiming school mathematics: the girls fight back, *Gender and Education,* 9: 285–305.

Bohan, J. (1997) Regarding gender: essentialism, constructionism and feminist psychology, in M. Gergen and S. Davis (eds) *Towards a New Psychology of Gender.* London: Routledge.

Brehony, K. (2005) Primary schooling under New Labour: the irresolvable contradiction of excellence and enjoyment, *Oxford Review of Education,* 31: 29–46.

Bricheno, P. and Younger, M. (2004) Some unexpected results of a learning styles intervention? Paper presented at BERA Annual Conference, Manchester, September.

Brighouse, T. (1997) Leading and managing primary schools: the changing world of the local education authority, in C. Cullingford (ed.) *The Politics of Primary Education.* Buckingham: Open University Press.

Browne, R. and Fletcher, R. (eds) (1995) *Boys in Schools: Addressing the Real Issues – Behaviour, Values and Relationships.* Sydney: Finch.

Burns, C. and Myhill, D. (2004) Interactive or inactive? A consideration of the nature of inter-action in whole class teaching, *Cambridge Journal of Education,* 34: 35–50.

Butler, J. (1990) *Gender Trouble: Feminism and the Subversion of Identity.* London: Routledge.

Carter, R. (2004) *Language and Creativity: The Art of Common Talk.* London: Routledge.

Castle, K., Ashworth, M. and Lord, P. (2002) *Aims in Motion: Dance Companies' Education Programmes* (Research Summary). Slough: National Foundation for Educational Research.

Charlton, T. (1998) Enhancing school effectiveness through using peer support strategies with pupils and teachers, *Support for Learning*, 13: 50–3.

Clarricoates, K. (1980) The importance of being Ernest ... Emma ... Tom ... Jane: the perception and categorization of gender conformity and gender deviation, in R. Deem (ed.) *Schooling for Women's Work*. London: Routledge and Kegan Paul.

Clarricoates, K. (1989) Dinosaurs in the classroom – the hidden curriculum in primary schools, in M. Arnot and G. Weiner (eds) *Gender and the Politics of Schooling*. London: Unwin Hyman/Open University Press.

Coffield, F., Moseley, D., Hall, E. and Ecclestone, K. (2004) *Should We Be Using Learning Styles? What Research Has to Say to Practice*. London: Learning and Skills Research Centre.

Cohen, S. (1972) *Folk Devils and Moral Panics: The Creation of the Mods and Rockers*. London: MacGibbon and Kee.

Collins, C., Kenway, J. and McLeod, J. (2000) *Factors Influencing the Educational Performance of Males and Females in School and their Initial Destination after Leaving School*. Adelaide: Deakin University.

Connell, R.W. (1995) *Masculinities*. Cambridge: Polity Press.

Connell, R.W. (2000) *The Men and the Boys*. Cambridge: Polity Press.

Connellan, J., Baron-Cohen, S., Wheelwright, S., Batki, A. and Ahluwalia, J. (2000) Sex differences in human neonatal social perception, *Infant Behaviour and Development*, 23: 113–18.

Connolly, P. (1995) Boys will be boys? Racism, sexism and the construction of masculine identities among infant boys, in J. Holland and M. Blair (eds) *Debates and Issues in Feminist Research and Pedagogy*. Clevedon: Multilingual Matters.

Connolly, P. (1996) Seen but never heard: rethinking approaches to researching racism and young children, *Discourse*, 17: 171–85.

Connolly, P. (1998) *Racism, Gender Identity and Young Children*. London: Routledge.

Connolly, P. (2003) Gendered and gendering spaces, in C. Skelton and B. Francis (eds), *Boys and Girls in the Primary Classroom*. Maidenhead: Open University Press.

Connolly, P. (2004) *Boys and Schooling in the Early Years*. London: RoutledgeFalmer.

Corden, R. (2000) *Literacy and Learning Through Talk*. Buckingham: Open University Press.

Covington, M. (1998) *The Will to Learn: A Guide for Motivating Young People*. Cambridge: Cambridge University Press.

Crick, R. (1998) *Education for Citizenship and the Teaching of Democracy in Schools.* London: QCA.

Crick, R., Tew, M., Taylor, M., Richie, S., Samuel, E. and Durant, K. (2005) *A Systematic Review of the Impact of Citizenship Education on Student Learning and Achievement.* London: EPPI-Centre (available at http://www.eppi.ioe.ac.uk, last accessed 7 September 2005).

Daly, C. (2003) *Literature Search on Improving Boys' Writing.* London: Office for Standards in Education.

Daniels, H., Creese, A., Hey, V., Leonard, D. and Smith, M. (2001) Gender and learning: equity, equality and pedagogy, *Support for Learning,* 16: 112–16.

Davies, B. (2005) Emerging trends in researching children and youth: a review essay, *British Journal of Sociology of Education,* 26: 145–53.

Davies, J. and Brember, I. (1993) Comics or stories? Differences in the reading attitudes and habits of girls and boys in years 2, 4 and 6, *Gender and Education,* 5: 3–20.

Day, C. (2004) The passion of successful leadership, *School Leadership and Management,* 24: 425–37.

Day, C., Harris, A., Hadfield, M., Tolley, H. and Beresford, J. (2000) *Leading Schools in Times of Change.* Buckingham: Open University Press.

Dearden, J. (1998) Cross-age peer mentoring in action, *Educational Psychology in Practice,* 13: 250–7.

Demos Learning Working Group (2004) *About Learning: Report of the Learning Working Group.* London: DEMOS.

DES (1978) *Primary Education in England: A Survey by HM Inspectors of Schools.* London: HMSO.

DfES (2002) *The Autumn Package, 2002: Pupil Performance Information.* London: Department for Education and Skills.

DfES (2003) *Excellence and Enjoyment: A Strategy for Primary Schools.* London: Department for Education and Skills.

DfES (2004a) *The Autumn Package, 2004: Pupil Performance Information.* London: Department for Education and Skills.

DfES (2004b) *Key Stage 2 to GCSE/GNVQ: The Value Added Pilot.* London: Department for Education and Skills.

DfES (2004c) www.standards.dfes.gov.uk/thinkingskills/resources. (last accessed 9 August, 2005).

DfES (2005a) www.dfes.gov.uk/rsgateway/DB/SFR/s000564/SFR08-2005v2.pdf (last accessed 20 April, 2005).

DfES (2005b) The Key Stage 1 (KS1) to Key Stage 2 (KS2) value added measure: http://www.dfes.gov.uk/performancetables/2005Tables.doc (last accessed 1 August 2005).

DfES (2005c) www.dfes.gov.uk/performancetables/2005tables/primary (last accessed 1 August 2005).

DfES (2005d) *Beacon Schools.* London: Department for Education and Skills.

DfES (2005e) Gender and Achievement website, http://www.standards.d-fes.gov.uk/genderandachievement (last accessed 6 September 2005).

DfES/London Challenge (2004) *Key Stage 3 National Strategy: Ensuring the Attainment of Black Caribbean Boys.* London: Department for Education and Skills.

DfES/NPDT (2003) *National Education Breakthrough Programme for Raising Boys' Achievement in Secondary Schools.* London/Manchester: DfES Innovation Unit/National Primary Care Development Team.

DfES/NHSS (2004) *Raising Boys' Achievement Toolkit.* London: Department for Education and Skills.

Downing, D., Johnson, F. and Kaur, S. (2003) *Saving a Place for the Arts? A Survey of the Arts in Primary Schools in England*, London: National Foundation for Educational Research, Local Government Association Research Series 41.

Driessen, G., Smit, F. and Sleegers, P. (2005) Parental involvement and educational achievement, *British Educational Research Journal,* 31: 509–32.

Drummond, M-J. (1993) *Assessing Children's Learning.* London: David Fulton.

Dweck, C.S. (1999) *Self-theories: Their Role in Motivation, Personality and Development.* Hove: Taylor and Francis.

Dyson, A., Howes, A. and Roberts, B. (2002) *A Systematic Review of the Effectiveness of School-Level Actions for Promoting Participation by All Students.* London: EPPI-Centre (available at http://www.eppi.ioe.a-c.uk, last accessed 7 September 2005).

Elkins, T. and Elliott, J. (2004) Competition and control: the impact of government regulation on teaching and learning in English schools, *Research Papers in Education,* 19: 15–30.

Epstein, D., Elwood, J., Hey, V. and Maw, J. (eds) (1998) *Failing Boys? Issues in Gender and Achievement.* Buckingham: Open University Press.

Epstein, D. and Johnson, R. (1998) *Schooling Sexualities.* Buckingham: Open University Press.

Essex Writing Project (2002) *More than Mulan: Using Video to Improve Boys' Writing.* Chelmsford: The English Team, Essex Advisory and Inspection Service.

Essex Writing Project (2003) *Visually Speaking: Using Multimedia Texts to Improve Boys' Writing.* Chelmsford: The English Team, Essex Advisory and Inspection Service.

Evans, A., Bolam, R. and Donovan, K. (1998) *Report on Combating Underachievement, Especially in Boys.* Cardiff: School of Education.

Evans, W., Flower, J. and Holton, D. (2001) Peer tutoring in first-year undergraduate mathematics, *International Journal of Mathematical Education in Science and Technology*, 32: 161–73.

Fennema, E. (1996) Scholarship, gender and mathematics, in P.F. Murphy and C.V. Gipps (eds) *Equity in the Classroom: Towards Effective Pedagogy for Girls and Boys*. London: Falmer Press.

Fielding, M., Bragg, S., Craig, D., Cunningham, I., Eraut, M., Gillison, S., Horne, M., Robinson, C. and Thorp, J. (2005) *Factors Influencing the Transfer of Good Practice*. Brighton: University of Sussex and Demos, DfES Research Report 615.

FitzGerald, M. (2005) White boys fail too, *The Guardian*, 1 June.

Fitz-Gibbon, C.T. (1996) *Monitoring Educational Indicators Quality and Effectiveness*. London: Cassell.

Foot, H. and Howe, C. (1998) The psychoeducational basis of peer-assisted learning, in K. Topping and S. Ehly (eds) *Peer-Assisted Learning*. Mahwah, NJ: Lawrence Erlbaum Associates, Inc.

Forman, G. and Cazden, C. (1985) Exploring Vygotskian perspectives in education: the cognitive value of peer interaction, in J. Wertsch (ed.) *Culture, Communication and Cognition: Vygotskian Perspectives*. Cambridge: Cambridge University Press.

Francis, B. (1997) Power plays: children's constructions of gender and power in role plays, *Gender and Education*, 9: 179–91.

Francis, B. (2000) *Boys, Girls and Achievement: Addressing the Classroom Issues*. London: Routledge/Falmer.

Francis, B. and Skelton, C. (eds) (2003) *Boys and Girls in the Primary Classroom*. Maidenhead: Open University Press.

Frank, B., Kehler, M., Lovell, T. and Davison, K. (2003) A tangle of trouble: boys, masculinity and schooling – future directions, *Educational Review*, 55: 119–33.

Freeman, S. (2005) Schools struggle to reach targets, *The Times*, 23 August.

Frosh, S., Phoenix, A. and Pattman, R. (2002) *Young Masculinities*. Basingstoke: Palgrave.

Galton, M. and Fogelman, K. (1998) The use of discretionary time in the primary school, *Research Papers in Education*, 13: 119–30.

Galton, M., Hargreaves, L., Comber, C., Wall, D. with Pell, A. (1999) *Inside the Primary Classroom: 20 Years On*. London: Routledge.

Galton, M. and MacBeath, J. with Page, C. and Steward, S. (2002) *A Life in Teaching? The Impact of Change on Primary Teachers' Working Lives*. Cambridge: Faculty of Education, University of Cambridge.

Gardner, C., Grove, J. and Sharp, D. (1999) *Solihull Boys Achievement Project*. Solihull: Solihull Metropolitan Borough Council.

Gardner, H. (1983) *Frames of Mind*. New York: Basic Books.

Gardner, H. (1999) *Intelligence Reframed: Multiple Intelligences for the 21st Century*. New York: Basic Books.

Gilbert, P. and Gilbert, R. (1998) *Masculinity Goes to School*. London: Routledge.

Gilbert, P. and Gilbert, R. (2001) Masculinity, inequality and post-school opportunities: disrupting oppositional politics about boys' education, *International Journal of Inclusive Education*, 5: 1–13.

Gillborn, D. and Mirza, H.S. (2000) *Educational Inequality: Mapping Class, Race and Gender: A Synthesis of Research Evidence*. London: Office for Standards in Education.

Gillborn, D. and Youdell, D. (2000) *Rationing Education: Policy, Practice, Reform and Equity*. Buckingham: Open University Press.

Gipps, C. (1996) Review and conclusions: a pedagogy or a range of pedagogic strategies? in P. Murphy and C. Gipps (eds) *Equity in the Classroom: Towards Effective Pedagogy for Girls and Boys*. London: Falmer Press.

Gipps, C. and Goldstein, H. (1983) *Monitoring Children: An Evaluation of the Assessment of Performance Unit*. London: Heinemann.

Gipps, C. and Murphy, P. (1994) *A Fair Test? Assessment, Achievement and Equity*. Buckingham: Open University Press.

Goldstein, H. (2001) Using pupil performance data for judging schools and teachers: scope and limitations, *British Educational Research Journal*, 27: 433–42.

Goodlad, S. and Hirst, B. (eds) (1990) *Explorations in Peer Tutoring*. Oxford: Basil Blackwell.

Gorard, S. (2000) *Education and Social Justice*. Cardiff: University of Wales Press.

Gray, J., Goldstein, H. and Thomas, S. (2003) Of trends and trajectories: searching for patterns in school improvement, *British Educational Research Journal*, 29: 83–8.

Gray, J., Hopkins, D., Reynolds, D., Wilcox, B., Farrell, S. and Jesson, D. (1999) *Improving Schools: Performance and Potential*. Buckingham: Open University Press.

Gray, J. and McLellan, R. (2005) A matter of attitude? Developing a profile of boys' and girls' responses to primary schooling, Unpublished paper available from Faculty of Education, University of Cambridge.

Gurian, M. (1998) *A Fine Young Man: What Parents, Mentors and Educators Can Do to Shape Adolescent Boys into Exceptional Men*. New York: Jeremy B. Tarcher/Putnam.

Gurian, M. (2001) *Boys and Girls Learn Differently!* San Francisco: Jossey-Bass.

Hall, C. and Coles, M. (1997) Gendered readings: helping boys develop as critical readers, *Gender and Education*, 9: 61–8.

Hall, C. and Coles, M. (1999) *Children's Reading Choices*. London: Routledge.

Hammersley, M. (2001) Obvious, all too obvious? Methodological issues in using sex/gender as a variable in educational research, in B. Francis and C. Skelton (eds) *Investigating Gender: Contemporary Perspectives in Education*. Buckingham: Open University Press.

Hammersley, M. (2002) *Educational Research and Policymaking in Practice*. London: Sage.

Hammersley-Fletcher, L. and Brundrett, M. (2004) Leaders on leadership: the impressions of primary school head teachers and subject leaders, *School Leadership and Management*, 25: 59–75.

Hannan, G. (1997) *The Gender Game and How to Win It*. London: G. Hannan.

Hannan, G. (1999) *Improving Boys' Performance*. London: Folens.

Hargreaves, D. (1967) *Social Relations in a Secondary School*. London: Routledge and Kegan Paul.

Hargreaves, D. (2004) Help us stop the pedlars of snake-oil, *Times Educational Supplement*, 17 September.

Harland, J., Kinder, K. and Hartley, K. (1995) *Arts in their View*. Slough: National Foundation for Educational Research.

Harland, J., Kinder, K., Lord, P., Stott, A., Schagen, I., Haynes, J., Cusworth, L., White, R. and Paola, R. (2000) *Arts Education in Secondary Schools: Effects and Effectiveness*. Slough: National Foundation for Educational Research.

Harris, A. (2003) Introduction: challenging the orthodoxy of school leadership: towards alternative theoretical perspectives, *School Leadership and Management*, 23: 125–8.

Hart, S., Dixon, A., Drummond, M.J. and McIntyre, D. (2004) *Learning Without Limits*. Maidenhead: Open University Press.

Head, J. (1996) Gender identity and cognitive style, in P.F. Murphy and C.V. Gipps (eds) *Equity in the Classroom: Towards Effective Pedagogy for Girls and Boys*. London: Falmer Press.

Head, J. (1999) *Understanding the Boys*. London: Falmer.

Hey, V., Creese, A., Daniels, H., Fielding, S. and Leonard, D. (2000) Questions of collaboration and competition in English primary schools: pedagogic sites for constructing learning, masculinities and femininities. Paper presented to the British Association Educational Research Conference, Cardiff, September.

Hoff-Sommers, C. (2000) *The War Against Boys: How Misguided Feminism is Harming Our Young Men*. New York: Simon and Schuster.

Holden, C. and Wilson, T. (2000) You can't read a book while you're on a bike. Paper presented to the British Association Educational Research Conference, Cardiff, September.

Hopkins, D. (2001) *School Improvement for Real.* London: RoutledgeFalmer.

Jackson, C. (2002) 'Laddishness' as a self-worth protection strategy, *Gender and Education,* 14: 37–51.

Jackson, C. (2003) Motives for 'laddishness' at school: fear of failure and fear of the 'feminine', *British Educational Research Journal,* 29: 583–98.

Jackson, C. (2004) 'Wild' girls? An exploration of 'ladette' cultures in secondary schools. Paper presented at British Educational Research Association Conference. Manchester, September.

Jackson, D. (1964) *Streaming: An Education System in Miniature.* London: Routledge and Kegan Paul.

Jackson, D. (1998) Breaking out of the binary trap: boys' underachievement, school and gender relations, in D. Epstein et al. (eds) *Failing Boys? Issues in Gender and Achievement.* Buckingham: Open University Press.

James, M. (1998) *Using Assessment for School Improvement.* London: Heinemann.

Jeffrey, B. and Woods, P. (1996) Feeling deprofessionalised: the social construction of emotions during an OFSTED inspection, *Cambridge Journal of Education,* 26(3): 325–43.

Jeffrey, B. and Woods, P. (2003) *The Creative School: A Framework for Success, Quality and Effectiveness.* London: RoutledgeFalmer.

Johannesson, I. (2004) To teach boys and girls: a pro-feminist perspective on the boys' debate in Iceland, *Educational Review,* 56: 33–41.

Jones, A., Payne, G. and Rainer, J. (1996) Drama, in J. Piotrowski (ed.) *Expressive Arts in the Primary School.* London: Cassell.

Jones, S. and Myhill, D. (2004a) Seeing things differently: teachers' constructions of underachievement, *Gender and Education,* 16: 531–46.

Jones, S. and Myhill, D. (2004b) 'Troublesome boys' and 'compliant girls': gender identity and perceptions of achievement and underachievement, *British Journal of Sociology of Education,* 25: 547–61.

Jordan, E. (1995) Fighting boys and fantasy play: the construction of masculinity in the early years of school, *Gender and Education,* 7: 69–85.

Kanaris, A. (1999) Gendered journeys: children's writing and the construction of gender, *Language and Education,* 13: 254–69.

Kehily, M.J. and Nayak, A. (1997) Lads and laughter: humour and the production of heterosexual hierarchies, *Gender and Education,* 9: 69–87.

Kelly, R. (2005), quoted in Ward, L., Catch-up lessons to help bridge class gap in schools, *The Guardian,* 27 July.

Kenway, J. (1995) Masculinities in schools: under siege, on the defensive and under reconstruction? *Discourse: Studies in the Cultural Politics of Education,* 16: 59–79.

Kenway, J. and Willis, S. with Blackmore, J. and Rennie, L. (1998) *Answering Back: Girls, Boys and Feminism in School.* London: Routledge.

Kershner, R. (2003) Intelligence, in J. Beck and M. Earl (eds) *Key Issues in Secondary Education.* London: Continuum.

Kimura, D. (2000) *Sex and Cognition.* Cambridge, MA: MIT Press.

Kruse, A-M. (1996) Single-sex settings: pedagogies for girls and boys in Danish schools, in P. Murphy and C. Gipps (eds) *Equity in the Classroom: Towards Effective Pedagogy for Girls and Boys.* London: Falmer Press.

Lingard, R. and Douglas, P. (1999) *Men Engaging Feminisms: Pro-Feminism, Backlashes and Schooling.* Buckingham: Open University Press.

Lloyd, G. (ed.) (2005) *Problem Girls: Understanding and Supporting Troubled and Troublesome Girls and Young Women.* London: RoutledgeFalmer.

Mac an Ghaill, M. (1994) *The Making of Men: Masculinities, Sexualities and Schooling.* Buckingham: Open University Press.

MacBeath, J. and Mortimore, P. (eds) (2001) *Improving School Effectiveness.* Buckingham: Open University Press.

MacBeath, J., Moos, L. and Riley, K. (1998) Time for a change, in J. MacBeath (ed.) *Effective School Leadership: Responding to Change.* London: Paul Chapman Publishing.

Mahony, P. (2003) Recapturing imaginations and the gender agenda: reflections on a progressive challenge from an English perspective, *International Journal of Inclusive Education,* 7: 75–81.

Maines, B. and Robinson, G. (1988) *B/G-STEEM – a Self-Esteem Scale with Locus of Control Items.* Bristol: Lucky Duck Publishing Ltd.

Majors, R. (2001) *Educating Our Black Children.* London: Routledge/Falmer.

Malone, M.J. (1997) *Worlds of Talk: The Presentation of Self in Everyday Conversation.* London: Polity Press.

Marjoram, T. (1980) Assessment, in C. Richards (ed.) *Primary Education: Issues for the Eighties.* London: Adam and Charles Black.

Martino, W. (1999) 'Cool boys', 'party animals', 'squids' and 'poofters': interrogating the dynamics and politics of adolescent masculinities in school, *British Journal of the Sociology of Education,* 20: 239–63.

Martino, W. and Meyenn, B. (2001) *What about the Boys?: Issues of Masculinity in Schools.* Buckingham: Open University Press.

Martino, W. and Pallotta-Chiarolli, M. (2003) *So What's a Boy? Addressing Issues of Masculinity and Schooling.* Buckingham: Open University Press.

MASA (Men Against Sexual Assault) (1996) *Boys-Talk: A Program for Young*

*Men about Masculinity, Non-Violence and Relationships.* Adelaide: Kookaburra Press.

Maynard, T. (2002) *Boys and Literacy: Exploring the Issues,* London and New York: RoutledgeFalmer.

Maynard, T. and Lowe, K. (1999) Boys and writing in the primary school: whose problem is it?, *Education 3 to 13,* June: 4–9.

McDowell, L. (1992) Doing gender: feminism, feminists and research methods in human geography, *Transactions of the Institute of British Geographers,* NS17: 399–416.

McEwan, A., Carlisle, K., Knipe, D., Neil, P. and McClure, B. (2002) Primary school leadership: values and actions, *Research Papers in Education,* 17: 147–63.

Millard, E. (1997) Differently literate: gender identity and the construction of the developing reader, *Gender and Education,* 9: 31–48.

Mills, M. (2001) *Challenging Violence in Schools: An Issue of Masculinities.* Buckingham: Open University Press.

Minns, H. (1997) *Read It to Me Now! Learning at Home and School.* Buckingham: Open University Press.

Mirza, H.S. (1992) *Young, Female and Black.* London: Routledge.

Morrison, I., Everton, T. and Rudduck, J. with Cannie, J. and Strommen, L. (2000) Pupils helping other pupils with their learning in primary and secondary school, *Mentoring and Tutoring,* 8: 187–200.

Mortimore, P., Sammons, P., Stoll, L., Lewis, D. and Ecob, R. (1988) *School Matters, the Junior Years.* London: Paul Chapman Publishing Ltd.

Mosley, J. (1996) *Quality Circle Time in the Primary Classroom.* Wisbech: LDA.

Mosley, J. (1998) *More Quality Circle Time.* Wisbech: LDA.

Moss, G. (1999) Texts in context: mapping out the gender differentiation of the reading curriculum, *Pedagogy, Culture and Society,* 7: 507–24.

Moss, G. (2000) Raising boys' attainment in literacy: some principles for intervention, *Reading,* 34: 101–6.

Moss, G. and McDonald, J.W. (2004) The borrowers: library records as unobtrusive measures of children's reading preferences, *Journal of Research into Reading,* 27: 401–12.

Moss, P. (ed.) (2002) *Feminist Geography in Practice: Research and Methods.* Oxford: Blackwell.

Myers, K. (2000) *Whatever Happened to Equal Opportunities in Schools? Gender Equality Initiatives in Education.* Buckingham: Open University Press.

Myhill, D. (2000) Boy zones and girl power: patterns of interaction and response in whole class teaching. Paper presented to the British Association Educational Research Conference, Cardiff, September.

National Statistical Bulletin/DfES (2003) *Statistics of Education: Pupil Progress by Pupil Characteristics, 2002*. London: National Statistical Bulletin/DfES www.dfes.gov.uk/rsgateway/DB/SBu/b000402/pupil_progress_final.pdf (Last accessed 2 May 2005).

National Writing Project (1990) *Perceptions of Writing*. Kingston upon Thames: Nelson.

Noble, C. and Bradford, W. (2000) *Getting it Right for Boys ... and Girls*. London: Routledge.

Noble, C., Brown, J. and Murphy, J. (2001) *How to Raise Boys' Achievement*. London: David Fulton.

North Somerset Education Department (2002) The *Numlit*, Summer, http://www.n-somerset.gov.uk/learning/national+strategies/literacy/numlitsummer2002.pdf (last accessed 9 September, 2004).

Nugent, M. (2001) Raising reading standards – the Reading Partners approach: cross-age peer tutoring in a special school, *British Journal of Special Education,* 28: 71–9.

O'Donnell, M. and Sharpe, S. (2000) *Uncertain Masculinities*. London: Routledge.

Ofsted (1993) *Boys and English*. London: HMSO.

Ofsted (2003a) *Improving City Schools: How the Arts Can Help*. London: Office for Standards in Education.

Ofsted (2003b) *Yes He Can: Schools Where Boys Write Well*. London: Office for Standards in Education.

Ofsted (2003c) *Expecting the Unexpected: Developing Creativity in Primary and Secondary Schools*. London: Office for Standards in Education (e-publication HMI 1612).

Ofsted (2004a) *Tuning in: Wider Opportunities in Specialist Instrumental Tuition for Pupils in Key Stage 2*. London: Office for Standards in Education.

Ofsted (2004b) *Reading for Purpose and Pleasure: An Evaluation of the Teaching of Reading in Primary Schools*. London: Office for Standards in Education.

Osborn, M., McNess, E. and Broadfoot, P., with Pollard, A. and Triggs, P. (2000) *What Teachers Do: Changing Policy and Practice in Primary Education*. London: Continuum.

Osler, A., Street, C., Lall, M. and Vincent, K. (2002) *Not a Problem? Girls and School Exclusion*. London: Joseph Rowntree Foundation.

Paechter, C. (1998) *Educating the Other: Gender, Power and Schooling*. Falmer: London.

Phillips, T. (2005) Opinion: African-Caribbean boys are still failing at school, *The Guardian,* 24 May.

Pickering, J. (1997) *Raising Boys' Achievement*. Stafford: Network Educational.

Platten, J. (1999) Raising boys' achievement, *Curriculum*, 20: 2–6.

Plewis, I. (1991) Under-achievement: a cause of conceptual confusion, *British Educational Research Journal*, 17: 377–85.

Plowden Report (1967) *Children and their Primary Schools*. London: HMSO.

PNS/UKLA (2004) *Raising Boys' Achievements in Writing*. London: Primary National Strategy/United Kingdom Literacy Association.

Pollard, A. (1987) Goodies, jokers and gangs, in A. Pollard (ed.) *Children and Their Primary Schools: A New Perspective*. London: Falmer Press.

QCA (2004) *English 2002/3 Annual Report on Curriculum and Assessment*. London: Qualifications and Curriculum Authority.

Reay, D. (2001) 'Spice girls', 'Nice girls', 'girlies', and 'tomboys': gender discourses, girls' cultures and femininities in the primary classroom, *Gender and Education*, 13(2): 153–66.

Reay, D. (2003) 'Troubling, troubled and troublesome?' Working with boys in the primary classroom, in C. Skelton and B. Francis (eds) *Boys and Girls in the Primary Classroom*. Maidenhead: Open University Press.

Renold, E. (2000) 'Coming out': gender, (hetero)sexuality and the primary school, *Gender and Education*, 12: 309–26.

Renold, E. (2001) Learning the 'hard' way: boys, hegemonic masculinity and the negotiation of learner identities in the primary school, *British Journal of Sociology of Education*, 22: 369–85.

Renold, E. (2003) 'If you don't kiss me, you're dumped': boys, boyfriends and heterosexualised masculinities in the primary school, *Educational Review*, 55: 179–94.

Renold, E. (2004a) *Girls, Boys and Junior Sexualities: Exploring Children's Gender and Sexual Relations in the Primary School*. London: Routledge-Falmer.

Renold, E. (2004b) 'Other boys': negotiating non-hegemonic masculinities in the primary school, *Gender and Education*, 16: 247–66.

Riley, J. (2001) The National Literacy Strategy: success with literacy for all? *The Curriculum Journal*, 12: 29–58.

Roberts, H. (1981) *Doing Feminist Research*. London: Routledge and Kegan Paul.

Rudd, P., Holland, M., Sanders, D., Massey, A. and White, G. (2004) *Evaluation of the Beacon Schools Initiative*. London: National Foundation for Educational Research.

Rudduck, J. (1994) *Developing a Gender Policy in Secondary Schools*. Buckingham: Open University Press.

Rudduck, J., Berry, M., Brown, N. and Hendy, L. (2003) Learning about improvement by talking about improvement, *Improving Schools*, 6: 246–57.

Rudduck, J., Berry, M., Frost, D. with Brown, N. (2000) Learning from other schools in a climate of competition, *Research Papers in Education,* 15: 259–74.

Rudduck, J., Chaplain, R. and Wallace, G. (eds) (1996) *School Improvement: What Can Pupils Tell Us?* London: David Fulton.

Rudduck, J. and Flutter, J. (2000) Pupil participation and pupil perspective: 'carving a new order of experience', *Cambridge Journal of Education,* 30: 75–89.

Rudduck, J. and Flutter, J. (2004) *How to Improve your School.* London: Continuum.

Safford, K., O'Sullivan, O. and Barrs, M. (2004) *Boys on the Margin: Promoting Boys' Literacy and Learning at Key Stage 2.* London: Centre for Literacy in Primary Education.

Salisbury, J. and Jackson, D. (1996) *Challenging Macho Values: Practical Ways of Working with Adolescent Boys.* London: Falmer Press.

Sanders, M. and Epstein, J. (1998) School-family-community partnerships and educational change: international perspectives, in A. Hargreaves, M. Lieberman, M. Fallon and D. Hopkins (eds) *International Handbook of Educational Change.* Dordrecht: Kluwer.

Sax, L. (2005) *Why Gender Matters: What Parents and Teachers Need to Know about the Emerging Science of Sex Differences.* New York: Doubleday.

Sennett, R. (2003) *Respect: The Formation of Character in an Age of Inequality.* London: Penguin.

Sewell, T. (1998) *Black Masculinities and Schooling: How Black Boys Survive Modern Schooling.* Stoke-on-Trent: Trentham Books.

Skelton, C. (1996) Learning to be 'tough': the fostering of maleness in one primary school, *Gender and Education,* 8: 185–97.

Skelton, C. (2001) *Schooling the Boys: Masculinities and Primary Education.* Buckingham: Open University Press.

Skelton, C. (2003a) Male primary teachers and perceptions of masculinity, *Educational Review,* 55: 195–209.

Skelton, C. (2003b) Typical boys? Theorising masculinity in educational settings, in C. Skelton and B. Francis (eds) *Investigating Gender: Contemporary Perspectives in Education.* Buckingham: Open University Press.

Skelton, C. (2004) Boys, identity and under-achievement in an individualised society. Paper presented at the British Educational Research Association Conference, University of Manchester, 16–18 September.

Skelton, C. and Francis, B. (2003a) *Boys and Girls in the Primary Classroom.* Buckingham: Open University Press.

Skelton, C. and Francis, B. (2003b) Introduction: boys and girls in the primary classroom, in C. Skelton and B. Francis (eds) *Boys and Girls in the Primary Classroom.* Buckingham: Open University Press.

Smith, A. (1997) *Accelerated Learning in the Classroom.* Stafford: Network Educational Press.

Smith, A. (1998) *Accelerated Learning in Practice: Brain-based Methods for Accelerating Motivation and Achievement.* Stafford: Network Educational Press.

Smith, E. (2002) Failing boys and moral panics: perspectives on the underachievement debate, *British Journal of Educational Studies,* 51: 282–95.

Smith, E. (2003) Understanding underachievement: an investigation into the differential attainment of secondary school pupils, *British Journal of Sociology of Education,* 24: 575–86.

Smith, S. (2004) The non-fiction reading habits of young successful boy readers: forming connections between masculinity and reading, *Literacy,* 38: 10–16.

Smithers, R. (2003) Education alliance urges test shake up, *The Guardian,* 3 December.

Smithers, R. (2005) Tests show gender gap widening at primary school, *The Guardian,* 24 August.

Southworth, G. (1998) *Leading Improving Primary Schools.* London: Falmer Press.

Spender, D. (1982) *Invisible Women: The Schooling Scandal.* London: Writers and Readers Publishing Cooperative.

Stanworth, M. (1981) *Gender and Schooling.* London: Hutchinson.

Stanworth, M. (1987) Girls on the margins: a study of gender divisions in the classroom, in G. Weiner and M. Arnot (eds) *Gender under Scrutiny.* London: Hutchinson.

Stoll, L. and Fink, D. (1999) *Changing Our Schools.* Buckingham: Open University Press.

Suffolk County Council (2002) *Learning and Teaching: A Discussion Paper.* February http://www.suffolkcc.gov.uk/documents/Education/learn-teach/Learning_and_teaching_discussion_paper.html (Last accessed 9 September, 2004).

Sukhnandan, L., Lee, B. and Kelleher, S. (2000) *An Investigation into Gender Differences and Achievement: Phase 2: School and Classroom Strategies.* Slough: NFER.

Sutherland, M. (1999) Gender equity in success at school, *International Review of Education,* 45: 431–43.

Swain, J. (2000) 'The money's good, the fame's good, the girls are good': the role of playground football in the construction of young boys' masculinity in a junior school, *British Journal of Sociology of Education,* 21: 95–109.

Swain, J. (2003) How young schoolboys become some*body*: the role of the body in the construction of masculinity, *British Journal of Sociology of Education*, 24: 299–314.

Swain, J. (2004) The resources and strategies that 10-11-year-old boys use to construct masculinities in the school setting, *British Educational Research Journal*, 20: 167–85.

Taylor, M. (2003) *Going Round in Circles: Implementing and Learning from Circle Time*. Slough: National Foundation for Educational Research.

Taylor, M. with Johnson, R. (2002) *School Councils: Their Role in Citizenship and Personal and Social Education*. Slough: National Foundation for Educational Research.

TEEP (2005) *Teacher Effectiveness Enhancement Programme News*, issue 7, summer, London: Gatsby Technical Education Projects.

Thomas, N. (1980) The primary curriculum: survey findings and implications, in C. Richards (ed.) *Primary Education: Issues for the Eighties*. London: Adam and Charles Black.

Thomas, S., Smees, R., MacBeath, J., Robertson, P. and Boyd, B. (2000) Valuing pupils' views in Scottish schools, *Educational Research and Evaluation*, 6: 281–316.

Thorndike, R.L., Hagen, E. and France, N. (1986) *Cognitive Abilities Test: Administrative Manual*. Windsor: NFER-Nelson.

Thorne, B. (1993) *Gender Play: Boys and Girls in School*. Buckingham: Open University Press.

Thornton, M. and Bricheno, P. (2002) Staff gender balance in primary schools. Paper presented to BERA Annual Conference, Exeter, 12–14 September.

Tinklin, T., Croxford, L., Ducklin, A. and Frame, B. (2001) *Gender and Pupils' Performance in Scotland's Schools*, Edinburgh: University of Edinburgh Press.

Titus, J.J. (2004) Boy trouble: rhetorical framing of boys' underachievement, *Discourse: Studies in the Cultural Politics of Education*, 25: 145–69.

Tizard, B. and Hughes, M. (1984) *Young Children Learning: Talking and Thinking at Home and at School*. London: Fontana.

Tizard, J., Blatchford, P., Burke, J., Farquhar, C. and Plewis, L. (1988) *Young Children at School in the Inner City*. Hove and London: Lawrence Erlbaum Associates.

Topping, K. (1990) Peer tutored paired reading: outcome data for ten projects, in S. Goodlad and B. Hirst (eds) *Explorations in Peer Tutoring*. Oxford: Basil Blackwell Ltd.

Topping, K. (1998) Introduction to peer-assisted learning, in K. Topping and S. Ehly (eds) *Peer-Assisted Learning*. Mahwah, NJ: Lawrence Erlbaum Associates, Inc.

Topping, K. and Bryce, A. (2004) Cross-age peer tutoring of reading and thinking: influence on thinking skills, *Educational Psychology*, 24: 595–621.

Topping, K., Campbell, J., Douglas, W. and Smith, A. (2003) Cross-age peer tutoring in mathematics with seven- and 11-year-olds: influence on mathematical vocabularly, strategic dialogue and self-concept, *Educational Research,* 45: 287–308.

Topping, K. and Ehly, S. (eds) (1998) *Peer-Assisted Learning.* Mahwah, NJ: Lawrence Erlbaum Associates, Inc.

Topping, K., Peter, C., Stephen, P. and Whale, M. (2004) Cross-age peer tutoring of science in the primary school: influence on scientific language and thinking, *Educational Psychology,* 24: 57–75.

Twist, L., Sainsbury, M., Woodthorpe, A. and Whetton, C. (2003) *Reading All Over the World: Progress in International Reading Literacy Study.* Slough: NFER/DfES.

Tymms, P. and Dean, C. (2004) *Value-Added in the Primary School League Tables: A Report for the National Association of Head Teachers.* Durham: University of Durham CEM Centre, available at http://www.naht. org.uk/userfiles/819714742/naht-value-added-report.pdf (last accessed 20th July 2005).

University of Durham Curriculum, Evaluation and Management Centre (2003) *MidYIS: Middle Years Information System.* Durham: University of Durham.

Van Houtte, M. (2004) Why boys achieve less at school than girls: the difference between boys' and girls' academic culture, *Educational Studies,* 30: 159–73.

Vygotsky, L. (1978) *Mind in Society.* Cambridge, MA: Harvard University Press.

Walford, G. (2005) Introduction: education and the Labour Government, *Oxford Review of Education*, 31: 3–9.

Walker, A. (1996) An ear for music, in J. Piotrowski (ed.), *Expressive Arts in the Primary School.* London: Cassell.

Walkerdine, V. (1989) *Counting Girls Out.* London: Virago.

Walkerdine, V. (1990) *Schoolgirl Fictions.* London: Verso.

Ward, L. (2005) Catch-up lessons to help bridge class gap in schools, *The Guardian*, 27 July.

Warrington, M. (1997) Reflections on a recently completed PhD, *Journal of Geography in Higher Education,* 2: 401–10.

Warrington, M. and Younger, M. (1999) Perspectives on the gender gap in English secondary schools, *Research Papers in Education*, 14: 51–7.

Warrington, M. and Younger, M. (2000) The other side of the gender gap, *Gender and Education*, 12: 493–508.

Warrington, M., Younger, M. and McLellan, R. (2003) 'Under-achieving boys' in English primary schools? *The Curriculum Journal,* 14: 139–56.

Warrington, M., Younger, M. and Williams, J. (2000) Student attitudes, image and the gender gap, *British Educational Research Journal,* 26: 393–407.

Weaver-Hightower, M. (2003) The 'boy-turn' in research on gender and education, *Review of Educational Research,* 72: 471–98.

Weinberger, J. (1996) *Literacy Goes to School: The Parents' Role in Young Children's Literacy Learning.* London: Paul Chapman Publishing Ltd.

Weiner, G., Arnot, M. and David, M. (1997) Is the future female? Female success, male disadvantage, and changing gender patterns in education, in A. Halsey, H. Lauder, P. Brown, and A. Wells (eds) *Education: Culture, Economy and Society.* Oxford: Oxford University Press.

Wells, G. (1985) Pre-school literacy-related activities and success in school, in D. Olsen, N. Torrance and A. Hildyard (eds) *Literacy, Language and Learning.* Cambridge: Cambridge University Press.

West, A. and Pennell, H. (2003) *Underachievement in Schools.* London: RoutledgeFalmer.

West, P. (1996) Boys, sport and schooling: an Australian perspective. Paper presented at University of Cambridge Faculty of Education, 7 November.

Whitebread, D. (ed.) (1996) *Teaching and Learning in the Early Years.* London: Routledge.

Whyte, J. (1985) *Girl Friendly Schooling.* London: Methuen.

Willis, P. (1977) *Learning to Labour: How Working Class Kids Get Working Class Jobs.* Aldershot: Saxon House.

Wing, A. (1997) How can children be taught to read differently? Bill's new frock and the 'hidden curriculum', *Gender and Education,* 9: 491–504.

Wise, D. and Lovatt, M. (2001) *Creating an Accelerated Learning School.* Stafford: Network Educational Press.

Wolfendale, S. (1996) Transitions and continuities in home-school related literature, in S. Wolfendale and K. Topping (eds) *Family Involvement in Literacy: Effective Partnerships in Education.* London: Cassell.

Wood, E. (2000) 'I don't want to stereotype but ...' the roots of under-achievement in the early years. Paper presented to the British Association Educational Research Conference, Cardiff, September.

Wood, E. (2003) The power of pupil perspectives in evidence-based practice: the case of gender and underachievement, *Research Papers in Education,* 18: 365–83.

Woodhead, C. (1995) Inspector attacks woolly teachers, *Daily Telegraph,* 27 January.

Wray, D., Medwell, J., Poulson, L., and Fox, R. (2002) *Teaching Literacy Effectively in the Primary School.* London: Routledge.

Wyse, D. (2003) The National Literacy Strategy: a critical review of empirical evidence, *British Educational Research Journal,* 29: 903–16.

Yates, L. (1997) Gender equity and the boys debate: what sort of challenge is it?, *British Journal of Sociology of Education,* 18: 337–47.

Young, J. (1971) The role of the police as amplifiers of defiance, negotiators of drug control as seen in Notting Hill, in S. Cohen (ed.) *Images of Deviance.* Harmondsworth: Penguin.

Younger, M. and Warrington, M. (1996) Differential achievement of girls and boys at GCSE: some observations from the perspective of one school, *British Journal of Sociology of Education,* 17: 299–313.

Younger, M. and Warrington, M. (1999) 'He's such a nice man, but he's so boring, you have to really make a conscious effort to learn': the views of Gemma, Daniel and their contemporaries on teacher quality and effectiveness, *Educational Review,* 51: 231–41.

Younger, M. and. Warrington, M., with McLellan, R. (2005a) *Raising Boys' Achievements in Secondary Schools: Issues, Dilemmas and Opportunities.* Buckingham: Open University Press.

Younger, M. and Warrington, M. with Gray, J., Rudduck, J., McLellan, R., Bearne, E., Kershner, R. and Bricheno, P. (2005b) *Raising Boys' Achievement.* London: DfES, Research Report 636.

Younger, M., Warrington, M. and Williams, J. (1999) The gender gap and classroom interactions: reality and rhetoric? *British Journal of Sociology of Education,* 20: 327–43.

# Index